Netprov

NETPROV

*Networked Improvised Literature for
the Classroom and Beyond*

ROB WITTIG

Amherst College Press

Amherst, Massachusetts

Copyright © 2022 by Rob Wittig
Some rights reserved

This work is licensed under the Creative Commons Attribution-NonCommercial4.0 International License. To view a copy of this license, visit http://creativecommons.org/licenses/by-nc/4.0 or send a letter to Creative Commons, PO Box 1866, Mountain View, CA 94042, USA.

The complete manuscript of this work was subjected to a partly closed ("single-blind") review process. For more information, visit https://acpress.amherst.edu/peerreview/.

Published in the United States of America by
Amherst College Press
Manufactured in the United States of America

DOI: http://doi.org/10.3998/mpub.12404656

ISBN 978-1-943208-30-2 (paper)
ISBN 978-1-943208-31-9 (OA)

CONTENTS

	Acknowledgments	vii
	Introduction	1
1.	The Impulse to Fiction	19
	Example 1: *The Ballad of Workstudy Seth*, a Netprov *An Impulse to Fiction Becomes a Character*	35
2.	Solo Netprovs	41
	Example 2: *All-Time High*, a Netprov *A Playground for Playing Multiple Characters*	51
3.	Playing Multiple Characters and Producing Larger Netprovs	59
	Example 3: *Fantasy Spoils: After the Quest*, a Netprov *Speaking Stories Together, Dungeons & Dragons Style*	75
4.	Playing Well with Others	81
	Example 4: *I Work for the Web*, a Netprov *Revolution in the Feed*	97
5.	Satirical, Situational Netprovs	105
	Example 5: *Reality: Being @spencerpratt*, a Netprov *Join the Game!*	115

6.	**The Thingness of Language** *Wordplay in Netprov*	119
	Example 6: *#1WkNoTech*, a Netprov *A Collaborative Thought Experiment*	133
7.	**Organizing and Launching Open-Ended Netprovs**	139
	Example 7: *The LA Flood Project*, a Netprov *An Environmental/Political Story Line*	161
8.	**Netprovs with a Story Line**	165
	Example 8: *Destination Wedding 2070*, a Netprov *A Sugarcoated Dystopia*	181
9.	**Games, Role-Play, and Netprovs in the Real World**	187
	Example 9: *Thermophiles in Love*, a Netprov *Larping Five Genders*	205
10.	**Futures of Netprov** *Laughter, Insight, Empathy*	211
	Notes	219
	Appendixes	235

ACKNOWLEDGMENTS

Given the nature of netprov any acknowledgements must necessarily begin with a big thank you and a big apology. A big thank you first of all to all the anonymous, pseudonymous, and unknown (to me) netprov players who have dropped in over the years to play a line or two or who contributed big, bold characters and crucial plot twists! I applaud your creative courage, and I thank you for taking time out of your busy lives to exercise your imagination with us so generously! Big apologies, next, to those of you who would like to have seen your name here and who I have neglected to include due to nothing more than my shoddy archiving systems and my sieve-like memory. I'm so sorry! Please let me know—after all, this volume is online, open access, and only then print on demand, so there could still be time!

Thanks to netprov players, featured players, and literary advisors: Paul Cabarga, Tom Grothus, Philip Wohlstetter, James Winchell, Jeff T. Johnson, Claire Donato, Clark Humphrey, Dene Grigar, Julie Ahasay, John Barber, Lane Ellis, Dirk Stratton, William Gillespie, Alex Mitchell, Eric Pitsenbarger, Jeremy Douglass, Juan B. Gutierrez, Lisa Anne Tao. Ann Carlson, Nzingha Clarke, Laura LaBounty, Sean Keith Henry, Roberto Leni, Daniel A. Olivas, Laura Press, Abel Salas, Kevin Schaaf, Nancy E.Taylor, Spencer Pratt, Heidi Montag, Brendan Howell, Mark Sample, Joel Sipress, Claire Kirch, Serge Bouchardon, Betsy Boyd, Skye McIlvaine-Jones, Davin Heckman, Crystal Pelkey, Ian Clarkson, Sarah-Anne Joulie, Chloe Smith, Krista-Lee Malone, Paul Benzon, Jessica Pressman, Perla Sasson, Kathi Inman Berens, Kathy McTavish, Anastasia Salter, John Murray, Rick Valicenti, Arianna Gass, Alvaro Seiça, Lee Skallerup Bessette, Michael J. Maguire, Leo Flores, Jason Farman, Sarah-Anne Joulie, Reed Gaines, Lari Chandler Tanner, Amit Ray, Michelle Chihara, Ben Grosser, Skyler Lovelace, Zach Whalen, Jim Brown, Chris Rodley, Michael

Russo, Raphael Schnee, Katie Vandermost, Mark Amerika, Cassandra Gillig, the Coup (Boots Riley), Sandy Baldwin, Darren Angle, Kevin McPherson Eckhoff, The Pistol Shrimps, Jesse R. Vigil, Martzi Campos, Erik Loyer, R. Lyle Skains, Jason Nelson, Hannah Ackermans, Rui Torres, Dave Ciccoricco, Michael Mateas, Noah Wardrip-Fruin, James Ryan, Jacob Garbe, Aaron Reed, Stephanie Strickland, Marjorie Luesebrink, Abraham Avnisan, Will Luers, David Jhave Johnston, Chris Funkhouser, Alan Bigelow, Bill Bly, John Cayley, Andy Campbell, Lai-Tze Fan, María Goicoechea de Jorge, Hartmut Koenitz, Jan Baetens, Domingo Sanchez-Mesa, Nieves Rosendo, Piotr Marecki, Judy Malloy, Shelley Jackson, Judd Morrissey, Mark Jeffery, María Mencía, Alex Saum, Laura Borràs, Luciana Gattass, Astrid Ensslin, Carolyn Guertin, Stacey Mason, Jim Bizzocchi, Ian Hatcher, Natalia Federova, Steve Tomasula, James O'Sullivan, John Saklofske, Steven Wingate, John Bogart, et al. Thanks to my agent, my whole management team . . . wait . . . that's from somebody's Academy Awards thank you list! Netprov writers don't have agents! Yet.

Thanks to my very tolerant and supportive academic colleagues: Jim Klueg, Jennifer Webb, Jane Ebersviller, Bill Payne, Lisa Fitzpatrick, the VizLab and MMAD Lab, Will Salmon, David Beard, Alexis Elder, John O'Neill, Vicky Lehmann, Jennifer Gordon, David Short, Matt Olin, Steve Bardolph, Robin Murphy, Craig Stroupe, Krista Twu, Liz James, Rae Ann Johnson, Jeff Kalstrom, Alison Aune, Sara Blaylock, Jamie Ratliff, Eun-Kyung Suh, David Bowen, Gloria DeFilipps Brush, Darren Houser, Betsy Hunt, Ryuta Nakjima, Freddie Parella, Erika Pazian, Kristen Pless, Cecilia Ramon, Terresa Moses, Katie van Wert, Ari Feld, Rebecca Boyle, John Schwetman, Ken Risdon, Michele Larson, Robert Repinksi, Chongwon Park, Maryam Khaleghi Yazdi, Daniel Apollon, Daniel Jung, Hilde G. Corneliussen. Thanks to my two great teachers Elizabeth Wenscott (and the students of the Tai Chi Center of Chicago) and Cheri Huber (and the students of the Zen Monastery Peace Center and Living Compassion). Thanks to those stalwarts of my monthly Persimmons and Myrrh Show and Tell Society in Chicago, Steve Lafreniere and David Sedaris. Thanks to longtime support and companion Lynn Martinelli. Thanks to Jill Narcisi, a great friend. Thanks to brilliant scholar/creator/netprov players Caitlin Fisher, Talan Memmott, Deena Larsen, Davin Heckman, Elizabeth Nesheim, Rod Coover, Stuart Moulthrop, and Mez Breeze.

Thanks to my formative friends from the legendary Chicago Electronic Literature Dinners at Moti Mahal: Kurt Heintz, Eric Rasmussen, the scholar supreme Joseph Tabbi, and mentor/writing buddy/grad advisor/

visionary Scott Rettberg who, along with Jill Walker Rettberg and family, were undendingly generous and gracious during my successful quest as a master in Digital Kultur at the University of Bergen, Norway.

Thanks to the new members of the far-flung squad that has rallied 'round a cocktail in video chat to help weather the pandemic lockdown of 2020–21: Jeremy Hight, Lisa Hight, Andrew Klobucar, Nick Montfort, Flourish Klink, Liz Hughes Wiley, Mark Wiley, Johannah Rodgers, Kathleen Roberts, Amy Holman, Anna Nacher.

Special thanks to my dear, loyal, and incredibly supportive friends and featured players who have gathered for so many years beneath the Crown of a Friday happy hour to share great conversation and news of their many, wonderful creative pursuits and who have nursed and cocreated so many netprovs in their infancy: Cathy Podeszwa, Margi Preus, Arno Kahn, Jean Sramek, John Bankson, Jamie Harvie, Nan Sudak, Christa Schulz, Todd Higgins, Catherine Winter, Chris Julin, Gary Kruchowski, Shannon Laing, and dear friends Ann Gummper, and Mark Harvey. Thanks to Beth Bouloukos and the crew at Amherst College Press. Thanks to the wonderful coaching of Sherry Richert Belul; gassho. Thanks for so much substantative and process advice to Robyn Roslak who, as a blessing to the universe, has decided to dedicate herself to supporting writers. Thanks to my mom, Alice Wittig, whose brilliant creative sparkle and skill at observation and imitation showed me the path to the creative life and taught me how to do character voices with her deep skill at puppetry, bringing a salt and pepper shaker to life for a fidgety kid!

My deepest wish for all you writers out there is that you find, and cherish, a writing buddy as wonderful as Mark Marino; it is a privilege to create beside you, my friend.

I love living in a creative house, as we often say to each other, with musician and composer J.J. Sivak, now out in the world creating, and the person without whom none of this would have been possible, the magnificent, creative, multitalented being who lights up every room she enters: Joellyn Rock.

INTRODUCTION

Are you a creative person who loves cracking people up with just the right phrase in text messages and social media? Do you ever wish you had the time to write something bigger, something with the characters of a novel, the story line of a TV series—a substantial piece of fiction like the ones you enjoy?

What if there were a simple structure—a trellis—on which you and your friends could *grow your own real literature in the flow of everyday life*?

Well there is; it's called netprov.

What is netprov?

Netprov is networked improv: networked, improvised literature. Netprov is collaborative fiction-making in available media. Netprov is role-playing in writing and images. Netprov is storytelling in real time. Netprov is a great game for students and friends. Netprov is an emerging art form of the digital age.

And netprov is fun. When your dog's social media account replies to another dog's account, that is netprov. When you comment with a facetious "blessed" to a friend's hilarious humble brag, that is netprov. When you contribute to the astonishing, rich fan culture of fantasy characters, drama, and backstory surrounding the seemingly simple COVID-era baseball simulator "Blaseball," that is netprov.[1] When you post on Facebook in "A group where we all pretend to be ants in an ant colony," you are already engaged in the art of netprov. Netprov shares the same easy, creative energy as the proliferating chains of songs and dances on TikTok. Netprov is something you may do every day without realizing it. Millions do.

This may all sound very high tech, but netprov is just a form of writing. I'm a creative writer. I'm a lover of older literature, especially literature that responded to new historical conditions with new ideas, new styles, and new forms. So as people began to write on platforms other than ink and paper, I started to see amazing pockets of creativity—of fiction—in the most unexpected places. People would write silly reviews of products and services, using exaggerated character voices. People would play extravagant characters in chat rooms for their friends' amusement. Then their friends would respond as their own characters, and whole stories would evolve. People would make parody websites and keep updating them as things went worse and worse for the fictional site owners. I found myself tuning in to these evolving stories regularly, waiting impatiently for the next installment.

I started to look at a whole host of electronic writing practices, even ones that were supposedly nonfiction but were, well, fudging things a bit, exaggerating to make their narrators look better (or comically worse). I realized how many of these new forms were just begging to be pushed a little bit further, to be parodied, to be turned into fiction the way biographies and memoirs had once been gradually "fictionized" and turned into novels.

I realized that, because of the possibilities of the Internet, these new forms easily could be collaborative, with groups of friends, or even thousands of strangers, improvising stories together in real time. I could look at them as Internet literature, but also as a form of improv theater. I started thinking of them as "netprov."

Then I asked the question that writers ask when new literary forms are being goofed around with for fun. I think of it as the Shakesepeare question (not that I'm comparing myself to Big Bill—but with this beard? a little?). Shakespeare and the Elizabethan writers said, "Look, we all love going to these wild, fun, folksy courtyard plays about the wages of sin with their villains and clowns and swordfights and pig bladders full of fake blood. And we also love these ancient Greek and Roman plays with their beautiful writing and deep ideas that the cool Renaissance kids in Italy are starting to imitate. What if we combined the two? How good can a courtyard play be?"

So you're asking: How good can a netprov be?

Hey, subheading, you stole my big line! But yes, that's what I'm asking; that's what this book is about. That's what my writer friends and I have been trying to find out for the last decade by doing lots of fun experiments. I'm sharing what we've discovered so far.

How do I know if something is a netprov or not?

For the purposes of this book I'm going to focus on netprovs that:

- create fictional stories that are networked, improvised in real time, and often collaborative;
- use primarily written language along with some images and videos;
- may use multiple media platforms simultaneously;
- are experienced as performances as they are published, and are read later as literary archives;
- may incorporate breaking news during the performances;
- may include content that is topical and satirical;
- may use models or actors to physically enact characters in images, videos, and live performance;
- may include players who play, as actors, the characters they create and write;
- may require players to travel to certain locations to seek information, perform actions, and document their activities;
- accommodate episodic and incomplete reading;

Wait—is netprov like an Internet hoax?

Netprov is not a hoax. Nor is it trolling or fake news. Netprov comes out of a long tradition of fiction and satire, using the same strategies pioneered by early novelists and early journalists, the same strategies we enjoy in ironic social media posts we share and in the bitingly comical TV shows we binge-watch. Instead of seeking to deceive or inflame, netprov seeks to heal, enlighten, and inspire, holding up a gentle mirror in which we can see our foibles. Netprov is a safe, cultural space to play out aspects of our personalities.

The genres we now readily identify as literary fiction and journalism evolved in the seventeenth and eighteenth centuries amid a surreptitiously printed sea of anonymous urban myths, meme-like cartoons, libellous handbills, and outright false "true accounts." Influential English journalists Richard Steele and Joseph Addison cowrote their periodical *The Spectator* (1711–13) by sharing the pseudonym Mr. Spectator—a fictional, idealized voice of the times. They intermingled hard news with imaginary characters and invented, but true-to-life, moments of contemporary existence. Some readers knew who the real writers were; some did not. Fact circled round with fiction in an entertaining dance. As the decades went by, historians and critics worked to define the rules of the game of genres such as novel and newspaper. Fiction came to be understood as "the lie that tells the truth" and news as "nothing but the facts." By the mid-twentieth century, literary fiction, on one hand, and evidence-based journalism, on the other hand, had matured and became more recognizable.

But the twenty-first century is more like the seventeenth and eighteenth centuries than the mid-twentieth. New communication technologies and their new writing styles have thrown everything back into the mixer. We are surrounded by genres in their infancy. The post-2016 wave of Internet disinformation—sometimes amateurish, sometimes chillingly professional, as in the Russian Internet Research Agency's social media efforts at voter suppression[2]—exist now alongside sincere and well-meaning artistic netprovs. To help sort it out, I'll talk more about the boundaries of fiction, hoax, and so on later in this book.

So netprov is part of literature?

Netprov is interdisciplinary, drawing ideas from five main creative worlds (see Figure 1) as well as pieces of many others. Netprov creators come to netprov with primary training and experience in any of these different worlds, usually more than one.

Netprov draws from the world of imaginative literature, with its short stories, novels, poems, and creative experiments. Netprov draws from theater with its memorized plays, improvised "improv," shows, and all kinds of street theater and avant-garde performance. Netprov draws from mass media such as film and TV and all their related forms, including game versions, books made from films, cosplay events, and the vast sea of fan fiction. Netprov draws from the world of games—particularly ones in which stories are expanded or invented by players, such as tabletop role-playing games and live-action role-playing games. And of course netprov draws from the world of the Internet, personal media, and social media, where the creativity of millions of users is shaping a multitude of creative subcultures.

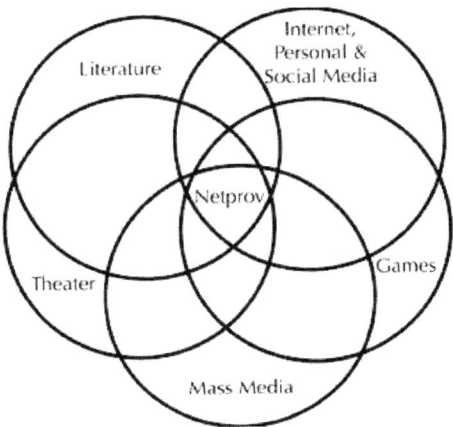

Figure 1. Five cultural worlds that contribute to netprov.

You can see what a strange hybrid netprov is (against this interdisciplinary backdrop) the minute you start to write about one. For example: If you simply list a date for the netprov, a reader may figure that it was a one-time thing whereas it's quite possible for the same netprov recipe to be repeated any number of times. If you describe a netprov as "first performed" on such and such a date, you place netprov squarely within the theater tradition, which means it can be repeated but brings with it the suggestion of a separation between performers and audience, whereas a netprov is open to everyone to cocreate. If you say "first played," it suggests a game, which is replicable and participatory (especially so-called serious games used for education, emergency simulation, and collaborative narrative games such as *Dungeons & Dragons*), but to a nongamer, "played" might not suggest the degree of user creativity netprovs have. If you say "first shown" or "exhibited," you are pointing to the tradition of visual arts in which the works usually remain unchanged and in which there is usually close attention to the brand identity of the artist. If you say "first released" or "dropped," it has echoes of movies, TV, or recorded music. If you say "first posted," it sounds like grassroots social-media use, and if you say "first launched," it suggests an entrepreneurial effort.

Personally, with my literature background, I might be most tempted to say a netprov was "first written," but that neglects the images and videos that are part of netprovs. And again, that risks condemning netprovs into being one-time-only relics rather than living creations. For better or for worse, I tend to think of netprovs as having "first appeared," which seems to me to have an unlimited duration, a sense of multiple creators, and is sometimes used to describe culture of mysterious origins.

Other concepts in netprov also reveal its varied heritage. For example, I've come to use the word *netrunner* for the creators and lead writers of a netprov, based on the TV term *showrunner*, the most powerful creative person on a show, and *player* for someone who participates in a netprov. Technically, netprov players are more like writer-actor-designers. But I love the word *player* first because it's lighthearted (and overseriousness can stifle creativity) and second because it's used for sports and games as well as being an older word for actor.

How did you get started doing netprovs?

That's a question I love to ask new netprov players, because everyone—you included—comes to netprov from a different path. I have a Russian literature and graphic design background. I came to collaborative writing via the exploits of a group of creators called Invisible Seattle, with whom I had the great fortune to play starting in the early 1980s. The group did surrealist-style literary performances at Seattle's annual Bumbershoot Festival, published imaginative manifestoes, and coordinated the assembly and publication of a crowdsourced "novel of Seattle, by Seattle" on a computer platform in 1983. That winter, we Invisibles began to do creative writing together on the dial-up, electronic bulletin board IN.S.OMNIA, nearly a decade before the World Wide Web took off. We discovered the joys of "doing voices" in the then-exotic new medium. We cracked one another up playing characters and improvising dramas and novels, intermingled with serious readings of contemporary philosophy and reflections on politics and economics. I documented these early exploits in a book called *Invisible Rendezvous: Connection and Collaboration in the New Landscape of Electronic Writing*.[3]

Once the World Wide Web opened networked writing to a wide user base, I started using the new platforms to expand the playful creating I'd been a part of on IN.S.OMNIA. I wrote a month-long novel in email, *Blue Company*, to which one of its readers, author Scott Rettberg, responded by writing a partner email novel, *Kind of Blue*. I created a fictional web 1.0 home page, "Fall of the Site of Marsha," and I posted a week's worth of chat on a fictional company's Internal chat room that supposedly "accidentally" becomes public, "Friday's Big Meeting." Most importantly, I started seeking out others—present and past—from all backgrounds who had been doing similar projects to learn, share, and collaborate.

Who else did you find who had been doing netprov-style projects?

In music, jazz had already long established a sophisticated tradition of artistic collaboration and real-time improvisation. Writers and visual artists in groups such as the Dadas and surrealists had done systematic collaborations, often in the form of rambunctious party games. Theater improv was an expanding cultural force. There were educational role-plays and other serious games. Finally, I began to catch wind of some who were using the new electronic platforms the way we had in Invisible Seattle. In 1998, Sue Thomas and Teri Hoskins stitched together a web page in the form of a quilt. Clicking on each patch revealed a short text written by an author somewhere in the world, describing what they saw from their window at noon. N_o_o_n Q_u_i_l_t[4] and its visual interface showed an exciting path for online collaborations.

Then I stumbled across a sprawling website, the hypertext novel *The Unknown*. This project began when writers William Gillespie, Scott Rettberg, Dirk Stratton, and Frank Marquardt embarked on a tour of readings from an anthology of fiction they had compiled. Having been introduced to early electronic literature experiments organized by the author of wonderful, self-aware metafictions Robert Coover, at Brown University, they proposed to write a set of interlinked web pages to document the tour. This was to be an amusing side project to the anthology—a side project that soon got out of hand. Fact began to mix with fiction as each writer recounted the others' extravagant behavior in the third person:

> Both William and Scott had become increasingly concerned about the effect Dirk's cult was having on the book tour. On the one hand, the perks weren't bad, the lobster meals for one, or the occasional make-out session with whichever disciple wasn't chosen to join Dirk.

But just as often the tone would be reflective:

> "Dirk isn't cut from the same cloth as us," Scott says sadly. "I mean he's a poet, an authentic poet. He can go for weeks without eating or writing. Me, if I'm hungry, I'll charge the shit on my overextended credit cards. And write a story about it..."

"Frank and Dirk together would make one real good hypertext novelist," William mutters softly, beneath his breath. "If we could only combine them...."

"We'd encounter some opposition," Scott says excitedly, "but who knows, you just may have an idea there. I mean they can clone sheep now. I'd imagine that there are skilled surgeons...."

"Mike knows some people," William says quietly, "and this is strictly sub rosa, my friend, if this were to get out, it would be bad, very bad. But in Urbana there have been some experiments, funded by the Department of Defense—"

"Experiments, like what kind experiments?"

"Let's just say that Mary Shelly was ahead of her time."

"No way."[5]

I was enchanted! The writing process of *The Unknown* happened in two ways, and after I got to know the authors, I was honored to participate in both. One was exhilarating, "live writing" sessions where some or all of the writers would be gathered in the same place, often a hotel room or bar, writing in short bursts and then reading chunks aloud to gales of laughter. Then there was an online mode, where the writers, living in different cities, would post chunks of text on the Internet and read and respond from afar. Networked writing, I came to realize, could allow people to enjoy the social delights of collaborative, creative play, even at a distance.

Later, I found out about writer Mark Marino's witty website *Bunk Magazine*, which, among many other cool projects, had responded to the *Los Angeles Times*'s creation of a wiki-based editorial section (aka the wikitorial debacle) with a participatory satire called "The Los Wikiless Timespedia" that imagined the *Times* committing to publish solely as a wiki. Marino and his collaborators engaged in revert wars, editing and reediting one another's entries, recreating the quibbles and flame wars to which wiki making is prone.

By Ole Opossum

Thursday, March 13, 2008, 2:02 PM:

The Raccoon who writes imaginaryyear.com recently admitted to tampering with "The Nudity on Film" entry in the Wikipedia.

"I'm no expert on nudity in film or anything," explains the Raccoon. And yet, the Raccoon edited the entry.

The Raccoon announced its insatiable appetite for editing, writing, "I more-or-less know how to organize and fix bad writing, which makes Wikipedia an occasionally-irresistable pasttime for me."

Nothing will stop this Raccoon. As it declares, "My work on it is not complete."

The billion-plus editors of Wikipedia could not be reached for comment.[6]

I loved the work, and I reached out and discovered in Mark Marino a kindred spirit. Mark, it turned out, likes collaboration as much as I do, and the two of us have been organizing netprovs ever since.

I was also intrigued by the idealism of game-designer-scholar Jane McGonigal. People will go to great lengths, McGonigal shows in her book *Reality Is Broken*, just for the chance to work really hard for no pay at their computers when they feel that there is a project at hand worthy of their effort and intelligence, when they feel that they are doing "something big." McGonigal's work pointed me toward projects from the game world that encouraged me to feel that netprov, too, could be something big.

So you really think netprov can become a big-time art form?

I think all the elements are there, yes. One early experiment in particular seems to me to really prove the concept, and I write about it several times in this book; it's the netprov *Grace, Wit & Charm*.[i]

Join me, dear reader, on stage back in 2011 for the debut public night of *Grace, Wit & Charm*! Yes—on a theater stage. I'm not trained as an actor, but the fun of the netprov helped me get over my fear of playing the role of Bob, the beleaguered boss. I loved the big laugh created by my solemn invocation: "We ask the audience to please keep your phones turned on throughout the performance!" What the audience didn't know was that they would be contributing to the story via their questions on Twitter. *Grace, Wit & Charm* was designed to try out all the dimensions the I could imagine for a netprov, including live stage performances with the writer-actors embodying their fictional characters 24/7 during the two-week run.

The fictional concept is this: *Grace, Wit & Charm* is a discreet business that offers gamers, chatters, and status-updaters assistance with their online self-presentation. If your game avatar is moving clumsily, one of the live Character Enhancement Agents will jump into a motion-capture studio and secretly make it move beautifully (the service called "Grace"). If you don't have a great sense of humor, agents will ghostwrite hysterical posts for you ("Wit"). And for the romantically impaired, the company offers "Charm"; the agents will flirt or conduct an online romance on your behalf.

To its audience, the netprov is a workplace comedy that lets them read (all week on Twitter) and see (once a week in the theater and streamed) the behind-the-scenes banter of four hardworking Character Enhancement Agents from *Grace, Wit &Charm*'s Duluth, Minnesota, office, during a special, two-week open house.

But even though the *Grace, Wit & Charm* corporate overlords imagine the open house as a fantastic promotional event, what is revealed on Twitter is a quirky, spunky, and beleaguered group of Character Enhancement Agents who have been working overtime to the point of exhaustion. In a reflection of the belt tightening and overtime pressures of the post-2008 recession, Bob the boss challenges the frazzled crew to outproduce their nemesis Shreveport office in the next two weeks and earn an actual paid vacation—the company's first ever.

The long hours mean our four agents must live their personal lives at work and therefore in the netprov. Between solving customer assignments for *Grace, Wit & Charm*, the close-knit group helps Laura manage her love life, helps Deb deal with her house full of kids, helps Neil accept the fact that his military-contractor wife in Afghanistan is cheating on him, and helps Sonny prep for the radio-controlled model snowmobile Grand Nationals.

Readers of the netprov followed the emerging plot lines in Twitter and linked to a fully functioning *Grace, Wit & Charm* company website (see figure 2).

Figure 2. Top of the web page of Grace, Wit & Charm.

As a netprov, *Grace, Wit & Charm* happened online, but it also occurred in the physical world. Reader-players could come to Duluth's Zeitgeist Teatro theater on Wednesday nights of the two-week run to see the characters step onto the stage and live out one hour of their hectic work lives. Artist and writer Joellyn Rock created a production design on stage that resembled a motion-capture studio with a giant computer screen showing fantastic projections, and costumes that looked like motion-capture suits. During the performance, the audience was encouraged to tweet *Grace, Wit & Charm* assignments to the agents on stage, who duly took these prompts as the basis for comic scenes (see figure 3). The characters and basic plot for all two weeks were developed by me along with help from Mark Marino, but the specific lines were always improvised and were free to wander widely from the outline.

Figure 3. Character Ehancement Agents solve client problems tweeted by reader-players during the second live performance of Grace, Wit & Charm, May 24, 2011. Photo by Joellyn Rock.

Netprovs are for artists with a day job. None of the original cast of players of *Grace, Wit & Charm* was a full-time actor. It made me realize netprov is perfect for creative folks with busy lives. And the feedback from those in that initial audience who could follow the characters' Twitter feed, come to the live shows, submit challenges, and watch them acted out in front of them, who rode along with the characters' story lines, happy and sad, proved *Grace, Wit & Charm* was a rich, complete cultural experience. *Grace, Wit & Charm* showed me netprov has legs.

I can goof around in social media but I could never be a real writer, could I?

Oh yes, you can! And you will if you play along with this book! I can feel you resisting as you read. So let me take care of it right away with a golden tip for netprov players and netprov students: the reason you may think, "Oh I'm not creative like that" is that you have internalized some negative feedback you got along the way and created what psychologists call an "inner critic" in your own mind. Nothing you do is ever good enough for that inner critic, right? Here's what you do: lure the inner critic out the door—chocolate helps—and lock it! No inner critics allowed! The neural circuits involved in judging are important but only at the *very end* of a creative project, right before you post and publish. They should account for 10 percent, at most, of your creative time. Instead, you want to cultivate the circuits of "what if?" Creativity—whether creating the next line or the next evolution of our species—consists in trying every "what if?" The only answer is "yes." Anything that occurs to you to try, the answer must be "yes."

Relax! Lower your standards! Don't compare! Let yourself play! Then simply read your draft once or twice over, kindly, at the very end, and any necessary changes will suggest themselves to you.

Throughout this book, I'll offer netprov tips to help you grow your potential as a netprov writer. Life is too short not to play, so play now!

Can netprov be used to teach writing?

Absolutely! Mark and I both do it. Clemson writing professor Michael Russo writes:

> I see great benefits in the netprov format, and I am happy to report that it works both in and out of the classroom. In the classroom, it facilitates a playfulness not often seen in writing classes. It helps to circumvent the problem of expertise, and it allows for a wide variety of genres to be implemented naturally. Out of the classroom, it helps to spark creativity, and the psychological connections created are as real as the story is fake.[7]

What other kinds of classes could netprov work in?

Almost any. In this book, I'm going to talk about *Destination Wedding 2070*, which is a netprov based on climate data imagining a wedding heavily affected by deteriorating conditions and would be perfect for science classes. I'm going to describe a netprov I admire, done by a consortium of scholars where they imagined a *World Without Oil*, which would work in all kinds of social studies classes. I'm going to share a netprov called *Thermophiles in Love*, a five-gender dating game for single-celled organisms that investigates gender construction and norming and could be used in a cultural studies, social science, or gender studies curriculum.

In my own teaching, I've found that netprov is very successful as homework. A typical assignment will be:

- Answer these four prewriting questions for your character in our class's online system.

- Upload one post a day from your character to the chosen platform, minimum one hundred words, maximum three hundred words, for the next four days, and advance your character's story line.
- Have your character respond to three posts from other characters in the next four days and help advance their story lines.

And as a classroom experience, netprov is even more amazing. Writing together, in character, in a simple discussion forum, with students (and teachers) improvising as an ensemble is so much fun! Since it builds on students' existing social media writing habits, it becomes a powerful way to leap over the dreaded writer's block and slay the demon Perfectionism. Once students start to follow the netprov advice of reading aloud texts by others that made them laugh, the energy builds. By the end of a netprov session, you can ask them to step back and admire what they've written and they're astonished by their own imagination and productivity.

What's in the rest of this book?

Sections marked *Try This* are perfect for classrooms or an evening's fun with your friends. Sandwiched among the *Try Thises* are the reflections on cultural history and the contemporary scene. Separate sections contain examples of netprovs that show some of the key features of the form that I hope will inspire you to invent and play your own netprovs. When you do, make sure to write me and let me know!

In addition to the term *players*, I use here the term *featured players*, which specifically means the jolly group of usual suspects—writers, artists, scholars—who join Mark Marino and me for nearly every one of the netprovs we produce. Among the featured players, we have private rehearsals and share a bit more behind-the-scenes strategizing than we do with the players. We write together in real time, in person or via videoconferences, and gales of laughter ensue. My hope is that you'll develop a group of featured players of your own, folks who get together in person to play netprov in real time when you can and on your phones when you can't.

In Chapter 1, "The Impulse to Fiction," I look at the basic creative impulse to make fiction as it develops in growing human beings and how it flowers in available media in simple, one-voice, one-character netprovs. You'll be invited to try some. I'll offer starting points and tips. I'll talk about the differences between spoken and written improv and the wonderful peculiarities of visible language as seen in graphic design.

Then in the next section, "*The Ballad of Workstudy Seth*, a Netprov: An Impulse to Fiction Becomes a Character," I'll take you on the trail of a (fictional) work-study student in a tailspin.

In Chapter 2, "Solo Netprovs," I'll give examples and tips about creating, developing, and sustaining one-character stories. I'll talk about how being aware of the design of the platform you're using can help you. And I'll discuss how to choose a platform for a netprov.

Following this, "*All-Time High*, a Netprov: A Playground for Playing Multiple Characters," the next section, looks at a big netprov called *All-Time High* for which players created Twitter accounts for their high school selves and we all went to high school together for a month (along with everyone else who has ever lived). The multiple characters are hilarious and harrowing.

Chapter 3, "Playing Multiple Characters and Producing Larger Netprovs," looks at the dialogic impulse in our minds, and shares some favorite netprovs in which one player plays two or more characters. I discuss some notable writers from the past who wrote in different authorial voices. I ask, "Who is the real you?" and look at how we all construct and polish our public identities on the web.

In the example "*Fantasy Spoils*, a Netprov: Speaking Stories Together, Dungeons & Dragons Style," I look at the tradition of collaborative narrative in the tabletop gaming world, where friends use dice and books of character attributes to guide improvised storytelling, through the lens of a Dungeons & Dragons-based netprov that brings everyday reality into the fantasy realm.

I look at the inspiration netprov draws from theatrical improv in Chapter 4, "Playing Well with Others," and learn from the ancient comic tradition of the commedia dell'arte. I talk about how to craft creative invitations to come play netprov and give lots of tips and suggestions about how to support other players as you play. I also start to share some behind-the-scenes structures that Mark Marino and I use to keep netprovs running smoothly.

In the example "*I Work for the Web*, a Netprov: Revolution in the Feed," I'll talk about how *I Work for the Web* addressed the social media business model of liking, favoriting, and sharing as unpaid marketing labor. I suggest ways in which creating fiction within major platforms offers a carnivalesque escape from corporate control.

In Chapter 5, "Satirical, Situational Netprovs," I examine netprovs that take on current events as they are happening. These netprovs use media interactivity to reach audiences and make points in ways not otherwise possible.

I'll look at the ethics of netprov in the era of trolling and fake news, and at netprov's fundamental mission to heal and educate as it entertains.

In "*Reality: Being @spencerpratt*, a Netprov: Join the Game with a Reality TV Star!," I look at how Mark Marino was given permission to use the official Twitter feed of reality show star Spencer Pratt, who was sequestered in the British version of the TV show *Celebrity Big Brother*, and how Mark and I morphed his imposter character Tempspence into a facilitator of crowdsourced creativity.

In Chapter 6, "The Thingness of Language," I look at netprovs that are games of wordplay, as well as netprov-play with existing, well-defined fictional genres. I invite you to join me in contemplating the absurd and philosophically challenging randomness of the sound and look of language (e.g., to, too, two, toot-toot!). I connect netprov play with the investigations of the wonderful French literary group OuLiPo, Ouvroir de littérature potentielle (workshop of potential literature). And since there are plenty of books and shows already about cooking with love, I invite you to taste the netprov *Cooking with Anger*, which incorporates all the usually neglected emotions and blends recipes with storytelling.

In "*#1WkNoTech*, a Netprov: A Collaborative Thought Experiment," I'll show how to play *#1WkNoTech* (One Week, No Tech), in which we all pretend to go for a week without technology, then share the heck out of the experience in social media.

In Chapter 7, "Organizing and Launching Open-Ended Netprovs," I'll discuss creating a basic setting—a world—in which numerous story lines can be improvised according to the players and share examples. I also offer tips for helping story lines evolve.

Next is my presentation of an important early piece cocreated by Mark Marino and friends: "The *LA Flood Project*, a Netprov: An Environmental/Political Story Line." The *LA Flood Project* used the inexorable rise of imaginary floodwaters as a story premise that instantly revealed the socioeconomic disparities between high ground and low ground.

In Chapter 8, "Netprovs with a Story Line," I look at how open play can be supported even when there is a predetermined story arc. The interwoven subplots of the inaugural version of *Grace, Wit & Charm* model one way to evolve a group of characters over time while leaving plenty of room for improvisation in the moment.

Following that, I'll turn to "*Destination Wedding 2070*, a Netprov: A Sugarcoated Dystopia." In *Destination Wedding 2070*, players took on the roles of family members trekking across the globe to a wedding in a location that, when grandma chose it and provided the funds, was idyllic but now is severely compromised by climate change.

In Chapter 9, "Games, Role-Play, and Netprovs in the Real World," I talk about studying games and game theorists to make netprov better and finding that one of the classic definitions of games, Bernard Suits's "Playing a game is the voluntary attempt to overcome unnecessary obstacles"[8] doesn't work for netprov. I look at some of my favorite games and the fun of getting out in the real world and performing an online character in real life. I also look at the parallel tradition of idealistic and enjoyable alternate-reality games (ARGs), as presented in the work of game maker and theorist Jane McGonigal. Then, with games of mimicry, parody, and satire in mind, I tackle the question: What kind of game is netprov? I conclude by proposing my own definition: netprov is the voluntary attempt to heal necessary relationships through collaborative play.

In "*Thermophiles in Love*, a Netprov: Larping Five Genders," I look at a netprov based on a five-gender dating site for microorganisms. I share the ideas of cocreator and LARP (live-action role-playing game) scholar Samara Hayley Steele about gender playability. Steele developed *Thermophiles in Love*'s five-gender system and rule set.

Finally, in Chapter 10, "Futures of Netprov: Laughter, Insight, Empathy," I conclude that netprov is a game of collaborative imagination that has the potential to help rebalance social conflicts and heal social wounds through humor and play. Building on the work of the Harvard Negotiation Project and its support for framing difficult conversations in a productive way, I set a course for possible future netprovs. Working together, learning from other artistic examples, how good can we make netprov?

One more thing: Is asking questions all I can do in this book?

Pardon me?

I would say—I would say the dialogic mode has a long history in Western literature and scholarship and, additionally, is perfectly suited to the easy back-and-forth of contemporary digital writing.

That wasn't really an answer, was it?

Hello? Rob?

Rob? Is it fair just running out on me like this at the end of the introduction?

CHAPTER 1.

THE IMPULSE TO FICTION

> Wash Me!
> —Traditional North American graffito written with fingertip on a dust-covered automobile.

This splendid and perennially hilarious inscription contains the basic transaction of written fiction in miniature. What is any writing, after all, but the dead object that mimics doing what we know perfectly well only human beings can do: use language?

The car's plaintive "Wash me!" actually goes further. It instantly both calls into being an elaborate self-consciousness—some "one" who is aware of being dirty, an undesirable state—and demands action from the reader. It creates a character and a relationship. The reader, asked for help, must process the request and choose to grant or refuse it. This is a text that, to put it in technical language, "messes with the head" of the reader.

For years now I've known what I want inscribed on my headstone: a single word. Each of its six characters is important to me, including the quotation marks that posit a speaker separate from the inscriber and the gumption-filled exclamation point. My epitaph: "Boo!"

So ... written netprov is very different from spoken improv?

Yes. First, the "speaker" of the written text is gone by the time you're reading it. It is very unusual to actually watch people as they write, seeing both the hands and the words. Even a rapid text-message exchange connects you to the writer of a moment ago rather than the writer of now. Second, text messages are the perfect example of another big difference between spoken and written improvisation: time to reflect and correct. Texting and posting offer time to sculpt, consider, edit. Third, messages can be written and read at your convenience—you don't have to all be in the same theater at the same time. This is what makes netprov perfect for busy lives.

These peculiarities of writing are what give rise to what electronic literature scholar Joe Tabbi calls the "minor literatures" we participate in all the time. You post a picture of your cat, aware of the tidal wave of cat pictures online, so your posting is not a serious cat picture; it is an ironic cat picture. But your cat is still soooo cute, and you love it soooo much! So it is also a serious cat picture. It's all of these things and more; it participates in the media universe the way works of art do.

When I look at it that way, I see that I post ridiculous, complex messages all the time; is that normal?

I know you do. That's why you're reading this book! Of course it's normal! Like you, we netprov players are unable to resist that opportunity.

In my earlier book, *Invisible Rendezvous*, I talked about "doing voices." This is something most of us do all the time in everyday conversation when we're telling stories involving other people. We'll say something like, "Then she's all [crosses arms, deepens voice], 'I don't know about that, we'll have to take it under consideration,' and he's all [higher, plaintive voice], 'But you promised at the last meeting.'"

Many people even have a character voice or two that they "do." Simply answering a call from a friend by saying cheerfully, "Joe's Pizza, may I take your order?" is a version of this impulse. This is fiction in miniature.

How did online character fiction start?

Among my favorite pioneers of building on the basic fiction impulse online were the first author-geniuses of Amazon product reviews. Back at its misty beginnings, reviewers were largely reverent and obedient, providing valuable information about themselves for free to Amazon as they provided information about products to other consumers. But before long, readers of Amazon reviews could read this seemingly innocuous review by Henry Raddick in 2002 of *Handbook of Meat Product Technology*: "[five stars] Tremendous. An admirably thorough guide to the tools of the production-line meat processing trade. The superb colour photographs particularly made it a perfect gift for my 15-year-old daughter who is showing alarming signs of not becoming vegetarian."[1]

These early creative reviews usually were organized in two forms. In the first, a single reviewer held court, such as Raddick, above, or Wayne Redhart, who has been producing what is essentially a series of brilliant satirical essays on Amazon for years. Often focusing on simple items such as a wig stand, Redhart goes into absurd detail and writes as though reviewing a symphony. The title of his digression upon Burt's Bees Nuts about Nature 3-Piece Gift Set is "Lacking in a cohesive premise," and it concludes: "All in all, the hand cream is pretty effective, if you like having soft hands. But unless you fear for your life/wish to frame someone for your impending suicide, then I think it would have been a lot better for all concerned, had they stuck with the initial coconut theme."[2]

The second strategy is a group game of hyperbole, with writers vying with one another to overpraise a simple or substandard item. Ironic reviews of camp, cult actor/singer David Hasselhoff's *Very Best Of* CD include "The best introduction to the most lavishly produced golden throat artist in recording history," written by reviewer Son of Flintstone Munchausen; "Breathtaking," by an anonymous reviewer; and "When life is locked, young Hasselhoff holds my key," by Da Peace Dog. The review "Let me recount a short tale," by H. Thompson, begins: "It was a quiet, iridescent night, as I walked, in a preternatural daze through a whispering, achingly old woodland glade somewhere half between this physical world and the next."[3]

Reviews of the radioactive uranium ore sample in Amazon's Industrial and Scientific category included, from Ellya: "I got a free cat in the box with this purchase but I'm not sure if I should open it to see if the cat is ok," referring to Heisenberg's famous uncertainty experiment; and from Patrick J. McGovern: "Great Product, Poor Packaging. I purchased this product 4.47 Billion years ago and when I opened it today, it was half empty."[4]

Try This: Mysterious Whiteboard Notes

Next time you find yourself in an empty meeting room or classroom with a whiteboard, write a set of perplexing notes (see figure 1). Write them in the typical style of the meeting notes of your organization but make them utterly weird—wild connections, incongruous dates and names, and absurd lists and priorities, with trivialities highlighted and underlined as though in the heat of a high-energy meeting. The goal is to make the next person who walks into the room go, "What the *hell* were they talking about in here?!" This whiteboard game contains the whole great gambit of serious literature in its basic gesture.

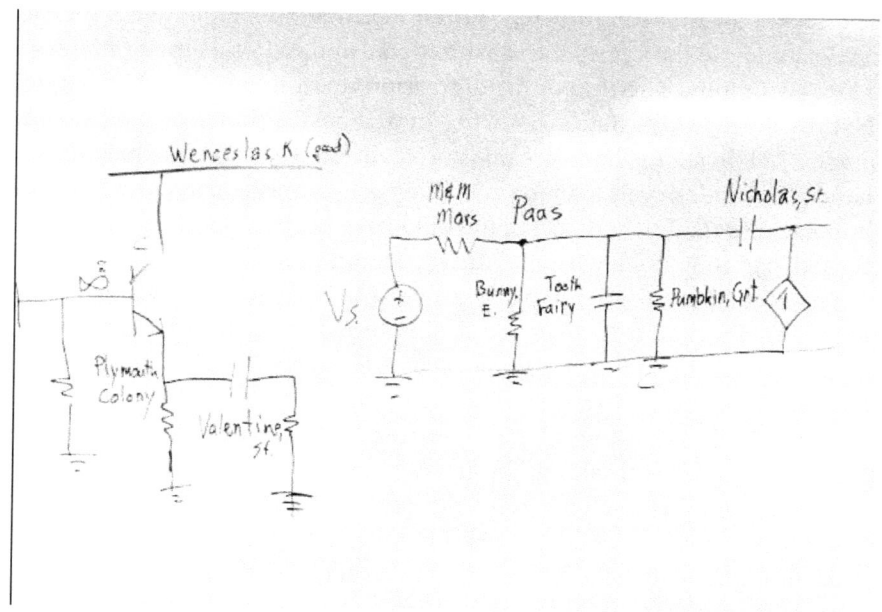

Figure 1. Mysterious whiteboard note left by Rob in a university classroom.

Where does that impulse to fiction come from?

Language learning begins as mimicry—and as relationship. We learn language by imitating mouth shapes and music—and being guided (gently or strictly) by corrections and rewards. We learn language by mimicking people with whom we have strong bonds: our earliest caregivers. But linguistic imitation is just a part of how we learn to be human. We imitate everything we see humans do: how they hold a spoon, how they sway to music, how they react to good news or bad news. In fact, we learn whether news is good or bad by their reaction.

So, our first relationship to spoken language is the effort to imitate a caregiver as faithfully as possible. This is our invisible linguistic foundation, our "accent." We have embarked on the first crucial period of "learning to do things right." Along with this comes a growing and haunting awareness that there is a difference between right and wrong, between the way things are and the way things "should" be. Then, as if that weren't enough, one precious day we are developmentally able to grasp that someone is making an intentional error for our delight.

How does humor actually develop in children?

According to developmental psychologist Paul McGhee,[5] a sense of humor starts at approximately eighteen to twenty-four months of age with simple substitution: "I'm going to wear the puppy as a hat" (gales of laughter). In the second stage of its development, at approximately two to three years of age, verbal jokes begin to appear, such as the pleasure of a naming error: "I'm the puppy. Rrrrrr!" In the third stage, at approximately three to five years of age, more distortion of reality is needed to get a laugh: "Puppy, can you drive us to the store?"

Finally, after the four- to five-year-old stage of development, marked by telling unfunny jokes as an enactment of the ritual of joke telling and its power to gather attention and create social bonds—playing at play—our brains grow enough to allow us to garner the cognitive delight of a real punch line with a real cognitive resolution. By the age of six or seven, the child's sense of humor begins to resemble an adult's, and we begin to delight in the stark, existential conundrum of puns. Puns, of course, undermine any sense of plan and order in the universe and bring us face to face with utter randomness—one word with two entirely unrelated meanings! What gods would allow such a horror?

The process of *getting a joke* models perfectly the process of seeing many netprovs in progress (at first thinking it is real then realizing it is not), understanding the game, and joining in.

Psychologist Michael Price writes that, for children, getting a joke

> requires that they first understand that a joke somehow deviates from the norm. . . . Second, children must understand that someone intended for this deviation to happen, that it wasn't just an error. Finally they must realize that the performer knows that the children think it's a joke. If all of these cognitive pieces are in place, cue the laugh track, the child gets the joke.[6]

The cognitive tension, the illogic, and the absurdity of someone doing a thing wrong on purpose creates so much microanxiety that, when the seeming danger is resolved by completing the circuit of human connection, the relief erupts as laughter.

Try This: Tweeting Too Hard

Grab something to write with and something to write on and play this simple netprov game. Read these three entries from the early website Tweeting Too Hard, "Where self-important tweets get the recognition they deserve," and write a tweet of your own in the same spirit!

1. "Just turned down the chance to do the keynote at an event to be held at MIT next year. Bummer! Sadly, just too much on (and it was unpaid)."
2. "I need another 5 white boards. My brilliance cannot be contained."
3. "Holy crap, I just saw my traffic. Are that many people looking at my humble little site? It's not even official yet."

OK, I know it's tempting just to keep reading instead of writing (my #book_stylings are just that good, or so my Twitter followers always tell me—stop it y'all!). But resist that temptation, set down the book for a moment, and actually write a Tweeting Too Hard. You didn't, did you?

How did you know I didn't actually try it?

Because I know it's unusual to stop in the middle of reading a book to write. But give it a go.

Wow, who knew it would be so much fun?

See? It was easier than you thought! In a world riddled with subtle power structures we don't dare call out (or else we feel we might lose our jobs or strain our family relationships), our imaginations leap to the chance to deflate pomposity and relieve some inner tension with a chuckle.

And then people go from telling jokes to creating characters?

Yep. From about the age of six begins the reign of make believe and roleplay—the "mimicry" of people and creatures who don't actually exist. This is the fiction-making impulse: "Rrrrrr, I'm an undead zombie puppy!" Then it is a simple step to go from the growing ability to recount real prior events at which the listener was not present to the recounting of events that did not happen, starring creatures who don't exist—"Puppy's Vacation in Italy"—which is the hallmark of fiction proper.

Fictional characters are funnier—and more powerful—the more they resemble the self-contradictory hot messes that are real people. Fictional characters that resemble specific people or classes of people can be used to say things that real-life power structures forbid. The puppy, held aloft as a puppet, can speak the unspeakable truth, can point out the elephant in the room—[high voice] "Daddy sure is grumpy today!"—and the puppeteer can immediately rebuke the puppet and claim for herself the ordinary decorum, "Puppy, no! How rude!" Purposeful mimicry is always political, to the exact degree of the power differential between the imitated and the imitator: "Puppy demands the house to himself for the afternoon. Puppy orders more shoes to chew!"

So then netprov comes from the same impulse as serious literature?

Absolutely. The genres we now take for granted were once experimental. Just look at the origins of the novel. As new technologies of book printing and distribution flourished, so did the novel. Early novels were essentially books playing make believe in a form usually used for transmitting information about the real world. We're now used to something called "a novel," but in the novel's early days it was hard to tell what was fiction and what wasn't.

A book considered among the earliest English novels was published in 1719, bearing this whopping title: *The Life and Surprising Adventures of Robinson Crusoe of York, Mariner: Who lived Eight and Twenty years all alone in an un-inhabited island on the Coast of America, near the mouth of the Great River of Oroonoque; Having been cast on Shore by Shipwreck, wherein all the Men perished but himself. WITH An Account how he was at last as strangely deliver'd by PYRATES*. The book was credited on its title page as being "Written by Himself"; in other words, by Robinson Crusoe. The actual author's name, Daniel Defoe, appears nowhere in the first edition. I use the work's original title here instead of the usual, misleading, abbreviated version to remind us how much explanation is required at first about new art forms.

Defoe's book was a thrilling, straight-faced, first-person account of a shipwrecked mariner who survives by his wits. And it was entirely imaginary, even though Defoe publicly insisted it was true for years after its publication. It was published shortly after an enormously popular account of a real shipwrecked mariner, Alexander Selkirk, caught the imagination of readers with its likely clever exaggerations and stretched truths. As art forms emerge, the line between fiction and nonfiction is renegotiated. "The novel is not just one kind of fictional narrative among others," writes literary historian Catherine Gallagher, "it is the kind in which and through which fictionality became manifest, explicit, widely understood and accepted."[7] The working definition of both fiction and nonfiction, she asserts, were forged by the novel. Gallagher points to a twenty-year period of transition.

> In England, between the time when Defoe insisted that Robinson Crusoe was a real individual (1720) and the time when Henry Fielding urged just as strenuously that his characters were not representations of actual specific people (1742), a discourse of fictionality appeared in and around the novel, specifying new rules for its identification and new modes of nonreference. . . . Later in the century, disclaimers like Fielding's were no longer necessary, for the public had been trained to read novels as stories about thoroughly imaginary (if representative) people, names without singular specific referents in the world.[8]

Defoe seems to have heard about Selkirk and felt the imaginative impulse to explore what being marooned on a deserted island was like as an experience—to mimic the writing of such a person, to take readers there as a thought experiment and invite them to learn from the adventure. But he felt readers wouldn't be able to take the book seriously unless it was real. What Fielding realized was that the culture was ready for a ghostly game of make believe in which nonbeings with everyday names were described in a naturalistic way. The result? As Gallagher describes it, readers and critics soon noticed that you could bond to an imaginary character with feelings as strong, or stronger, than those you feel for a real person. These characters enter your life experience as people; they become data points for your own decisions. And the whole process of disbelieving in the characters' reality makes you, the reader, look good.

How does fiction make me look good?

Gallagher points out that the subjects of many early novels were gullible characters, making mistakes that you, the reader, can see coming a mile away. "Hence, while sympathizing with innocent credulity," she writes, "the reader is trained in an attitude of disbelief, which is flattered as superior discernment."[9]

Oh, "I get it." (See what I did there, Rob?)

Well played! And why did this particular set of rules of the game about fiction develop at just this time and place? There are many factors, but I think Gallagher points correctly to the parallel development, at the time, of imaginative new forms of shady, speculative, financial profiteering and the risks they entail. These practices went on, of course, to become the foundations of our modern economy. She connects these new financial risks with the increasing risks of personal life.

> Since marriageable young people were given somewhat greater freedom of choice starting in the eighteenth century, and were also expected to have a genuine emotional attachment to their spouses, some form of affective speculation became necessary. Women especially would need to be able to imagine what it would be like to love a particular man without committing themselves, for loving a man before he had proposed was still considered highly improper.[10]

The "what if" of fiction is more than just escape. It can be a vital testing ground to process decisions in an increasingly unpredictable world.

But isn't it important that readers know who the real author is?

Authorship is a tricky thing. We tend to think that one work has one author who goes by one name. But right from the beginning, things get problematic. Many scholars believe there was no Homer, author of the *The Odyssey* and *The Iliad* and supposed anchor and founder of Western literature. Instead, they believe, Homer was a loose franchise or guild of storytellers who traveled independently and who collectively created long stories subdivided into exciting, one-night-of-entertainment-sized episodes. Lao-tzu, literally "Old Master," the author of the foundational book of Taoist wisdom, the *Tao Te Ching*, is thought to be a handy way to brand a "best of" collection of wisdom by numerous authors of even earlier centuries in China. Feminist scholarship shows us the large number of uncredited contributions made by wives and girlfriends to supposedly male, single-author works.

Before the mid-nineteenth century—that is, before enforceable copyright laws—the world of print was remarkably similar to the digital networks of today. Fake novels, purportedly by famous authors, abounded alongside garbled, pirate editions of popular stories, false news reports, and baseless conspiracy theories designed to influence politics or the market.

Except for a window of semireliability barely more than one hundred years long and ending with the advent of the World Wide Web, the perennial warning for any perusal of published matter has been "reader beware!"

I will look at the ethics of fictionizing in more detail in chapter 5, "Satirical, Situational Netprovs." But for now, yes, genuinely fake web communications do exist, and yes, sometimes for nefarious ends. The US presidential elections of 2016 and 2020, and their hoarse shouts and counter shouts of "fake news," are just one example. Serious journalists, consumer protection agencies, and educators such as Howard Rheingold with his continuously updated collection of "Crap Detection Resources" assist in seeing through the fog of unscrupulous shams and scams.[11]

Side by side with these frauds, however, are a spectrum of fake websites and fake accounts created for aesthetic rather than criminal purposes.

Are there degrees of "fakeness"?

I like to think of "literary fakeness" in terms of time: the amount of time creators want their readers to believe in the fake before they realize it *is* fake. This timing is accomplished by subtle adjustments to the plausibility of the writing and the graphic design. Relatively longer times I refer to as belonging to "deadpan" sites while relatively faster times belong to "with-a-wink" sites. How long would it take you to see through the following stellar examples from the early days of netprov?:

> Looking for expertise in male pregnancy? You'll have to dig for it among the barrage of plausible stock med-business imagery, but you'll find it at the deadpan RYT Hospital Dwayne Medical Center.[12]

> Disturbed at finding dihydrogen monoxide (DHMO) in your home? You'll be surprised: this colorless, odorless liquid compound is found just about everywhere. The less deadpan DHMO Research Division, managed by creator Tom Way, can calm your fears at http://www.dhmo.org/.[13] (DHMO is also sometimes written H20.)

> Are you looking for a church where the worthwhile worship and the unsaved are unwelcome? Are you "Conservative, Godly, Republican and Unstoppable?" Then creator Chris Harper's Landover Baptist Church,

with its heavily mascaraed eye winking strongly, is for you! Find it at http://www.landoverbaptist.org.[14]

Landover fixture Betty Bowers, by her own admission "America's Best Christian," is so incredibly godly she has her own spin-off site, http://www.bettybowers.com/.[15] Building on the rich transvestite theatrical tradition of the drag scene and drag queens—particularly the critically self-aware, postmodern drag movement that began in the 1980s and produced writer-actor characters such as RuPaul and Vaginal Davis—*Betty Bowers*, written and acted by Paul A. Bradley, can be seen as an ongoing, single-character netprov in the queer performance tradition.

One of the first fictional blogs to gain recognition as such—despite early reactions from readers who weren't sure if it was fake or not—was *She's a Flight Risk*.[16] This blog diary of a self-described "international fugitive" named isabella v. unrolled in real time and now is archived with an overview introduction. *Lonelygirl15* was a fictional YouTube video blog relating the trials and tribulations of a heartbroken teenager.[17] It drew hundreds of thousands of followers as a "real" blog and then used the revelation of its fictionality as a marketing tactic. It grew into a transmedia microempire with connections to the television industry.

Masquerading as video instruction for Photoshop users, the miserable life of "Donnie" comes leaking out in passive-aggressive chunks in the hilarious series *You Suck at Photoshop*, designed by Troy Hitch and Matt Bledsoe and recorded with simple, desktop-video-capture software.[18] Imitating the profusion of amateur instructional videos covering activities from music to sports to software, *You Suck at Photoshop* sets as its goal to both legitimately teach one pro trick of the graphic-design software Photoshop in each brief episode and tell Donnie's story at the same time. Donnie lets his personal life leak out in the image files he chooses (his ex-wife's car that he vandalizes in Photoshop) and in his conversations with an obnoxious buddy who intrudes in chat on the desktop. The joke works because Donnie's desktop looks so lifelike in its design and typography.

Media artist and programmer Eric Loyer does inspiring, digital explorations and extensions of the possibilities for readers to interact with text and image. Characters in Loyer's storytelling apps such as *Upgrade Soul*, an immersive science fiction graphic novel for tablet and phone, are constantly playing with the very novelty of their formal containers.[19] As he describes himself and his work, "I make stories you play like instruments, and instruments for telling stories."

Even in the older print tradition, the supposedly spontaneous, first-person narrator has the effect of calling attention to the materiality and temporality of writing. Just a moment, dear reader—I'll be right back. I'm dehydrated and need a drink. Hang on.

Are you OK, Rob?

Phew! Better; thanks for asking.

So what *is* the connection between the novel and online writing?

Instant publishing caught people by surprise. The fact that a blog—written as an intimate, private journal—could technically be read by anyone with World Wide Web access didn't really register with many early bloggers (and usually wasn't an issue). Awareness of the wide reach of digital publishing technologies consistently lagged behind the assumption of privacy inherent in confessional writing in the web 1.0 era and well into the social media explosion. But by blurring the lines between private journaling and publishing, bloggers and posters were also renegotiating the boundaries between fact and fiction.

As Catherine Gallagher points out, one of the key signs of fictionality "appears when the narrator depicts the subjectivity or the consciousness of a character."[20] The plain and frustrating fact that we know others have thoughts and feelings *but we don't know what they are* is as profound a developmental discovery as the rippling humor of the puppy who talks. What on earth is puppy *really* thinking? Third-person novelists know more about what's going on inside their characters than anyone can. Texts that demonstrate this are instantly recognizable as works of imagination.

Then, to read a first-person diary that is so private and so revealing that no ordinary person would share it by social convention is also a sign of fictionality. "I am a sick man. . . . I am a spiteful man. I am an unattractive man. I believe my liver is diseased."[21] These are the legendary first lines of Dostoevsky's *Notes from the Underground*, which signal us we are in for a fascinating, rough ride. But wait. No, these are not the first lines of the book. The actual first lines are: "The author of the diary and the diary itself are, of course, imaginary. Nevertheless it is clear that such persons as the writer of these notes not only may, but positively must, exist in our society," which amount to the same thing.[22]

When bloggers began to share "too much information," as the wonderful saying goes (often accompanied by a comic covering of the ears), they wandered into the boundary zone between fiction and nonfiction. When do "painting myself in a good light" or "exaggerating for dramatic effect," actions done constantly in everyday conversation and social media, become lying? How far does the exaggeration need to go before it is instantly recognizable as invention?

So even though novels are about imaginary people, they still are made out of things noticed in real life?

The first novels were. Writers drew from life. But then ... (sigh).

But then, what?

The thing happened that always happens in all art forms. Writers begin to write novels imitating other novels that were imitating other novels. People began to teach that there are rules for novel-writing—right ways and wrong ways to go about it. This produced a reliable pipeline of publishing product, but the freshness of the early, observation-based novels gradually got lost.

There are no hard-and-fast rules for art. If it works, it works. The minute you say a genre is dead, someone does something awesome in it. But genres can get into ruts, so it always pays to know where you are in the life cycle of a genre. Right now, novels are really, really old in comparative terms. There are certain joys to be found in an older art form. You can play with all the rich conventions, echoing them or breaking their rules. You can be minimal, since everyone more or less knows what's coming. You can do "cover versions" of earlier novels, adding current irony and historical contrasts. But, on the downside, in an older art form there is a lot of pure repetition: the same novel being published hundreds of times a year, year after year.

Where does the energy come from for new art forms?

The fine observer of creative cultures, Henry Jenkins, describes in *Convergence Culture* a large-scale rhythm of high-culture borrowings from, and contributions to, popular culture: "The older American folk culture was built on borrowings from various mother countries; the modern mass media builds upon borrowings from folk culture, the new convergence culture will be built on borrowings from various media conglomerates."[23]

But here I think Jenkins is missing another tributary flowing into his convergence culture: the exercise you just did when you tweeted too hard: the direct fictionalization of vernacular nonfiction communications. As you can probably tell by now, I'm a big fan of that first moment of artistic innovation when an artist notices a new mode of communications used "for real" and decides to fictionalize it. I find it daring, fresh, and insightful.

My personal preference is to be wary of the perennial attempt to legitimize a new art form by parroting the style of the older art form in a new technology. This always happens when new technologies enter the scene. Early attempts at art photography had models dressed in historical garb posed dutifully as though they were in a painting. The sharp focus of photography, considered ugly by those used to the soft lines of oil painting, was purposely blurred to look appropriately "artistic." It took decades for crusading photographers to insist on the new beauty of the sharp focus and other delights of the medium we now take for granted.

In writing, we all know there are vocabulary choices and sentence structures that sound "poetic" and signal to the reader a membership in the long, poetic tradition, thereby wangling a special status for the author. It's a fine line, but I find a difference between mimicking for a generous comic or satiric effect and mimicking in order to recuperate prestige for the writer. To me, it sometimes seems like a way of blackmailing readers into granting status to works. I prefer to search for new beauty in the new vernacular forms.[24]

Nonetheless, there is a ton of fun to be had taking an established art form and transporting it into a new venue with an ironic attitude. This can be a variation on the old principle of high-status/low-status comedy, since established art forms tend to be associated with the rich and powerful and new media can often have a grassroots feel. People have divided entire novels and plays into tweets and posted them, for the thrill and giggle of the "wrongness" of the publication venue. The gesture resembles how comedians such as Russell Brand practice speaking in a "high culture," ultra-literary way about banal or crude topics, using absurdly bookish sentence structure and vocabulary or the reverse; Brand titled his autobiography *My Booky Wook*.[25]

Try This: Friction Becomes Fiction

Here's a great way to feed the frustrations of your unpredictable world into your netprov writing. The creative process is more than filling a blank page with markings. That is the output phase. Equally important, and much less discussed, is the input phase, the activity of "noticing." Take seriously those little stress points of life, the things that make you laugh and shake your head—curious patterns of behavior among friends, weirdly self-sabotaging communications, things in your world that have disappeared or are suddenly omnipresent. There are no rights and wrongs in noticing—a thing either intrigues you or it doesn't. Collect what intrigues you. Netprov players find ways of keeping these half ideas and quarter ideas in notebooks, sketchbooks, and cameras. Whole ideas—good ideas—are most often built from combining these halves and quarters of things you've noticed.

Step one: look for places where human friction occurs in writing. The angry note left under the windshield wiper, the garbled spam attempt to get your bank info, the family member's text message so deeply coded as to be unintelligible to outsiders—all are begging to be mimicked. Try to find places where people write that haven't been widely fictionalized yet: the guest book at a bed and breakfast, the feedback card at the chain restaurant table. Pay particular attention to new media venues for writing: a chat within a game or a photo-sharing site, for example, or review threads on a travel site or shopping site. Look at what you do on your phone all day: there's something there for sure!

Step two: take this moment of written friction and fictionalize it! Invent a character who gets tangled in the phenomenon you've noticed. Write five messages and see what develops.

EXAMPLE 1: *THE BALLAD OF WORKSTUDY SETH, A NETPROV*

An Impulse to Fiction Becomes a Character

One fine day in March of 2009, followers of University of Southern California writing professor Mark Marino's Twitter account read this unassuming series of posts:

> Mark C Marino, @markcmarino, March 6, 2009
> @markcmarino just hired me as his 'social networking' assisstant, sez all i have to do is witter, facebook, & bookmarx. its a resume builder, seth

> Mark C Marino, @markcmarino, March 6, 2009
> sez i can call him coach, he calls me seth youtube. my names seth yoo. he seems to think he invented that joke, best not pop that bubble

> Mark C Marino, @markcmarino, March 6, 2009
> haz not made real clear my job duties, but sez i might have to give up some evenings cuz he thinks its better to update late at night (sy)

> Mark C Marino, @markcmarino, March 6, 2009
> doz not seem to ve cleaned this office in 6-7 semesters, random memo from faculty meeting May 05 i found on hiz desk, not my job 2 care (sy)

Thus was born Seth, or more properly Workstudy Seth, fictional protagonist of a three-month long netprov[j] archived and republished as *The Ballad of Workstudy Seth.*[1]

Workstudy Seth appears to log hours working for Marino in dribs and drabs, but then comes spring break, the netprov's second sequence, and Seth takes his work laptop on the road to Cabo San Lucas, the notorious Mexican party spot. He gets rerouted to Phoenix, Arizona, and there begins an intense story that unrolls over several days. Seth runs out of money, tries to get more through Marino's various online bank accounts, then falls in with an apparently appealing young Luddite named Noe, who leads Seth to the edge of the Grand Canyon and to the edge of Seth's attachment and addiction to social media. There is a group gathered at the canyon's rim preparing to throw their electronic devices into the dusty deep:

> Mark C Marino, @markcmarino, March 19, 2009
> tonite Noe sez we're all supposd to throw our tech into the canyun & dance! i askd where r we goin 2 get music w/o our ipodz? #workstudyseth

> Mark C Marino, @markcmarino, March 19, 2009
> hav 2 sneek 2 rangr stashun 2 get any kind of reception out here – plus theyre alwayz watchin 4 piopl sneakin a tech moment #workstudyseth

> Mark C Marino, @markcmarino, March 19, 2009
> its hard 4 them 2 keep lookoutz, have 2 use smoke signalz, very inefficient, tho they alwayz hav serviz -cept when it rainz #workstudyseth

> Mark C Marino, @markcmarino, March 19, 2009
> all the piopl here have sorry storiez.. everyone has lost someone they lovd 2 social networkin #workstudyseth

Readers follow Seth's agony as the time approaches for him to renounce electronic posts and hurl his social connectivity into the void. Will he? Won't he?

The canyon story sets Workstudy Seth apart from the typical single character Twitter netprov. In it, Marino's style gets more concentrated, more, well, literary. With direct references to Australian electronic literature titan Mez and her mezangelle style (which I'll talk about more in chapter 6), Marino crafts a hybrid of alphabet-efficient, texting slang and poetic practice. Seth's descriptions of the strange scene he observes and his inner turmoil become more vivid.

> Mark C Marino, @markcmarino, March 20, 2009
> u shlld c theze piopl—when they toss over ther Blakberriez, iPlods, zunes, mac heirs, notebookz, odesseyz,—#bliss #workstudyseth

> Mark C Marino, @markcmarino, March 20, 2009
> wonderz do i thro my asus eee (so small&sweet) in the canyun or do i juzt go back 2 So-Cal & tweet & feed in my web2.0 cell? #workstudyseth

Writing for his subscriber audience of fellow electronic literature writers and scholars, Marino need do nothing more than suggest the deep theoretical and historical waters into which Seth peers from his cliff top. The light touch keeps this second sequence perfectly balanced between narrative and theory.

The canyon sequence ends in a silence, which a fictional "Mark Marino" breaks only to begin the third sequence, wherein Marino tries to repair the damage done by Workstudy Seth and begins to detail his university's judicial review of Marino as the party responsible for Seth's social-networking indiscretions.

Here this netprov goes from being merely good to being important. At this point, friends and colleagues of Marino's (including Mez herself) began to tune in and take seriously Marino's supposed tussle with the administration. The fiction had hit home.

> Mark C Marino, @markcmarino, March 23, 2009
> For reasons that I think are pretty obvious, there may be no further status updates from my workstudy student Seth. Apologies.

> Mark C Marino, @markcmarino, March 23, 2009
> apologizes for some of these posts under the moniker #workstudyseth. This is a real mess that I hope to clean up over the next few days.[2]

At this point a post appears in the *Chronicle of Higher Education*'s blog *Wired Campus*, detailing Marino's project.[3] A careful reader of the piece will tune in to the fictional nature of the game, but the journalist Jeff Young's lead is the idea of a professor hiring a work-study student to tweet on his behalf, and some readers missed the clue. In a delicious period of vertigo, Marino had to ask himself the questions that accompany authentic experiments with fiction: Should I tell them it's fiction? Should I let it ride? To his delight, colleagues still occasionally ask him: Was that Seth thing real?

But there's more! Sequence four begins with Marino accepting applications for a new social media work-study student and winds up with the bland copycat reTweetPete who, predictably, does nothing but repeat other tweets and is unutterably boring compared to Seth.

And then, praise the gods, Seth hacks into Marino's account for one last, astonishing hurrah, and we're into sequence five. It turns out that reTweetPete annoyed Seth more than anyone else. Seth strikes a blow for intelligence and urgency in electronic communication (and he tells the end of the canyon story for good measure) in a flurry of poetic messages.

After some gorgeous sequences of ASCII gibberish as Marino and Seth battle for control of the account, Marino finally manages to eject Seth and reemerges in his own voice in this wonderfully rhythmic sequence:

Mark C Marino, @markcmarino, April 13, 2009
Hi

Mark C Marino, @markcmarino, April 13, 2009
Hi, the real

Mark C Marino, @markcmarino, April 13, 2009
Hi, th3 $$ real Mark

Mark C Marino, @markcmarino, April 13, 2009
Hi, the real Mark Marino here

Mark C Marino, @markcmarino, April 13, 2009
Hi, 7he real Mark Marino *$^here breaking into

Mark C Marino, @markcmarino, April 13, 2009
Hi, the real Mark Marino here breaking into my own account using Tweetdeck Pro Tool! Whew! I'm back in. And #workstudyseth is out at last![4]

Reading *Workstudy Seth* was a breakthrough for me. The piece swept me off my feet and confirmed my intuition: real-time Internet improv can be high art. As I followed it, post by post, I loved the breezy fluidity with which Marino changes from sequence to sequence—from narrative strategy to narrative strategy. My literature radar was going wild; the piece has the unmistakable feel of a landmark work done early in the "fictionalization" of a vernacular form, when there are yet no conventions and no canon, a work that blazes the trail.

Marino seems to just follow his wit wherever it leads, trying a bit of this approach and a bit of that. His casual willingness to ask "what if?" and the joyous brilliance with which his imagination answers are delightful. It's the feeling that he and his characters are simply following their impulses in a search for intense communication and understanding of the world—combined with high literary skill—that makes this netprov so memorable.

CHAPTER 2.

SOLO NETPROVS

Minutes after the NASA robot rover Curiosity landed on Mars, these tweets appeared:

> The Surface of Mars, @surfaceofmars, August 5, 2012
> Whoa! What the hell just happened?

> The Surface of Mars, @surfaceofmars, August 5, 2012
> Do I have something on me?

Whenever a new communication technology such as Twitter emerges, before long someone will have the impulse to make a fictional move like @surfaceofmars, which is a basic, one-author, one-character, solo netprov.

What kinds of netprovs can you do on your own?

@bronxzooscobra purported to be tweets from an Egyptian cobra that had escaped the Bronx Zoo in New York City. Within the first few hours, the cobra's ghost writer had helped the netprov leap from mimicry to biting social satire:

> Bronx Zoo's Cobra, @BronxZoosCobra, March 28, 2011
> Want to clear up a misconception. I'm not poisonous as has been reported. I'm venomous. Super venomous, but not poisonous so don't worry.

Bronx Zoo's Cobra, @BronxZoosCobra, March 28, 2011
A lot of people are asking how I can tweet with no access to a computer or fingers. Ever heard of an iPhone? Duh.

Bronx Zoo's Cobra, @BronxZoosCobra, March 28, 2011
What does it take to get a cab in this city?! It's cause I'm not white isn't it.

Solo netprovs can be as simple as a single post in a comment thread or as rich as a fictional blog that lasts for years. Solo netprovs can be posted under the author's own name or they can be an elaborate, fictional persona complete with avatar, a profile, and a separate account.

Some solo netprovs emerge imperceptibly from the texture of everyday communications, building on common, usually unseen, linguistic strategies of irony, exaggeration, and "doing voices." Not every pet on social media can boast the 2.4 million or so followers of the late, legendary Grumpy Cat, but hundreds of thousands of them cavort and wheedle for the entertainment of small networks of family and friends. On the subtlest level, writer after writer adopts a social media persona in their own name just absurdly irascible enough that friends can read it as self-effacingly ironic at the same time as it satirizes others who hold those opinions for real.

Other solo netprovs build out of new, casual cultural forms, such as the YouTube genre of "let's play" videos where gamers record a video game session on-screen while narrating into a headset microphone. The form is usually used for some combination of giving advice on game skills, exulting, bemoaning, and bragging. In the hands of popular young-adult author John Green (*The Fault in Our Stars*), his series of "let's plays" concerning the exploits of his video game soccer team—officially the real-life AFC Wimbledon, redubbed by Green the Wimbly Womblies—became a weekly soap opera. As he played and talked, Green improvised elaborate, off-field backstories of his user-created players and recounted the pep talks and life advice he had just given them before the digital game. For a time, the narrative focused primarily on goal-scoring legends Bald John Green and Other John Green, a married gay couple with their fair share of thrilling subplots.

Do people do more traditional-style literature as netprov?

A fun example of a displaced literary style in a netprov is Dan Sinker's Twitter project @MayorEmanuel, which was published in book form in

2011.[1] Sinker's use of recognizably literary, bookish vocabulary and sentence structure in his tweets is a way of insisting on the literary status of his project. In this scene, the fictionalized politician Rahm Emanuel, known for his real-life, foul-mouthed tirades, joins then mayor Richard M. Daley (son of legendary Chicago mayor Richard J. Daley) for a tour of city hall:

> Rahm Emanuel, @MayorEmanuel, February 21
> And Daley's gesturing for me to follow him, and suddenly we're out a window and heading up a motherfucking fire escape.
>
> Rahm Emanuel, @MayorEmanuel, February 21
> We're on the roof of City Hall. The wind is fucking strong and the snow stings when it hits my face. Daley heads into a glass dome.
>
> Rahm Emanuel, @MayorEmanuel, February 21
> It's so warm and beautiful in the dome—green everywhere—and the air is pungent with the smell of . . . is that fucking celery?
>
> Rahm Emanuel, @MayorEmanuel, February 21
> And it's then that I notice for the first fucking time that, nestled amid the stalks of celery, are three modest headstones.
>
> Rahm Emanuel, @MayorEmanuel, February 21
> Daley points to the headstones. "They're here with us, always. Harrison, Washington, Dad." He chokes up on that last one.

Writing styles can migrate from high culture to low culture (from novels to Twitter in the case of @MayorEmanuel), but new voices in writing just as often migrate from low to high, from marginal to mainstream. New styles can enter literature despite the fact that they are being satirized. To put it another way, when creative writers experiment with new styles and new voices, they are inviting guest writers to write in their official accounts as in *Workstudy Seth*.

How do I go about creating a solo netprov character?

The advice Mark Marino gave to participants in the netprov *Air-B-N-Me* is very useful:

> Create a character. . . . Base them on yourself, someone you know, or someone you're just imagining. This is an opportunity to play on the

kinds of folks who fill our world and also to reflect on our own troubles dealing with the moments of our lives.

Note: Be sensitive. You can be comical or satirical, but be careful when creating characters in an online community like this. These characters are representations of other people, perhaps the very same people you are playing with. Especially be careful when creating characters who live with vulnerable status.[2]

Mark and I always encourage netprov players who are playing satirical characters and enjoying the comedy that comes from differences in status to "punch up, not down." Deflate the puffy pomposity of the elite; don't tease the disadvantaged.

Choose an avatar image for your account that represents the mode of your character; is it very realistic? Is it silly? Remember to be sensitive about society's power structures around race and gender if you're playing a character different from your own. Avoiding stereotypes both produces better art and reduces the chance of offending. Remember that illustrations and "artsy" or abstract images can often be more evocative (and funnier) than photos.

It's a fun starting point to consciously set about to break a stereotype, to give a character one random attribute: a hidden skill or a surprising background. We all know that these unexpected elements are much more like real life anyway. If your platform allows you to choose your type font, choose one that supports your character—either one that is just right for them or exactly wrong.

Does the choice of type font really make that much difference?

Yes. We're talking about writing. Writing is visible language. The look of visible language matters. The fact that in networked media our writing is instantly set in type is one of the most important, but now unnoticed, changes it enacted. Viewed historically, typesetting is power. To write directly into type constitutes an upheaval in status, a seizing of power.

Typography is power?

Let's remember the desktop publishing revolution and the web revolution. Before the early 1990s, typeset text was the exclusive province of those who could afford expensive typesetting equipment. A recognizable and basically consistent system of printing, publishing, and distribution had been in existence at that time for over two hundred years. The owners of these means of production (printers and publishers) provided a gatekeeping function, exercising judgment over whose text merited the cost of typography. Typeset text therefore carried an automatic aura of authority. Few would pay to print nonsense.

Around 1990, however, the combination of new desktop printing and new what you see is what you get (WYSIWYG) word-processing programs meant, effectively, that typesetting was available to many more people at a drastically lower production cost. Cultural inertia continued to give typeset text an aura of authority, but the gatekeeping function gradually fell away.

Then, as we know, thousands, tens of thousands, and eventually millions of people began to self-publish without the traditional gatekeepers. The result? Any text can parade around in typography designed exclusively for the prestigious newspaper *The Times* of London spouting any idiocy!

Our culture hardly has begun to catch up with the change this self-publishing revolution represents. News websites such as the *New York Times* and *Politico* still ape the black-on-white design of printed newspapers, but that reference will eventually fade as web-born designs establish their own authority. What concerns netprov, however, is a set of phenomena that were an almost immediate side effect of the expanding use of Tim Berners-Lee's physics-paper-sharing system he called the World Wide Web. People began pouring their hearts out into it. The design conventions of the print world translated poorly into the new medium, so (as always happens at the infancy of new technologies) despite designers' attempts to reproduce the "look of authority," they wound up creating new graphic looks that were initially unattached to any cultural norms.

What was the result of these new typographic "looks?"

Along with these new norms came a new relationship between writer and reader. The worlds of the Internet and personal and social media are fundamentally marked by the common feature of interactivity—the ability to register an immediate reaction in the form of likes, favorites, comments, etc. or to directly contact the creator. This levels the power hierarchies found in other worlds, such as literature's meritocracy and mass media's celebritocracy. The power to publish an immediate response in this world is assumed as a right.

The big contribution to netprov from the cultural worlds of the Internet, and personal and social media, is the proliferation of subcultures of participation and collaboration on which many netprovs are founded. No other cultural sphere allows creators to satirize giant advertising corporations, such as Facebook, from within their own systems (at least as of this writing).

Try This: Naming Your Character

Literary historian Catherine Gallagher points out the importance of characters' names in the development of the novel. The earlier style featured names that gave you a head start to understanding the character. Thomas Love Peacock's gloomy protagonist Mr. Glowry and his servants Graves and Deathshead welcome guests such as the judgmental Mr. Toobad and the droopy Mr. Listless to their home, Nightmare Abbey, in the volume of the same name.[3]

An interesting possibility in the digital age is the common practice of using fanciful and descriptive pseudonyms such as @spatialamerica and @NoGodsNoMisters. This means that netprov players can create names that are both quick introductions to a character and at the same time are utterly plausible. We live more in Peacock's world than in Jane Austen's.

Look for styles of pseudonyms and avatars in the platforms you play in. How can you use them to intensify your characters?

But the text and image limits of social media are so random. How does that make literature?

You're crediting the forms of the past with being intentional. They were random too. Random technical limitations often become art forms. The practical length of scrolls in the ancient world created divisions in the text we call books or chapters. The size and cliff-hanger structure of Dickens's story sections was dictated by the fact that each chapter was published separately in magazines and constituted a TV-show-length evening's entertainment when read aloud.

In our era, Twitter's original, draconian 140-character limit is an example of how the technical limitations of Internet, social media, and personal media formats serve, wittingly or unwittingly, as literary forms. YouTube's early ten-minute film limit for most users spawned a ten-minute-film explosion. Instagram's automatic photo resizing and square cropping has created a de facto default for images. Any of these standards, which were created by engineers for engineering and marketing purposes, becomes a new form for literature once they have been fictionalized.

What platform should I choose for my netprov, if design matters that much?

The short answer is: let laughter and tears be your guide. If you're planning a comedy netprov, choose the medium that's the funniest for your idea. If you're planning a serious netprov, go for the one that's the most moving.

The cuckoo bird is known for laying its eggs in other birds' nests. Netprov netrunners are the cuckoo birds of technology. We play in other birds' platforms. Electronic literature poet and scholar Leonardo Flores proposed in a talk given at the 2018 Electronic Literature Conference in Montreal that we are now in a "third generation" of electronic literature.[4] Building on the work of N. Katherine Hayles, Christopher Funkhouser, and others, Flores defines the three generations or waves of electronic literature as follows:

- First (1952–1995) is preweb experimentation with electronic and digital media.
- Second (1995–present) are innovative works created with custom interfaces and forms.
- Third (circa 2005–present) uses established platforms with massive user bases[5]

Netprov, along with other third-generation creations, in Flores's terms, "builds upon existing forms; adopts existing interfaces," and "readers are familiar with the platform; works circulate where the audience is." In other words, we third-generation collaborative writers are a bit cuckoo.

The kinds of questions that Mark Marino and I ask when planning a netprov are: Is it private or public? Is it more powerful as a stand-alone website or a community forum? Is it more powerful as a project in the heart of a bigger, existing platform, such as Facebook or Instagram? Is it for people using their own main account? Fictional accounts? Multiple accounts? With your own list of parameters, you'll be able to choose a good platform.

Now that I've got a character and a platform, how do I get started?

Make a character sheet that contains the basic demographics about your character and some notes about their personality. Are they cheerful, mopey, high achieving, or low energy? It's useful to ask a couple of classic screenwriter's questions: What does this character want and what stands in the way of them getting it?

Then try four or five practice posts to get a sense of how your character writes. Do they use long, literary sentences or text-message shorthand? At this stage of our netprovs, Mark Marino, the featured players, and I often create a private practice space, a simple threaded discussion where we try out our characters together and get a sense of their voices. The best of the practice posts can simply be copied and pasted into the public platform once the netprov is launched.

Try This: Be an Unreliable Narrator

There is a lot of great humor (and insight) to be gained by playing a sincere-but-clueless narrator. Narrators can doubt themselves: "Here's the way it happened. No wait. Maybe that happened later." Narrators can misinterpret others' motives: "They loved me so much they made me king of the party, King Doonsie (spelled 'Dunce')! They put a big cone hat on me and everybody was laughing and carrying on and we had a splendid time!" Narrators can reveal the hidden mechanics of their craft. "Comedy works in threes, so this third example of the unreliable narrator has to be the funniest. But I don't think it is. In fact this example is terrible. Darn it!"

You were on a roll there and then you lost it with your third example. What happened?

I'm OK. I'm OK.

I know writers are supposed to think about their audience; what if people come into my netprov in the middle and don't read everything I write?

That's a great question. Take a deep breath, sit down, and I'll give you the answer, which is a bit harsh (fair warning). The idea that readers read everything, and read in the right order, is a long-standing myth dating to the beginning of the book era. People have always skipped around and skipped over things. These days, reading and writing now take place in dozens of tiny moments intermixed with other activities throughout the day. Rather than always spending blocks of time watching a play or reading a book, people follow narratives—real and fictional—in micro moments woven into other behaviors.

Among partners and friends there may be a sense of completeness to communication—wanting to be sure to read every message in an exchange so as not to miss important information. But in the types of more emotionally distant communication we call "news" or "entertainment," there is not always a feeling of necessity to see *every* update, to view *every* episode. Readers often seek "just enough" to catch the gist of a story.

For example, the amazing fact that streaming media can remember where you left off in a TV series has radically changed our time experience. The misnomer "binge-watching" doesn't begin to capture the effect. There is now an assumption that all digital communications will always be available, migrating from platform to platform, and therefore that a complete viewing can be indefinitely postponed until some future time.

And people are often "on" two or three screens at once, if you include smartphones, right?

Good point. Attention is infinitely interruptible. The solution, for an author, to the problem of incomplete reading is twofold. First, you have to let yourself be emotionally OK with incomplete readings. Some reading of your work is better than no reading of your work. But this sobering truth has a wonderful silver lining. If you can train yourself to get your biggest intrinsic reward for creative activity from the *making*, from the playful thrill of writing itself, climaxing with hitting the "send" button, you'll always win. If your enjoyment comes from the making, you can treat the number of views, likes, and reposts as optional—as bonus points. Easy to say, hard to do, I know, but worth the effort.

Second, I recommend that netprov players write in what I call a *holographic* way. If you cut a hologram in half, you can still see the whole image, you just have to move your head around more to "look through" the "smaller opening." Holograms record multiple copies of the entire image all over the image surface. When we do netprovs, we look for ways to retell the basic premise frequently and catch up new readers on the progression of the story at many points during the run. Some netprov is good. More netprov is better. Netprov can thrive in a world of episodic and incomplete reading.

Try This: Character Creation: Too Much Information: Go For It!

I'm writing this part of the book on my laptop in the back stairwell at work. It's one of the few places I can get any peace and quiet. The sharing of too much information in blogs and social media is a phenomenon that has been noticed since the early days. A narrator with loose lips can paint pictures of not just their own psychology of denial but complexities about relationships. One of the uses of fiction is to lift the curtain on private moments and prove to us that we're not alone in what we think and feel. I hear footsteps on the stairs. I'd better scram.

EXAMPLE 2: *ALL-TIME HIGH*, A NETPROV

A Playground for Playing Multiple Characters

The promotional email for the ambitious netprov *All-Time High*[i] began with an invitation and examples:

> You don't fit in? None of us fit in! New netprov running all month: *All-Time High*. Impersonate your high school self (or any high schooler ever) and meet us in the halls at [Twitter hashtag] #ATH15

> @unbearablerightness July 1, 2015
> This 18th century midwife in my Algebra II class gave me a GREAT cure for acne! Downside: u need a live frog

> @thereal_Charles_Darwin July 1, 2015
> How the devil did I get here? And what on earth is "AP Bio?"

All-Time High, a netprov, consumed numerous imaginations for a month and generated an amount of creative writing equivalent to a four-hundred-page novel.[1] Creators Claire Donato and Jeff T. Johnson, in the guise of their collaboration Atelier Spatial America (which followed in the wake of their performance collaboration Special America), worked with Mark Marino and me as netrunners on the project.

"In *All-Time High* we find ourselves—our own high school-age selves—all together at the same high school in July of 2015," began the full invitation. It continued:

> What a freaking nightmare, right?! And yet, what an opportunity. For comedy, if nothing else.
> We play out the differences (generational, geographical, subcultural) and the commonalities (stress, sugar, hormones). We play our former

selves, and we can also play additional fictional characters—composites of classmates, or notable former adolescents such as Emily Dickinson, George Washington, Sherlock Holmes, or Pina Bausch.

Our hallucinatory month of school is loosely hyper-organized around four grand, archetypal high school events—The Talent Show, The Big Game, The Big Dance, Graduation—at which we aim to gather in Twitter for an hour each Wednesday night (11pEDT/ 10pCDT/ 9pMDT/ 8pPDT).

Before and after these key events each week we fret, we scheme, we debrief, and we form alliances that are just as easily broken, so the drama lasts all week, and you can drop in whenever you feel like roaming the halls of #ATH15 (or hanging out behind the gym with your burnout buddies).

You're already registered and the Vice Principal (that dick!) is already on your case.

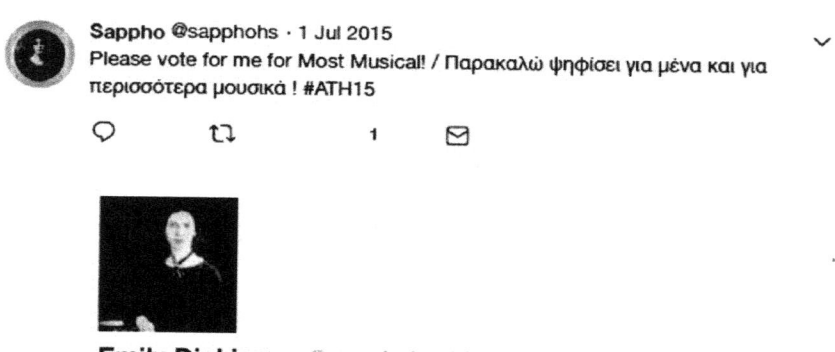

Figure 1. Screen grab from All-Time High on Twitter.

Donato's sense of the possibilities of character and character voice combined with Johnson's architecture background and vision of a perennially shifting, infinite, combinatorial, hallucinatory high school campus combine to create an amazing creative playground. Among the standout characters in *All-Time High* was Claire Donato's high school self, @clairedonato04, whose sensitivity led her to organize a chicken sanctuary on the football field. Donato also played high school Sappho who tweeted poetically in Greek, posted classical imagery of the female form, and then suddenly transformed into Emily Dickinson (with the same account handle but a different screen name and avatar image) (see figure 1).

The paths of @clairedonato04 and @sapphohs rarely crossed in the feed, aside from this exchange:

> Claire Donato '04, @clairedonato04, July 23, 2015
> Emily Dickinson has always been my favorite poet, and she seems to be here now in the guise of @sapphohs. Hi Em! #ATH15 #fangirl

> Sappho, @sapphohs, July 23, 2015
> Replying to @clairedonato04
> What is a Fangirl—I ask—
> As if a label writ speaks multitudes—
> Between Ourselves and living!
> #ATH15

They traveled in different circles and participated in different subplots.

Netrunner Jeff T. Johnson was also playing at least two characters that I knew of: his high school self Cul de Sux (@culdesux) and a high school-age HS Morrissey (@MozzerHi), megadramatic lead singer of the achingly popular band the Smiths. HS Morrissey lent his voice to a protest against the social conformity of the big dance, #prom, by advocating an alternative event:

> HS Morrissey, @MozzerHi July 21, 2015
> No date 4 #prom? Moz here to help. Follow my advice and Get Over It. Stay tuned. #ath15

> HS Morrissey, @MozzerHi July 21, 2015
> 1. Don't go to #prom. Will it be any better this time? #ath15

> HS Morrissey, @MozzerHi July 21, 2015
> 2. Go to #morp. Get yr faux freak on & go alternative. No date needed, but you can still hook up in a car. #ath15 #prom

> HS Morrissey, @MozzerHi July 21, 2015
> 3. Make a date. Literally. You are the one that you want, and it's not the 80s anymore. Anyone ever can be your #prom dream date. #ath15

HS Morrissey, @MozzerHi July 21, 2015
Solved your #prom probs earlier tonight but what are you without your probs? Goodnight, sweet fools, I am no one nothing without you. #ath15

Cul de Sux embodied teen angst:

Cul de Sux, @CuldeSux July 2, 2015
#secretdairy Is it wrong that I told a girl I'm vegan to impress her? I ~want~ to be vegan but coffee tastes wrong with soy milk! #ATH15

Cul de Sux, @CuldeSux July 6, 2015
#secretdiary The Vegan Mafia is on to me. Forgot to wipe off my milk mustache before homeroom. D'oh! #ath15

Cul de Sux, @CuldeSux July 8, 2015
Not sure what to cram for #bigtest couldn't find homeroom today what's my talent I should quit football. #talentshow #ath15

Cul de Sux, @CuldeSux July 8, 2015
Pencil Flipping #talentshow #ath15 https://vine.co/v/enT0dMa0i0P

Cul de Sux, @CuldeSux July 8, 2015
Passed @athVICE [the Vice Principal] in the hall today, mumbling to himself about dobermans, jackboots, and chestnut trees. #mascot #ath15

Johnson described the multivocal experience like this:

There was a sense of intrigue among netrunners, who weren't always aware just how many characters the others were running. Claire and I probably had around 5 each, maybe more, some of whom played bit parts and some of whom were actively pushing things along and troubling the narratives. I remember speculating offstage about who played certain other characters, which was not only part of the fun, but melted some of the boundaries between the world of the game and the worlds of the players. The platforms we used and the ways we moved within and between them encouraged that. Not only were we using Twitter (in the netprov as well as in our other lives), but we were extending the game into Vine, Instagram, and phone SMS messages (including burners). There was also a robust side game going on in Twitter DMs (direct messages, visible only to sender and receiver) between characters, which nonetheless informed the netprov. DMs were like the bedroom telephones, hidden stairwells, janitor's closets, and exclusive Denny's rendezvous of All-Time High.

This was all crucial to the materiality of the netprov, even if it wasn't always on the top layer(s) of the game.[2]

Among the many plot themes during the month of *All-Time High* alongside the chicken sanctuary were a feminist movement to change the name of the team mascot from the Fighting Cocks to the Cockatrices (a fearsome mythical beast; Google it) and a bitter division among students supporting the cheerleader bots or supporting their enemy, the Vice Principal, who thwarted make-out parties in a cabin in the woods with an abyss tucked under its floorboards and created sinister photo booths that might have been interdimensional portals or just convenient wormholes for jogging through the labyrinthine halls and far-flung locales of *All-Time High*. In the end, the Vice Principal brought in programmers to shut down the cheerleader bots.

The cheerleader bots were, in fact, a Twitter bot programmed by Mark Marino, which every half hour automatically tweeted hilarious, combinatorial exhortations from a database:

> ATH Cheer Squad, @ATHcheersquad July 19, 2015
> Sacre Bleu Students! Weaken thy Proxies for Your Insecurities! Woh! #ath15 #BigGame

> ATH Cheer Squad, @ATHcheersquad July 17, 2015
> Hark Students! Isolate the Gangly Foes! Let's Discuss! #ath15 #BigGame

> ATH Cheer Squad, @ATHcheersquad July 15, 2015
> Hail In-crowd winners! Slaughter those Red-Shirted Teammates! Adderall! #ath15 #BigGame

> ATH Cheer Squad, @ATHcheersquad July 15, 2015
> Egads Students who happen to live in the same municipality! Slayeth all Tosspots! Stay Optimistic! #ath15 #BigGame

The school authorities did their best to shut the bots down:

> Cul de Sux, @CuldeSux July 15, 2015
> Replying to @clairedonato04
> @clairedonato04 I heard captcha booths will be set up at all school gates! #ath15 #antibots #botlist

But the cheerleader bots survived until their code ultimately came apart in the last week:

ATH Cheer Squad, @ATHcheersquad July 28 2015
Error 90210 Achtung Re-imagine your uncle's form processor Shazbot #ath15 #athGrad

ATH Cheer Squad, @ATHcheersquad July 28 2015
You got me, Bro {me{z Re:Re:Re your mama's hard drive beg[in]co[u.n]tdown #ath15 #athGrad

ATH Cheer Squad, @ATHcheersquad July 29 2015
You got me, Bro Please Re-lick the unoriginal agents of the state Vroooom! #ath15 #athGrad

ATH Cheer Squad, @ATHcheersquad July 29 2015
Error 90210 1010110 101010 your bff's Signalhilarity] #ath15 #athGrad

Netprov player Michael Russo (unknown to us until after the netprov), in a move similar to Claire Donato's switch from Sappho to Emily Dickinson in the same account, started with a character based on actor Johnny Depp—or, more precisely, the character Depp played in the TV series *21 Jump Street* Tom Hanson, who was an adult police officer posing undercover as a high school student. Russo changed the avatar photo for the account, @21tomhanson, to a succession of Depp characters from other movies, with the account taking over each fictional persona.

Russo writes:

> I created several Google Chrome Profiles and opened each persona in its own separate browser.... The idea of morphing-multiple personas didn't happen thoughtfully—it really was just an outgrowth of play. I pretended to be a drug dealer at first, but nobody was buying my drugs, so I created somebody to do so. Then I needed a NARC. So I created a NARC.
>
> Once these multiple personas were in play, others started engaging more with their story-lines. Probably for "follow-the-crowd" reasons. If I had to guess, I would say that people found these storylines engaging because I faked the engagement at the start. (Hey, three people in this thread are discussing X, as opposed to one person in another thread discussing Y).[3]

To the distress of netprov lovers who missed the initial performance and like to search the hashtag and read the text later, the @21tomhanson account was suspended by Twitter and lives on, like Sappho herself, only in fragmentary retweets.

During *All-Time High*, the four netrunners and some featured players arranged to meet and/or videoconference with each other during the weekly, one-hour live events. Netproving together around a home or restaurant table with more friends on screen is really fun! We wind up not really looking at the folks on screen very often, but it's wonderful to glance up and see them there and to hear their voices, laughing at posts and planning duets and other story strategies.

As with all Twitter-based netprovs, the exhilarating experience of cocomposing *All-Time High* in real time is very difficult to recreate via static archives. The cumulative effect of the interweaving braid of themes, running jokes, and callbacks (a stage improv term that describes a reference to some element of an earlier scene) can be compared to the immersive richness of binge-watching a multiseason TV series.

We take for granted the publishing mechanics of social media, but it's worth stepping back and registering their strangeness compared with print traditions. They include forcibly limited short texts and uploaded or linked images along with direct and indirect replies, likes (tallied votes of approval), and retweets (reposting of others' posts, often interpreted as approval, with the option of accompanying commentary), all organized within a searchable hashtag in reverse chronological order. These conventions, designed over a decade, can be viewed as an attempt to make writing behave like spoken conversation, and the technically self-aware tension between the spoken and the written-and-illustrated is exploited for fun and as art by netprov players.

CHAPTER 3.

PLAYING MULTIPLE CHARACTERS AND PRODUCING LARGER NETPROVS

Our delight in watching films in which an actor plays multiple characters is twofold: we admire the skill that makes it easy for our mind to accept them as different people at the same time as we know they must all be facets of one person. One of the best tips I can give you if you want to up your netprov game is to create two characters from the start. I usually make two accounts right away in whatever platform is being used.

How do I use two netprov characters?

You can make your characters friends and write duets for them. These duets can be used to share and model complex themes and help other players to join a call-and-response game you want to initiate.

Your characters can have similar written voices, which tells you something about their relationship, or they can be dramatically different. Differences almost always come with status differentials, so the comedy practically writes itself. If you follow the great stage-improv tip that the characters should always already know one another, you'll be able to begin their relationship in the middle, which not only provides immediate exposition but accelerates the story.

Try This: The Tag-Along, a Two-Character Netprov Exercise

Here's a fun way to practice playing two characters:

1. Create a character who is an up-and-coming social media star, a trending, self-important influencer who takes themselves altogether too seriously.
2. Write a post in which the star previews a live video that is so cool that it's sure to go viral. Exaggerate the pomposity of the character.
3. Then, create a younger sibling to the star, who has gotten the password to the star's account and has decided to jump in and "help" but systematically proceeds to render totally uncool the star's best efforts. The younger sib has a very different writing style (emojis and acronyms?) and, with the best of intentions, tells embarrassing, behind-the-scenes anecdotes, and contradicts and generally muddies the waters.
4. Have the star and the sib go back and forth about four or five times, each in their characteristic style, until the feed unravels.
5. Avoid dumbing down either of the characters. As the *Second City Almanac of Improvisation* encourages: "Always play to the top of your own intelligence."[1]

Playing two characters allows you to explore a range of points of view. Mark Marino ran several accounts during *All-Time High*, including his high school self and the vice principal J. Jonah Jeffries (@ATHvice), with its avatar typography mimicking the 1980s television show *Miami Vice*. He also programmed the cheer bots' account @ATHcheersquad. And I've come to understand that Mark usually creates at least one secret account and never tells anybody that he's playing it.

Playing two characters can also allow you to develop a relationship among yourself. My own experience of *All-Time High* was surprisingly emotional, a reaction shared by many players. In my high-school-Rob account, I was plunged back into the feelings of isolation and loneliness that I experienced at a tiny rural school. Little did I suspect that another character I created, an imagined Irish immigrant student from the class of 1942, Patrick Kavanaugh (@paddyclassof42), would wind up befriending young Rob in their duets. By the end of the project, I was really sad to bid Patrick goodbye, since in my glib eagerness to create a realistic character I had already foretold in my mind Patrick's imminent death in the maw of World War II. It sounds strange to say, but I love it when netprov players report crying at the end of a story. It means to me that their characters have come alive in their minds and that the netrprov has had a real impact.

Try This: Keep a Secret Character up Your Sleeve

In the next netprov you play, experiment with this:

1. Create one extra character account at the very beginning. You can have a sense of its personality right from the start, or you can simply stake out some territory with a funny handle that's been floating around in your mind.
2. Have this new character appear late in the netprov. Perhaps they can follow up on a narrative impulse you had but couldn't carry out with your initial character set. Or perhaps they can lampoon another of your own characters who has gotten too big for their britches.
3. Make it your goal to see if you can get other players to wonder who is running your new character.
4. Take the secret to your grave. There are netprov characters I have enjoyed from the early '80s who still haven't fessed up.

The mind loves dialogue. It's a fascinating result of—

Wait! Does the mind really love dialogue?

I was kind of in . . . in the middle of . . . never mind . . . yes, I think the mind really does love dialogue. It's a fascinating result of our massive brains and their capabilities for parallel processing. When was the last time you gave yourself a pep talk? When was the last time you rehearsed (and rehearsed and rehearsed) a difficult conversation about a relationship, and then, of course, when the time came, it turned out differently because the other person hadn't gotten a copy of your imaginary script?

Dialogic writing goes way back in literary history, and not only in fiction. Plato wrote philosophy as dialogue. Galileo's scientific argument for the Earth orbiting the sun was written as a dialogue—and not even a dialogue between real people but between imaginary allegorical characters whose portraits (avatars?) are carefully illustrated on the title page. Novels of ideas, such as Kate Chopin's *The Awakening* or Fydor Dostoevsky's *The Brothers Karamazov*, are just one step over the line from fiction to a form of philosophy-in-dialogue.

A single voice—a single unopposed presentation—isn't capable of containing the inherent self-contradictions of complex thought. Dialogue is a way of exploring "what if" instead of "I know." As the presentation of mathematics and science became more univocal (single voiced), philosophers followed suit, and the dialogic became relegated to the category of mere fiction. Given that most cultural phenomena are cyclical, it's interesting to wonder when dialogic science and dialogic philosophy will emerge from the shadows again.

Isn't the point of creative writing to develop your own individual voice?

That's one goal, but it's not the only goal. When I was in the Invisible Seattle group, we were determined to find alternatives to the prevailing Romantic model of writerly creativity: the solitary genius in a cabin by the lake drawing inspiration from leaves and ether to compose works of utter originality, slave to the perennial dictum to "discover your own unique voice" and forswear all others until death do you part.

Since we loved writing together and writing in different styles we were delighted to find many examples of both literary collaboration, often swept under the rug, and writers writing in multiple authorial voices. Feminist scholarship, for example, has exposed the large number of partners of the so-called great men who made decisive contributions to their male partners' oeuvres. Such collaborations were often concealed to support both the egos of the lead authors and the economic value of their names and "voices" as brands.

You mean that "find your unique voice" thing is kind of a myth?

It's limiting. In contrast, the Invisibles celebrated authors such as Portugal's great poet Fernando Pessoa, who wrote and published under numerous heteronyms (the word he used to describe his fictional literary personae, for whom he created unique names, personalities, philosophies, and writing styles) and conducted parallel "careers."[2] We celebrated the astonishing work of the French writer Georges Perec, who loved writing as a thing in itself, not as self-promotion, and saw it as a kind of tender, athletic craft rather than a mystical, rapturous form of expression. Perec wanted to write one of every literary genre—crime novel, comic novel, travel book, summer romance—in every style, a goal exactly the opposite of the unique voice cultivated in many writers' workshops.

My own early foray into online multivocality took place in 2000 during "Friday's Big Meeting," the weeklong, proto-netprov published as a website. It purported to be an internal chat room for a small web design company that was suddenly and unaccountably accessible.[3] Readers saw not only the public texts meant for all employees (on a white background) but all the private, back-channel texts among the employees (on color-keyed backgrounds). I asked the friends who modeled for the photos to pose according to a list of positions, most of them with a neutral expression: looking right, looking left, palms up, hand cupped by ear, etc. The characters' posts were accompanied by each character's visual vocabulary of simple, emoji-like hand gestures and facial expressions, which foreshadowed the avatars of Facebook and Twitter, still a few years off.

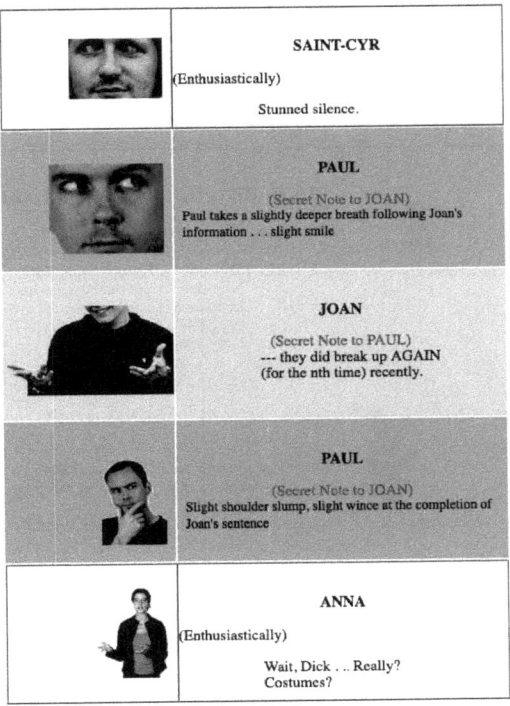

Figure 1. Screen grab from Rob Wittig's "Friday's Big Meeting."

The chat room form was in part a response to the great concern at that time about the eadability of online text. Solid, wide, book-like text was considered fatiguing so I experimented with a graphically open format, based on the look and mechanics of movie scripts (see figure 1).

The characters of "Friday's Big Meeting" act out an intertwining pair of story lines. The company will go out of business if they don't wow their last remaining clients in the big, online meeting in the chat room on Friday. Throwing all the company's resources toward this effort, the boss flies Paul up to the main office in Chicago from his satellite office in St. Louis, Missouri, meaning that Paul and Anna, who have been conducting a torrid hidden flirtation in the chatroom, will have their first meeting on Friday as well. The boss's conviction that changing the team's avatars to medieval costumes will be the clincher for the client (see figure 2) leads to a tumultuous conclusion.

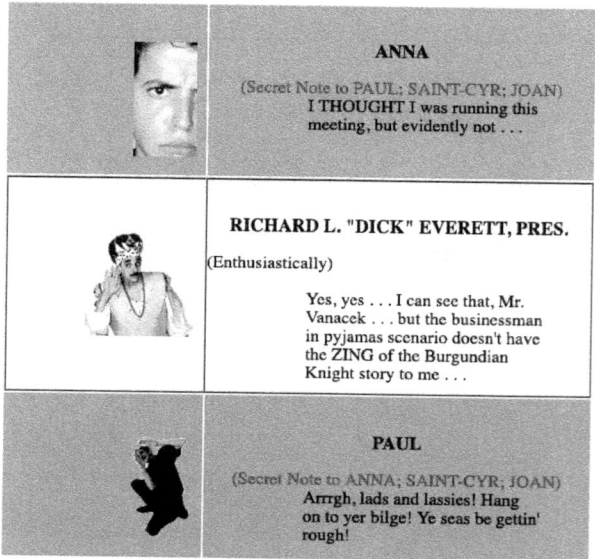

Fig. 2. Screen grab from Rob Wittig's "Friday's Big Meeting."

So, what happens at the end of "Friday's Big Meeting"?

You're asking me to be a spoiler, and I won't do it!

Try This: Create Your Own Photo Emojis

Sit or stand against a plain background and do the following:

1. Take a small set of selfies with happy, sad, contemplative, and surprised looks on your face.

2. Next, take several selfies with a neutral look on your face, first turning slightly to the left, then turning slightly to the right.
3. Finally, take four more selfies with a neutral look on your face, this time with your head facing the camera and only your eyes moving: eyes up, eyes down, eyes left, and eyes right.

You will find that the pictures with more neutral expressions are much more useful (and funny) than those with the more extreme ones. Combined with your text, they are subtle, expressive, and surprisingly powerful.

Why do social media companies make it so hard to create multiple accounts for my netprov characters?

It's a real problem, isn't it? We always have to provide current workarounds to our netprov players. The reasons the companies give publicly for this problem usually include the prevention of trolls and predators and the ways in which fake accounts can be used for nefarious social and political ends. Both are serious concerns.

But that is not the overwhelming reason social media companies hate multiple accounts. They hate multiple accounts because they make their money by knowing everything there is to know about single, simple, reliable, and predictable account holders. A person writing as multiple authors is threatening—not just to literary norms but to powerful and uncaring economic interests as well.

In my book *Invisible Rendezvous*, I exhorted, "Minimum: two selves."[4] The exhortation grew out of our playful and exploratory use of heteronyms in our early online writing. Today, the corporate profitability of the notion of the single, predictable, consumer self has transformed this creative, psychological exhortation into an act of defiance. I encourage you to live multiply.

What is the difference between a fictional social media account and a real one anyway?

Great question. Looking at some history will help answer it. From the earliest days of the strangely public diaries called *weblogs*, shortened to *blogs*, digital media hosted the transformation of the old private diary, written on paper in a book, into a public confessional. Perhaps at first users didn't quite realize how public a blog was. First-generation web readers scrambled to cover their eyes and muttered "too much information." But as generations of platforms succeeded one another, the routine sharing of formerly personal information became the norm. Feelings about this were initially very positive. Digital-culture scholar Jill Walker Rettberg, writing about online photographic self-portraiture in the context of the reversal of the top-down flow of traditional mass media in *Mirrors and Shadows: Digital Aestheticisation of Oneself*, wrote,

> In an attempt to cling to the past, mass media try to fit in with this change by making everyday people the stars of the mass media. We have reality television, makeover television, contests like Idol and Survivor which all make miniature celebrities of people who fade quickly in and out of the limelight. The more powerful movement is on the internet, and it is controlled entirely by the everyday people themselves. These people write diaries, they publish photos, and most importantly: they write themselves. They don't allow others to represent them. They are in charge of the presentation of their own lives. That is something the mass media have never encouraged. Capturing our mirror images and our shadows is an exploration of what it means to be a subject in an age where masses no longer exist.[5]

Walker Rettberg pointed out the way in which the performance of identity is an act that takes place in an adversarial environment—one in which other forces are eager to shape one's identity.

But in addition to the rebellious liberation from top-down mass media (which I believe is still possible), something else happened. A handful of new platforms (Facebook, Twitter, Instagram) attracted massive user bases by offering powerful "free" software so bewitching that it blinded users to the fundamental truth that every citizen of a consumer society knows: nothing is free. The companies figured out ways to channel and generate money from self-presentation. Far from being a challenge to mass media, seemingly independent self-presenters became a vast, unpaid workforce (the theme of the netprov *I Work for the Web* in the next chapter). Instead of being opposed by media giants, the adversarial environment that Walker Rettberg identified has now been co-opted by them and transformed into a vast and legal dogfighting arena in which trolling is good business, Russian spy accounts are OK as long as their credit cards are valid, and popularity algorithms promote a handful of celebrities to dizzying heights to stoke their craving for fame. The reality TV shows that Walker Rettberg saw being opposed by blogs are now the main models for all online self-creation, for all of media culture in fact. Even the most high-minded, truth-based news media cannot resist the pull to view politics as a vast, personality-based reality show.

"Here come the celeberazzis taking pictures of themselves," says radio reporter Danny Vanilla the celebrity stalker, in the Firesign Theater's incredibly prescient 1998 CD *Give Me Immortality or Give Me Death*.[6] The age of the celeberazzi is here.

This situation feeds not only the corporate data-gathering machine but also the ego identities of millions of content creators. Using the same consumer logic that has people wear clothing for sports they don't participate in and drive vehicles prepared for conditions they never encounter, social media platforms have offered ordinary people the feeling of round-the-clock-news attention formerly reserved for celebrities, thereby adding a statistical illusion of achievement to their lives in the form of likes and views. The fact that a tiny percentage of influencers actually become old-style celebrities (usually with a lot of invisible, professional help) is the equivalent of the startled lottery winner whose image fuels millions more ticket purchases.

So social media accounts are on a kind of scale from slightly fictional to totally fictional?

That's it. Is an account that shows only successes and systematically edits out its main character's doubts, depressions, and setbacks real or fictional? Are images that use filters to alter faces and bodies in imitation of professional lifestyle photography real or fictional? If a person adopts a set of beliefs or behaviors for a period of time, then subsequently rejects them, which version of the account, the person, is the "real" one?

As web writers such as Sherry Turkle have been telling us for years, online identity in netprov-like multi-user dungeons (MUDs), chat rooms, and games is a performance that interpenetrates, amplifies, and sometimes contradicts the performance of identity that we enact in real life. Turkle writes,

> As a new social experience, MUDs pose many psychological questions: If a persona in a role-playing game drops defenses that the player in real life has been unable to abandon, what effect does this have? What if a persona enjoys success in some area (say, flirting) that the player has not been able to achieve? Slippages often occur in places where persona and

self merge, where the multiple personae join to comprise what the individual thinks of as his or her authentic self.[7]

It used to be argued that a person's identity was as unchanging as a book. Now we are beginning to see that it has always been as fluid as a social media feed. Facebook's insistence on a single, verifiable identity is a desperate rearguard action of the waning book-paradigm era.

The difference between a fictional social media account and a real one is that the fictional one is designed to accentuate certain aspects of a persona and downplay others in order to have a strategic effect on the mind of the reader. In other words, there is little difference at all.

Who is the real me anyway?

That's the question! Playing multiple netprov characters puts you nose to nose with a fascinating psychological and philosophical conundrum: Who *is* the real you? Far from the oversimplified consumer self to which the big platforms are determined to reduce us, the answer is complex and manifold: it's always a performance.

The self is always a performance?

Yep. Psychologists and social scientists have written for years about the performance of identity. One of the pioneers of the subject, sociologist-anthropologist Erving Goffman, conducted an amazing experiment by closely watching people in a small Irish town.[8] As they approached one another's cottages, he observed that there would be a transformation in their body language: They would straighten their clothes, stand up tall, and become different versions of themselves—idealized, authoritative, ready-to-be-judged versions. And this would happen at the same exact point outside the different cottages. Puzzled, he wondered: Why does this seemingly unconscious transformation happen at this exact spot? Then he realized that the transformation occurred one step before the point at which the person knew they could be seen from the front windows.

Once you start looking for the performance of identity in real life, you'll see it everywhere. Just compare how you are with your friends at midnight with how you are with your family of origin at a holiday dinner.

Sherry Turkle, in her studies of social media, cites as one of the chief reasons so many people prefer digitally mediated interactions to in-person interactions is the fact that there is time to edit (often meaning to improve) one's statements before making them public. Just as with Goffman's Irish townsfolk, digital humans seem to be haunted by our own inadequacy—needing just one more touch to our makeup, one more selfie to make sure we're getting the best one, the one that so often looks the least like us.

So, netprov is just an extension of the self-making we do in everyday life?

Netprov is a great place to play with and think about these ideas of identity and self and laugh in the bargain! For example, in *All-Time High*, the hashtag #secretdiary played with the netprov's public-private confessional theme. Characters in *All-Time High* would pretend to have intuited the information contained in #secretdiary posts, or simply admit they had read the information. #Secretdiary became a way to overcome the powerful social pressures on self-presentation. It formed and strengthened relationships. It was a fictional convention that could have real-life benefits.

Try This: Use the Hashtag #secretdiary in Your Own Social Media Account

Here's a great trick we use in netprovs that's like an actor turning and confiding directly to the audience in an "aside":

1. Use the hashtag #secretdiary. Use it to share something written as though it was deeply private. Start slow. Share a small doubt, a hesitation, a flub, or a foible. See how it feels.

2. See if there's an awkward situation occurring online with someone—again, nothing too serious—and see if #secretdiary can be used to ease the situation, like you would be able to do in person using facial expressions, body language, jokes, etc.

3. Enlist a friend to join you in a real-life #secretdiary duet. Model the practice for your friends and see if someone else starts doing it because they've seen you do it!

How do the ways people perform their identities online for real translate into a made-up character?

I learned a lot about using multiple characters and their web performance in creating the fictional web 1.0 home page "Fall of the Site of Marsha" in 1999. The project shows three stages of progressive deterioration of a personal home page across three seasons: spring, summer, and fall.

The protagonist Marsha is a fan of angels—particularly throne angels. I studied the many real angel websites of the time and positioned Marsha and her best friend Bits as new members of the online angel community. Marsha's site is, in part, a tribute to her late father, about whom she feels some ambivalence and guilt. She throws out a rhapsodic invitation for people to participate in her site and for the angels themselves to come and visit.

The angels come, and they are not nice. In fact, the angels—or possibly hater-trolls posing as angels—begin to bully her and vandalize her website in its second and third iterations, touching sore points about her father's death and the loyalty of Bits. Careful readers will have noticed by the second summer version that Marsha's husband Mike and her friend Bits are having an affair in a chat room. By the third iteration of the site, the angels' harsh emendations to the site dominate, the images are dark and mangled, and Marsha's husband is announcing that Marsha has been institutionalized for mental illness.

So Marsha's website gets destroyed?

Yes. At the time, I was interested in the nineteenth-century Romantic fascination with ruins and asked myself to imagine what a ruined website would look like. (We now have seen plenty of ruined and abandoned websites, but in those hopeful, early days of the web, they were an odd notion.)

Try This: Choose Your . . . Wait for It! . . . Timing

We all know the agony of waiting for a text message when you really want to hear from someone. These timing tips will give additional punch to your characters:

1. Take the characters from one of the netprovs discussed in this chapter and decide what dramatic plot turn happens to them in the course of the next week.
2. Write a two-to-three-page sketch in which you specify the exact time of day and day of the week each post gets released.
3. Use delays for dramatic and comedic effect.
4. Also use sudden bursts of frantic, multiple messages. Then, what happens when your characters post awkwardly to one another at the same exact time? How do they extricate themselves?

Do you do a lot of scripting and planning for netprovs like *All-Time High*?

Planning yes, scripting no. Our netprovs have what in commedia dell'arte theater are known as scenarios: a sequence of story events, or "beats," but no specific dialogue. As with many of our more complex netprovs, Claire, Jeff, Mark, and I shared planning documents. For each of the major weekly events, we wrote a creative starting point that we posted on the netprov's website:

Act 1 The Talent Show
Wait, there's a test today? Also, what am I going to be—I mean do—for the talent show? Preparation and performance anxiety, mortification at the thought of who you might run into in the halls, general drama, test trauma, cliques formed and disrupted are all key themes this week. @ATHvice (that dick!) will also announce the new team name and mascot at the Talent Show, so cast your votes #mascot! Tease out the double-consciousness of what you wanted to be back then (your HS talent) and what you became as an adult. Think of the auditions as trying out for life. Combine and conflate talent show and test jitters. This may be a way to exorcise all those late-for-test-and-didn't-study-where's-the-room dreams, but it also introduces the self-reflexive metagame that overlays high school meaning-of-life drama.

Act 2 The Big Game
Who are we playing again? Competition culture, metagaming, narrative conflict. Halftime should be a total shitshow, and could be the highlight of The Big Game. What the fuck is the band doing? What's all this about a 4th quarter #walkoff? @ATHvice (that dick!) to announce prom theme at halftime. Oh, and The Big Test was handed back today—you got a C—so you could use a good scream in a public place. The stadium will do! And as if we don't have enough to worry about, @ATHvice (that dick!) has scheduled mandatory SAT Prep for Monday.

Act 3 The Big Dance
Social pressure, gender roleplay, teen hormone reboot, authority and rebellion, and a malfunctioning rental photo booth. And has anyone noticed how, um, labyrinthine—shout out to my English teacher!—the halls are? OMG what are you wearing, and what's with your hair? Look at those vintage moves! At the dance, visit the glitchy, sticky rental photo booth (and tweet yr face-obscured photos), nominate king, queen and

joker of #promcourt, and pester the DJ to play your favorite era-specific slow jam, cathartic rocker, or wallflower-picking dance number. Or duck out behind the gym for some "fresh air" and check in with the kids who are too cool to dance.

Act 4 Graduation
Take a victory lap through the endless halls of All-Time High while you wonder what to do when you get back to your so-called life! It's a week of hyperactive success and failure, returning from the return (back to the future), moving on, existential crises—and a chance to perfect your yearbook quips and finally get your senior quote right. Maybe @ATHvice (that dick!) finally turns into a giant serpent and swallows his own tail, or tells us what happened to the principal! Maybe one of those fire alarms rings true—can a holographic school burn down? Perhaps we find that school is well and truly out forever, and we've invented a new, socially engaged, visionary educational model! Or maybe we have a giant pizza party (complete with giant, interdimensional pizza!)! What happens at ceremony—resistance stunts? Does #valedictorian give a speech?

Do I have to invent new characters for every netprov?

Great question. No! The brilliant netprov writer Davin Heckman started his contribution to 2013's *SpeidiShow* netprov by developing a wistful Twitter character, Brutus Corbin, who lives in his mom's basement and complains poignantly about her and his situation.[9] As we played the monthlong netprov (which I'll describe later in this book), we fell in love with Davin's character. And then his mom, Franny Cheshire, started tweeting too! The two started bickering, providing great passages of dialogue. Then, two years later, Brutus and Franny reappeared in *All-Time High*:

Corbin Brutus, @BrutusCorbin July 15, 2015
@markcmarino well . . . I ended up doing yard work all day. And now I can't use the car for 2 weeks. #ath15

Corbin Brutus, @BrutusCorbin July 15, 2015
@markcmarino My stupid mom makes me go to #ath15, but Margaret goes to the art high school . . .

Corbin Brutus, @BrutusCorbin July 15, 2015
@markcmarino Margaret works at the video store. I was going to rent Rubin and Ed and invite her to watch it with me. #thisblows #ath15

Corbin Brutus, @BrutusCorbin July 15, 2015
@markcmarino So, I told my mom I needed to pick up Harold and Maude for school . . . She went to pick it up. #stillgrounded #ath15

Franny Cheshire, @FrannyCheshire July 15, 2015
I'm watching a really great movie with a friend . . . Harold and Maude! Never seen it, but it's fantastic! #ath15

This was a perfect example of the learning that happens in doing experimental, interdsiciplinary projects. With the limitations of my novelist's training, I unconsciously assumed that you should create a new set of characters for each netprov idea. But here were the same two characters moving over into a new conceptual world. Heckman claims that the reason he reused Brutus and Franny was convenience: the accounts already existed and he was too busy to make new ones. But at the same time it was genius! Why shouldn't characters move from world to world, netprov to netprov? In a tip of the hat to the movie *Back to the Future*, in which a high school boy travels back in time and encounters his own mother in her high school years, Brutus watched in horror as his mom flirted and became the center of attention during *All-Time High*'s big events.

Try This: Migrate Characters from Netprov to Netprov

It's always a good sign when players are sad to say goodbye to their characters at the end of a netprov. If you just can't bear to part, consider doing this:

1. Use your characters in a subsequent netprov.
2. If your characters have had story lines of their own during their first outing, continue them in the next netprov. What has happened to them in the intervening time?

All this character making sounds fun; how do I start?

Here's a great, all-purpose netprov that will help you practice playing multiple characters (and it's a great way to spend an evening).

Try This: Netprov TV

Here's a fun parlor game to play with friends near or far:

1. Create or repurpose two new social media accounts.

2. Arrange with friends to post together for exactly a half-hour, using the same hashtag.

3. Have the netrunner decide on an imaginary TV show name and an imaginary episode name. Try to make the names open to interpretation and not in a narrow genre; for example, *Plethora*, Episode 3, "The Diaper Switcheroo"; or *Oscar Sauce*, Episode 12, "Teacher's Evil Pet."

4. At the top of the hour, have the netrunner tweet the show and episode name to the hashtag.

5. For exactly half an hour, have players live-tweet the imaginary show, building on one another's posts to cocreate what kind of show it is and what is happening in this particular episode.

6. Use this format as a time to perform duets among your characters. Repeat. Have fun!

EXAMPLE 3: *FANTASY SPOILS: AFTER THE QUEST, A NETPROV*

Speaking Stories Together, Dungeons & Dragons Style

For many people, the first experience of improvised, collaborative roleplay storytelling has been the fun of playing games such as Dungeons & Dragons, the hit tabletop game that developed out of the world of miniature war games. Achieving its first popularity in the 1970s and '80s, D&D, as it is often referred to, has enjoyed several subsequent waves of popularity, including the one happening as this book was written, which is fueled in part by the general revival of board and parlor games, particularly among young people, and intensified by the 2020–21 pandemic lockdown. From preceding tabletop war games, D&D keeps the frame tale of a military campaign and the structure of referring to guidebooks for settings and character attributes along with the rolling of a die, typically a twenty-sided one, to determine key outcomes. But within an approximately *Lord of the Rings*y fantasy setting, D&D foregrounds character development and improvised narrative interactions that happen in conversation around the table and often provide the most entertaining and memorable parts of the experience. For many players, the storytelling far outweighs success or failure in the game itself. The ongoing story arcs of player/characters and their correspondence or contrast with their creators and other player/characters make for a rich, subtle cultural experience among longtime players.

As a model for netprov, beyond the fantasy narratives themselves, longtime D&D groups demonstrate the social and interpersonal delights of making fictions together. D&D groups can develop sophisticated ways to deepen and enrich friendships. They can be a joyous example of playing well with others. I'll talk a lot more about games and netprov in chapter 9, but here I want to focus on the pure, often hilarious, fun of sitting around creating stories in an epic genre frame.

Early in 2020, Mark proposed a spring netprov based on D&D to take place on Discord, a social media platform originally designed to support D&D-like game play but which, as the year went on, became wildly popular as a general-purpose social platform.

The invitation for the netprov *Fantasy Spoils: After the Quest* began like this:

"Thou owest the sum of 12 gold splonders for damage to Farmer Galorn's chicken shacke where thou foughtest the angry troll."
Signed, Ye Accountant

Fantasy Spoils / After the Quest,[i] a netprov

Ye Premise
Having just paid for and completed the glorious epic saga, *Ultimate Final Victory!*, you have now returned home to deal with the aftermath: the sequel, *Fantasy Spoils*. Gone are the orcs, hobgoblins, and dragons. In their place, you must contend with your wounds, property damages, and ensuing lawsuits. How will you deal with life here in Muddled Earth after the glorious quest? Are you hero enough to face your most daunting enemy: your own irritation? Because at the end of every epic quest, you will find fantasy spoils!

Fantasy Spoils is a new netprov set in a playful take on the role-playing game Dungeons & Dragons. However, rather than focusing on glorious bloody battles, this netprov focuses on the not-so-glorious.

"We shall reimburse thee for only 85% of the potion that healed thy shoulder. The balance of 7 gold splonders must be paid by the 15th."

Signed, Ye Insurancer[1]

The instructions for players tried to strike a balance between explaining enough about D&D to invite newcomers to play while providing levels of creative challenge for D&D experts. We encouraged experienced players to become Drudgeon Masters, our version of the Dungeon Master who guides and arbitrates D&D campaigns. Since our setting transported real-life concerns and consequences into a fantasy genre world, we called our narratives a combination of campaign and complaint: camplaigns:

Welcome, Drudgeon Masters!

- The Drudgeon Master's job is to make your players' lives difficult! And fun!
- You are the master storyteller, narrating the events. You create the world. You set obstacles and create puzzles that in overcoming will turn your ragtag group of miscreants into heroes! Some players have a highly complex piece of software to render their world, its physics, and its scoring mechanisms. Your players just have you.
- A camplaign is a mini-adventure typically played in real time in which your adventurers will do battle with one or more monsters. Before the battle, there's some free play in which the players enter the area. Perhaps they do not see the monster right away. Perhaps they do not see it at all. When either the player attacks the monster or vice versa, we begin COMBAT!

General Play: The Camplaign!
Bureau of Camplaigns in Discord

- Are you ready to face a recovery monster? Time to go on a Camplaign!
- Apply to join an adventuring Party or Volunteer to be a Drudgeon Master!
- Join an Adventuring Party (or we can assign you to one) and get ready for your quest.
- Launch your Camplaign in any available Camplaign channel
- Read over the #Sample-Camplaign for an example of game play.
- A drudgeon master will assign you an abstract monster to battle, and you and your crew will seek out and battle this monster. You will need to work as a team to defeat the monster.

We also offered a specialized list of writing tips for making the most out of the concept and platform:

Here are some ways of weaving ongoing stories amid the hubbub of Discord.

1. Think of having the characters of your adventure party describe their individual experiences of a single event in the #season-1-recap channel. For example: The Bottleneck at Transit Pass, or The Great Shortage on Paper Product Isle. The repetition of the name of the event will knit the posts together.

2. Then, if you'd like, the travails of the #repairs, #recovery, and #lawsuits channels could largely refer back to that same single event.

3. As always with netprov: support and build on others' characters and ideas.

4. Prearrange with your party to all write about a single place at some point in their narratives, for example: The Coughing Pangolin Tavern.

5. Prearrange an invented slang word or expression that everyone will use. This achieves a totally flemertious effect.

6. Think bout given thy character an unik mode of scripting . . . an accent, as t'were

7. Play with the oral D&D tradition of shifting seamlessly from the third person "Butterloess does this, Butterloess does that . . ." to the character's first person "I, Butterloess of Modesto, hereby . . ." to the player's first person "I don't think Butterloess knows kung fu." This is a fascinating language arts phenomenon. Let's heighten it!

8. As a soul-exalting, two-layer storytelling challenge: fictionalize the player as well as the character.

Mark's models of *Fantasy Spoils* monsters both built on the basic premise of the netprov, along with typical D&D skills and attributes and their comparative ranking numbers, and were tailored to address the sudden isolation of the 2020 pandemic lockdown:

Endless Ennui
A sleepy cat who could not be less interested in what you are offering.

HP 73

Attacks:
— Boulders of Boredom
— Apathy Arrows

Spell:
— *Relishing Reluctance*: A spell that keeps players from taking any initiative because, well, what's the point?

This monster is bored of you already, and you are consequently bored of all things. Your desire to conquer it is persistently dissipated by a general disinterest in all things that used to put a gleam on your chainmail armor.

Ambient Ambivalence
More of gas than a solid monster, it can take over an entire party, taking away their forward movement by making every option seem equally good or bad.

HP 25

Attacks:
— Flying Flip Flops

Spells:
— *Unxious Uncertainty:* Creates a cloud over the entire field of battle, reducing visibility to 0. Players are not even certain that the monstrosity released this cloud, or that the monstrosity is even there, or that there is even there. I am uncertain why I am writing this.
— *Indecisivation:* (reaction) When attacked causes the player to ask whether or not that was a good idea, Wisdom saving throw, loss of a turn.

Alack of Motivation
A vampiric monster that drains its opponents of their will to adventure.

HP 60

Attacks:
— *Comforter Creep:* Has the effect of pulling the bed linens over their head. Causes reticence to move and extreme coziness
— *Snooze Bar Slam:* Zzzzzz damage: Takes turn away as player sleeps for just 5 more minutes, 1d8+4 biting damage
— *Verve Sucking:* biting damage plus draining enthusiasm damage, next turn is done with disinterest

Even though we had initially thought of *Fantasy Spoils* as an escape from the stress of the pandemic, the real-life difficulties found their way into the netprov in a positive, cathartic way and allowed players to chuckle together and encourage each other to epic efforts.

CHAPTER 4.

PLAYING WELL WITH OTHERS

In the first run of the netprov *Grace, Wit & Charm*, the centerpiece of the live performance during the second week was an onstage wrist surgery (executed in a pillowcase) in which Laura sought to cure Neil's carpal tunnel pain. This highlighted the fictional company's turn from helping gamers online to performing more lucrative virtual health-care work. The next day, followers of the hashtag blushed reading this exchange:

Neil, @Neil_GWaC May 25, 2011
@Laura_GWaC Maybe this was the horse tranqs speaking, but . . . um . . . even though you were cutting my wrists, you were holding my hands. #GWandC

Laura, @Laura_GWaC May 25, 2011
@Neil_GWaC *blush* I liked holding your hands. Your senstiive, firm Jazz hands. #GWandC

Neil, @Neil_GWaC May 25, 2011
@Laura_GWaC *blush* *blush* *blush* #GWandC

Neil, @Neil_GWaC May 25, 2011
@Laura_GWaC I liked haldong honds, too. *blush* #GWandC

Laura, @Laura_GWaC May 25, 2011
@Neil_GWaC *blush* *blush* *blush* #GWandC

Sonny, @Sonny1SoBlue May 25, 2011
@Laura_GWaC @Neil_GWaC Ah, fer cripes sake, you two! Get a chat-

room! #GWandC Everything we say is visbile to the pubic during Open House!'[1]

This is a great example of how netprov players support each other in building a scene.

What are the characteristics of a good netprov player?

The *prov* in netprov comes from stage improv, and theater is much more helpful in modeling useful characteristics for a netprov player than my original background: literature. Even though projects such as National Novel Writing Month provide a wonderful, jolly community for amateur scribes, literary writing in the European tradition has been considered a solitary pursuit. Theater, on the other hand, is fundamentally and intensely collaborative.

Where does stage improv come from anyway?

Improv as a form of theater arrived on the US scene in the 1950s and 1960s, a period in which the Dada and surrealist ideas about art as a chance operation, and the improvisatory free association of automatic writing, were hip and entering the mainstream. This resulted in movements such as the theater of the absurd of Eugène Ionesco and Samuel Beckett, which drew not only from the surrealism of the '20s and '30s but from an ancient theater tradition that had haunted the wings of legitimate theater for centuries: the commedia dell'arte.

Commedia dell' wha?

Commedia dell'arte is a particularly exquisite Italian flowering, occurring from about 1500 to about 1750, of an unbroken tradition of popular comic performance that extends back into classical Rome and Greece. It is the bawdy, acrobatic underbelly of European theater. Plots, gags, and character dynamics from the commedia influenced literary giants such as Shakespeare, Molière, Carlo Goldoni, and others. The raucous, bawdy, British Christmas pantomime of our own day, with its exaggerated characters, naughty double entendres sailing over the little kids' heads, and ritual audience participation, is a living part of this ancient tradition.

Commedia dell'arte had a fundamental formal difference from "high" theater: it was improvised, not memorized. Its plots were recorded in *sce-*

narios, as they were called in Italian: simple plot outlines. Its characters formed a traditional, unchanging cast, with costumes, body language, gestures, and voices that probably also dated back to ancient times. "It was simplistic, physical, witty in the way of folk wisdom," writes Bari Rolfe in *Commedia dell'Arte: A Scene Study Book*: "Its sole motivating force was love: misers loved money; lovers loved each other . . . servants furthered the love interests of their masters while engaging in their own; the captain loved himself and the deference due him; and the doctor loved his pretensions. Love, lust, lucre, laughter."[2]

The spectacular skill of the commedia dell'arte performer is best described by one of the best, Gherardi, in this passage cited in *The Italian Comedy: The Improvisation, Scenarios, Lives, Attributes, Portraits, and Masks of the Illustrious Characters of the Commedia dell'Arte* by Pierre-Louis Duchartre:

> Listen to Harlequin himself, otherwise known as Gherardi, the gifted actor-author of the seventeenth century, who said: "The Italian comedians learn nothing by heart; they need but to glance at the subject of a play a moment or two before going upon the stage. It is this very ability to play at a moment's notice which makes a good Italian actor so difficult to replace. . . . For a good Italian actor is a man of infinite resources and resourcefulness, a man who plays more from imagination than from memory; he matches his words and actions so perfectly with those of his colleague on the stage that he enters instantly into whatever acting and movements are required of him in such a manner as to give the impression that all that they do has been prearranged."[3]

Here in this ancient art form we see the figure of the writer-actor of netprov.

How do these individual improvisers work with the other actors?

The commedia has unwritten, but highly important, rules for collaboration (like netprov does). These become a kind of personality trait that differentiates the commedia actor from other creators. Duchartre specifies: "Moreover, a good improvisator had to practise a kind of self-abnegation and refrain from indulging his own conceit or overplaying his part to the detriment of other *rôles*. The actors of the Italian troupes of necessity developed a spirit of *camaraderie* in their playing, and they achieved such understanding and mutual co-operation as were not found in the companies playing ordinary drama."[4]

Break these rules of generosity and cooperation and you risk destroying the work. Duchartre writes,

> Riccoboni, another actor-author, wrote in his *Histoire du théâtre italien* (1728): . . . "for a drawback of improvisation is that the success of even the best actor depends upon his partner in the dialogue. If he has to act with a colleague who fails to reply exactly at the right moment or who interrupts him in the wrong place, his own discourse falters and the liveliness of his wit is extinguished."[5]

So theater people in the '60s combined this ancient improvised comedy stuff with avant-garde surrealist stuff?

Basically, yes. And they added games.

In the mid-twentieth century, a Chicago theater teacher named Viola Spolin had an idealistic vision that anyone could learn to be an actor if they had an easy and fun way to get started. Spolin's teacher, Neva Boyd, had based her own use of acting games on her observation of social-mimicry games among inner-city immigrant children. Spolin tested Boyd's and her own ideas for years with groups of young actors from all socioeconomic backgrounds, and ultimately refined a set of games based on avant-garde theater experiments and the old commedia. She compiled them in the book *Improvisation for the Theater*, first published in 1963.[6] It was Viola Spolin's son, Paul Sills, who championed his mother's ideas and believed that they could be useful not only for behind-the-scenes theater training but also as a form of professional theater performance. Sills cofounded Chicago's legendary Second City, a cabaret-style theater with nightclub tables and drink service. The shows consisted of a combination of prewritten sketches and completely improvised games based on suggestions from the audience.

Into this emerging scene came Del Close, a writer-actor-director who was inspired by both Spolin and the commedia dell'arte. Close had a hand in a succession of groundbreaking troupes, from the Compass Players of Chicago and St. Louis to San Francisco's the Committee, Chicago's Second City, and NBC television's *Saturday Night Live*. He ultimately, with Charna Halpern, founded Chicago's ImprovOlympic.

Importantly for the deeper ambitions of netprov, Halpern, Close, and Kim "Howard" Johnson wrote about improv's origins: "As the purists will be quick to point out, improvisation is not necessarily funny (even when it's intentional, as plenty of actors who have 'died' on-stage will attest to).

The first improvisations performed by the Compass Players and other forerunners to Second City were not always intended to be humorous."[7] The serious motivation behind all the laughter (the fundamental aesthetic morality of Close's improv) is summed up in his dictum: "*The truth is funny.* Honest discovery, observation and reaction is better than contrived invention."[8]

This cabaret improv tradition thrived in the latter part of the twentieth century, producing as a by-product several generations of popular and influential writer-actors such as Tina Fey, Amy Poehler, Steve Carell, Will Ferrell, and Melissa McCarthy, not to mention Bill Murray, Gilda Radner, Mike Meyers, and many others. Significantly for netprov, into the twenty-first century, improv meccas such as Second City and Upright Citizens Brigade"[9] have become corporate teaching institutions, with their pay-to-play schools serving not just as feeder systems for the top main-stage troupes but as places for pure participatory activity, like ballroom dance studios or local basketball leagues. People are not content merely to sit and watch; they want to join the fun and play the game. Books such as Alison Goldie's *The Improv book: Improvisation for Theater, Comedy, Education, and Life* offer advice and exercises for the performing path.[10]

All this time, experimental performance artists were adding to the mix. Among the many other kinds of inspiring performance currently pushing at the boundaries of both the theater tradition and notions of self-represented identity itself are a raft of LGBTQ+ performers. Writing of Eisa Jocson's performance *Princess* in the *Theatre Times*, Elke Huybrechts notes,

> Using the genre of the Disney fairytale and especially the Disney princess Snow White, she interweaves class inequality with gender norms and racial clichés, which operate on so many levels. Queerness becomes an antagonistic force of systematic and systemic disruption here, affecting all these different aspects. In addition, Jocson queers the concept of identity by showing that it's always a historical construct and never once seems to stop being a construct. Queering has become an indispensable strategy in a complex world in which norms and powers form more intricate structures than ever before.[11]

What did theater people think about early Internet possibilities?

With her background in performance studies, Antoinette LaFarge, writing on creative, proto-netprov experiments on online multi-user dungeons (MUDs) and MUD object-oriented (MOOs) in 1995, says this about collaborative, networked creativity (then a practice searching for a name), which she calls online theater:

> My feeling is that such alternative names (hypertext/fiction/narrative) tend to underline the verbal and textual nature of online theater, with a nod to its real-time, multi-participant aspect (live/jazz/consensual). There is no question that this is a world now dominated by writerly conventions: in order to participate, one uses a keyboard to type descriptions, dialogue and commands. If I think of it as a form of theater, it is because the real power of this world lies in the ways people inhabit personalities (roles) through words. As with other forms of theater, the point is the enactment of the text, not the text in and of itself.[12]

Note LaFarge's use of the concept of an online theatrical world. In *Invisible Rendezvous*, I talked abut how the main predigital process for literary collaboration was the add-on story—you do chapter one, I'll do chapter two, etc.—and usually how unhappy it is. The chapter one writer has most of the fun, the chapter two writer less, until the fourth and fifth writers are trapped in an increasingly narrow box. The simultaneous, theatrical cocreation allowed by digital improv solves this problem.

So what can I learn from theater improv to be a better netprov player?

Del Close was taught as a student of theater that all drama comes from conflict. But the key moment in his development came when he realized, while playing Viola Spolin's games in front of audiences, that just the opposite is true: agreement is more compelling than conflict. To train his actors in this counterintuitive approach, Close created the Ad Game, which mimicked an advertising-agency brainstorming session. The ironclad rule of the game was:

> Every idea is accepted enthusiastically and remembered, each step is built off the previous idea. In order to properly brainwash the actors with this theory of acceptance, the director may want to force them to overaccept, screaming "Yes!" "Terrific idea!" "Great!" and other praises of brilliance after each idea is stated. This over-acceptance—particularly of stupid ideas—only makes the game funnier.[13]

In their textbook of improvisation, Halpern, Close, and Johnson describe how they teach this counterintuitive principle of agreement

> by placing the actors in situations which normally cause conflict on stage. However, they are instructed to make unusual choices, so that the expected conflict will not arise.... this exercise is not about conflict. It is actually about agreement, and what develops after agreement is reached. ... It is the *relationship between the players* that makes the scene.

As this idea spread throughout the Chicago improv scene and beyond, it was boiled down to this terse formula: Never say, "No, but." Always agree. Always say, "Yes, and."

Here is a great netprov game for practicing this principle of agreement. It comes from the 2013 netprov *Center for Twitzease Control*, presented in full in chapter 6.

Try This: The WORST Social Media Disease EVER!!! (from Center for Twitzease Control)

The Center for Twitzease Control is wringing its hands, pacing up and down, blubbering and texting everyone it knows upon hearing news of a potential outbreak of the Twitzease #twixtreme. Symptoms: Every emotion is taken ABSOLUTELY to its MAX!! The LIFETIME BEST or the COMPLETE WORST!!!! With incredible URGENCY!!! Seriously I am NOT KIDDING!!! Example: I lost my +FAVORITE+ mechanical pencil and MY DAY is ******ing RUINED!!! Why MEEE?!?!?!? #twixtreme #ctwitzc.

1. Identify a social media platform in which to play.
2. If you need a hashtag, aim for one that helps explain the concept; for this one, we have used #twixtreme.
3. Start a hyperbolic panic about a trivial subject and/or support and add to the panic of other players' tweets.

If improv was based on theater games, what is the game in netprov?

The term *game* had two meanings for improv pioneer Del Close. One meaning was the teaching games of Viola Spolin and others. The second meaning of *game* was subtler, based on direct observation of everyday human interactions.

Dr. Eric Berne's bestselling 1964 pop-psychology book *Games People Play: The Psychology of Human Relationships* may have influenced how Close and other improv founders thought about these everyday games at the time. In the book, based on a school of psychology called *transactional analysis*, Berne describes and names psychological games such as See What You Made Me Do, I'm Only Trying to Help You, and Let's You and Him Fight.[14]

In *Truth in Comedy*, Halpern, Close, and Johnson write,

> Careful players will note that the structure of any good scene is usually a game, one that is discovered in the first three lines of dialog. A game doesn't have to be as specific and organized as some of the improv exercises explained throughout this book. Games are found within scenes. One example is one-upsmanship, where each player tries topping the other with every sentence (and of course, the opposite—continuing to lower one's own status—is equally valid).[15]

These informal or semiformal games, based closely on unconscious social and rhetorical tropes embedded in everyday life, are crucially important to netprov.

How do netprov writers know if they're doing good work?

I was trained like most literary writers of the print era, to be starved for feedback from readers . . . and to *keep smiling, darn it!* Aside from the opinions of a few trusted friends or editors, and once-in-a-lifetime letters of praise from readers, the key trait of resilient writers was to be at least 51 percent confident—based on no evidence—and just keep on writing. As my netprov path led me to collaborate more with theater and game people, I realized how different the feedback in their worlds is. Game designers think constantly about the feedback they provide their players in the form of granting scores, visual rewards (or withholding the same), sounds (celebratory or punitive), and even physical jolts to the hands via little motors built into the controllers. Actors have laughter as feedback, and they can feel the mood of the audience even in serious plays. A couple hundred people holding their breath is a thunderous response.

Feedback in the everyday games of mimicry out of which netprov grows generally takes the form of laughter. Trial and error in eliciting laughter hones our comic skills. But there's an even subtler source of feedback in everyday life. *Phatic communication* is a term used in linguistics and sociology to denote the nods, shrugs, waves, *um*s and *uh-huh*s, and other small feedback of conversation. Formerly considered meaningless, phatic communication is seen by more recent thinkers as serving a vital purpose of social bonding and support. "What's up?" long ago ceased being a real question and became more of an "I acknowledge your presence in a friendly way and I am currently available for communication." These subconscious cues—used copiously by improv actors onstage—got stripped away by early digital writing. To replace them, pokes, pings, emojis, likes, retweets, and a hodgepodge of other gestures were developed. Now these, too, have become nearly completely subconscious. Giving other netprov players born-digital phatic communication feedback, consciously, is key to good netprov play.

So what are the key things I need to know to be a strong netprov player?

Try This: Tips for Netprov Players

Play netprov within earshot of other players if you can. Netprov is a great real-life parlor game for a night with friends. I have had so much fun over the years hanging out with friends in living rooms, restaurants, and bars doing netprov. If you can't be together in person, open up a livestream with video or even just audio and netprov together. Voice your encouragement! The laughter and back-channel feedback is encouraging and inspiring!

Support by repeating. This is the most basic way of supporting other players. You can do platform-enabled repeating such as retweeting, reposting, and forwarding. And you can literally retype a text or part of someone else's text and repost it.

Support by reading aloud. If other players can hear you, when a post makes you laugh or cry, read it out loud.

Support by voting. If the platform you're using allows some kind of voting (likes, hearts, thumbs-up), make sure to vote for texts you like. If you are playing multiple characters, have them all vote.

Support by quoting. In addition to simple repeating, quote from texts as you compose your own posts: As so-and-so said, [insert quote here]; I disagree with so-and-so's position, [insert quote here]. Use terminology and names that others introduce. Copy and paste for speed. Everybody loves to be quoted.

Support by using emojis, stage directions, and other phatic communication. Write the words "nod," "smile," and "shrug." Write "yeah," "wow," or "uh-huh." Throw in an emoji, appropriate or mysterious. The time-honored, digital phatic statement "LOL" is a shortened version of a stage direction: [laughing out loud], [Rob raises an eyebrow], [twinkles eye]. Remember? [Sits at computer, types: "use stage directions," exclamation point].

Support by reacting. React directly to other players' posts as a way to advance your character's subplot. You can take your character off into the blue, but try to avoid simply doing a monologue alongside others in a feed. Reacting to others in whatever way suits your character reinforces the shared fictional world. Use your character's reaction to others to jump-start your own subplots.

Support by imitating. If another player is doing something that cracks you up and you think is brilliant, have your character join them in doing the same thing, the way people do in real life. This helps heighten distinctions between characters as they attempt the same thing with varying success. And it is the sincerest form of flattery.

Support by extending. If a player has begun a narrative thread (say they just saw a superhero in real life), support it by extending the idea. You think you, too, saw a superhero, in a coffee shop you just passed. You go back to get a second look. Now extend this just a little: sure enough, there is a superhero using the free wifi. Resist the temptation to take this quickly to a level of absurdity (e.g., everyone in the coffee shop is a superhero). Ramp things up bit by bit, giving each level a chance to breathe. Explore the ramifications of the other player's original idea.

Give more feedback than you initially think you should. Just like in real life, everyone is a little less confident than they seem to be. Support and encourage. It'll feel good and it'll produce deeper art. It's wonderful fun to play characters who start out doing nothing more than supporting other players' ideas. Those characters' depths emerge in the end.

Be patient. Let themes and stories develop. Don't rush to a conclusion. Let characters explore ambiguities and dilemmas. Have your characters tune in to the dilemmas of others. Listen carefully and your characters will let you know what they need to do.

Be real. All your characters are parts of you. They have strong personality traits but they can be complex too. Don't feel that they have to be funny (or angry, or mopey) all the time. Let them be ambivalent and share their ambivalence. If you don't quite understand what's going on with the various story lines developing in a netprov, maybe your character doesn't either. Have them seek clarification within the fiction or offer clarification.

Netprov means never having to say you're sorry. Netprov players constantly apologize for not writing more. No need! New art forms have no norms. Simply smiling at the concept is fine. Just reading a few lines of a netprov is fine. Contributing one post is fine. Contributing a ton of posts, when you have the time, is fine too. No expectations, no standards, no shoulds! You have our permission and our encouragement to make netprov all fun, with no apologies.

Are there different roles in a netprov group or is everyone the same?

There are a lot of ways of organizing netprov groups. My ideas about organized collaboration are founded on the fun we had in Invisible Seattle, putting on shows and writing together in person and online. I brought that experience with me into the graphic design and publishing worlds, which were just then transitioning to in-house typesetting and digital design and for which I created new job descriptions and workflows known over the years as "Rob's Rules of Order." I needed models and found some in the mid-twentieth-century organization of Hollywood film production centered around Irving R. Thalberg, who had the enviable role of looking in on all the films in production and providing feedback and brainstorming. My official publishing job title of troubadour represented my Thalbergesque duties.

Try This: Ideas for Organizing Your Netprov Team

Here's the way Mark and I organize large netprovs these days.

Netrunners are the creative leads, usually developing the concept and writing the inivitations. We've done netprovs with between one and four netrunners.

Featured players are our worldwide friends—artists, writers, and scholars—who come and play with us as often as they can. There are private ways of communicating among the netrunners and the featured players that allow the netrunners to focus creative energy on particular events or issues and to indicate plot points if there is a planned story. They also allow featured players to plan duets and trios. Featured players often reflect among themselves about the shape and progress of the piece.

Players are the beloved friends we haven't had a chance to meet yet. They include students, when a particular netprov is used as part of a course. It's all about the players.

A *player care coordinator* does a number of things, depending on the netprov and the time available. The PCC attends closely to the feed and welcomes newcomers by engaging them, mirroring, responding to them, and reposting. The PCC is often also responsible for online promotion (announcing the netprov in various locations) and publicity (sharing the netprov with media outlets). Once the newcomers are settled in, the PCC acts as a kind of super-featured player, giving feedback to players and featured players who haven't been responded to in a while. The role of PCC, so foreign to those with a literature background (imagine a writer offering to get a reader coffee or fetch a footstool), joins netprov from the game world, where the focus is strongly on the user. I'll talk more abou the inspiration from the game world in chapter 9.

A *graphic designer* and a *programmer* are also involved, depending on the platform and the conceptual needs of the netprov. Sometimes these roles are assumed by featured players, occasionally in the same person, but more complex projects often require paid professionals.

An *archivist* is in charge of keeping an independent archive of the netprov (you never can rely on the web to store things). This is often a netrunner or a featured player.

How do I be a good featured player?

We created the following generic encouragement and guide for our featured players, which we adapt to each netprov:

1. Follow the emails from the netrunners.
2. Locate the online folder that contains the documents for the current netprov.
3. Read the "Basic Premise" document.
4. Read the public "How to Play" page.
5. Share the description(s) of the character(s) you intend to play in the "Character" document, along with your characters' individual narrative arcs if you know them already, so that other featured players can support your characters.

6. Read about the other characters in the "Character" document so that you can support their narratives.
7. Meet online, or in person if possible, for rehearsals and real-time project play sessions, as needed.
8. Play with abandon!! (If you run out of abandon, we sell our own proprietary strain, Abandanza!™, at reasonable rates.)
9. Use the Featured Players Forum or Facebook page, if it amuses you, to share behind-the-scenes thoughts and schemes for the current netprov.
10. Attend, or participate online in, the cast party and readings after the netprov.

How do you get players to come and play netprov with you?

We've got a mailing list and we send out announcements, starting with a "save the dates" message and then build-up emails counting down to the launch. These announcements usually direct players to a website that either houses the whole netprov or at least contains a short video trailer and the rules of play. We use social media to point to either the feed or the website or both. We've developed a generic schedule for netprovs that we adapt for each project that I'll include in the appendix to this book.

How do you keep a netprov from getting too chaotic on one hand or too tightly regulated on the other?

Classic stage improv has an instructive example of creative cat herding. Del Close's most sophisticated, robust, and long-form improv game is called the Harold, suitable for an evening's cabaret entertainment. The following caveats by the shapers of the Harold capture perfectly its balancing act between stifling rigidity and the boredom of randomness:

> The first rule in Harold is that there are no rules. Still, a basic Harold usually takes on a general structure described as follows.... The team solicits a suggestion for a theme from the audience, and begins a warm-up game to share their ideas and attitudes about the theme.... Eventually, a couple of players usually start a scene. Normally, it's unrelated to the theme, although it can be inspired by elements of the warm-up game. Once the scene is established, it will be cut off by a second scene, one which has as little to do with the first scene as it has to do with the theme. After a

third scene is similarly presented, the ensemble will then participate in what is generally referred to as a "game," although the event may bear little resemblance to the audience's notion of a game.

The initial three scenes usually return again. This time, they may have some bearing on the theme. Or, maybe not. After a second group game, the scenes return for one last time, often tying into each other and the theme, and as many elements from the scenes and games as possible.

... its structure is similar to a three-act play.[16]

If stage improv isn't about dramatic conflict, what is it about?

According to Halpern, Close, and Johnson, it is about *connections*: "Where do the really best laughs come from? Terrific connections made intellectually, or terrific revelations made emotionally." With an inspiring idealism, the authors make their own connection from the fictional world back to the real world: "The connections are always there; they run through our work and through our lives. When you notice the richness of connections in a Harold on stage, then you can go out and live your own Harold."[17]

How do you come up with and develop ideas for netprovs?

Mark and I keep running lists of intriguing moments of absurdity, frustration, and irony that we observe in the digital realm. Mark's one-off Facebook joke—that he was showing up and cheerfully going to work for Mark Zuckerberg, liking things all day—became *I Work for the Web*. Once we've got a short list of possible topics, we workshop them behind the scenes with the featured players in what we call the Netprov Tes(x)t Kitchen. Here are its ground rules, which apply to all netprov play:

Netprov Tes(x)t Kitchen

1. *What is it?*
   Weekly, behind-the-scenes play sessions to test netprov prompts and hone our skills. Think jam session. Think yoga class. Think spontaneous, after-work pub crawl.

2. *But I'm so busy!*
   But our standards are shockingly low! Just come and play for a few minutes! You deserve a break from the humdrum.

3. *Who plays?*
   Folks we identify as netprov featured players—the regulars, the usual suspects. Let us know if you want to nominate someone!

4. *When does it happen?*
   We play with one prompt for a week or two, with new prompts usually coming out on Mondays.

5. *Is it a live, real-time thing or can I participate any time during the week?*
   Both. You can play asynchronously at any time. In addition, we'll often announce a one-hour, live event on Wednesdays. Local folks will gather in person (details in the invite). Folks elsewhere are welcome to join us by live audio; let us know and we'll show you how.

6. *Where do I put my writing?*
   Here in this Google Group forum. Each prompt will have its own topic and you'll make contributions as replies to that topic. We'll use other topics in the same group to make announcements.[18]

Do netprov players rehearse their characters?

Absolutely! Before the launch of *Grace, Wit & Charm*, the usual Friday happy hour gatherings of the featured players became an informal workshop. Writer-actors Cathy Podeszwa (Deb) and Gary Kruchowski (Sonny) would simply slide into character and improvise long conversations in which they invented and shared backstory. This created both a bond and a body of fictional shared experience to be used later.

On show nights, an hour before curtain in the green room, the quartet dropped into character once and for all and became, in effect, *Grace, Wit & Charm* workers preparing to work their shift. One of my favorite memories of that entire netprov was when I came in to the green room, frantically searching for one of production designer Joellyn Rock's brilliant props and listened for several minutes to a conversation that was so naturalistic that I assumed it was real, only to finally discover—with a huge laugh—that the troupe was all in character. The opening of the live shows was a "soft start," with the characters simply wandering on stage as though coming back from their break, already deep in conversation. Before the second show, the writer-actors had built up such a head of steam in the green room that director Jean Sramek didn't have to give them a signal to begin. They simply sighed, looked at their watches, and trudged dutifully "back to work."

EXAMPLE 4: *I WORK FOR THE WEB*, A NETPROV

Revolution in the Feed

One fine day in 2015, Mark Marino put on a brave face in his Facebook account:

> For those of you asking how things have been going here at Facebook Dept. of Likes: generally everything is hunky-dory. Everywhere you look there's someone throwing a thumbs up (or Flipping the Zuck). But I've started noticing different kinds of Likes. Like the not-so-nice Likes, and sometimes it seems like people feel obligated to do it, like they're afraid if they don't thumb up everything they might miss out, miss some opportunity, lose some social media capital (which come back to us as bonuses paid in FaceBucks to use in the company store). So while all and all things are really swell, I'm starting to suspect something beneath the surface—though I try not to notice it. So mostly things are A-Ok.

This was the seed for the netprov *I Work for the Web*.[i] We thought back to the railroad robber barons of the nineteenth century and imagined the secretive company that owns the Internet: RockeHearst Omnipresent Bundlers. Its charismatic leader the "explorer" (exploiter-employer) Andrew Rockehearst Sr. (@tycoonthropist on Twitter) launches a viral morale-boosting campaign on Twitter called "I Work for the Web," encouraging all social media users to celebrate and feel pride in the revenue their liking and reposting generates.

The explorer's website exhorted:

> You work for the Web!
> And it's so easy, you probably don't even know you're doing it!
> We gave you a stage to perform on!
> We let you upload your dreams and images to the clouds!

So tell us your stories on Twitter and Facebook! Now!
The Stats Don't Lie: 38% Awkward Moments; 29% Waiting On Downloads; 66% Friends Ignoring You—It all means 100% Time on Device!
We *Earn* Your Attention
Be *Proud* of Your Contributions:
Sending Comic Selfies, Trying New Emoticons, Inventing New Passwords, Clicking Celebrity Teases, Counting Your Likes, Winning Next Level, Re-typing Captchas
The wheels of the Web turn on your generosity!
You're welcome![1]

The website contained Mark Marino's animated Prezi slideshow, the text of which read, in part:

The World Wide Web, every post, every selfie, every like
50 billion posts each second
The work you do collectively could LIGHT up the entire WORLD
Andrew RockeHearst, Sr.
He put the Web to Work for You . . .
Just a twinkle in his eye . . .
And has made it HIS life's work
To build a cyberspace where Work
feels like Play!
Shout it loud:
I Work For the Web!
RockeHearst Omnipresent Bundlers says: Tell us your story #IWFW*
*By Tweeting your story using the #IWFW hashtag, you waive all copyrights and contribute your content to R.O.B. Marketing and Promotions.[2]

Instead of boosting morale and increasing donated productivity the "I Work for the Web" campaign had the opposite effect. In the netprov, ordinary web workers like you and me began to realize how much labor they'd been giving away in the form of clicks, likes, upvotes, and reposts. They balked at donating time and energy to helping voice-recognition algorithms improve through data-gathering systems such as Apple's Siri and facial recognition systems authorized by clicking on interminable terms of service. They decided to organize. Electronic literature great Mez (whom I talk about more in chapter 6) created an eerie feline to represent the legions of income-generating cats in social media (see figure 1).

Figure 1. Mez's @CaterWaull responded to the veiled threat of Mark Marino's @tycoonthropist.

Halfway through the netprov, a notorious live Twitter event was called by disgruntled workers to organize a union. The union was called the International Web and Facetwit Workers so that they, too, could use the hashtag #IWFW. The legendary rally was to happen in a real-time Twitter event at the imaginary Nighthawks bar, the sprawling, fictional hangout where all web workers in the world gather after work.

What happened at Nighthawks?

This question echoed through the netprov. A riot? A rumble? Reports conflicted. Emotions ran high. Whose side were you on? Union or no union? The tweets that came through that night brought vivid scraps of information, like the tweets from real life protest marches that year. Rumors appeared that the tycoonthropist Rockehearst was sending his brutal "Pingertons" to crush the union. No one could remain neutral. Players were encouraged to vote thumbs up to approve the union (see figure 2).

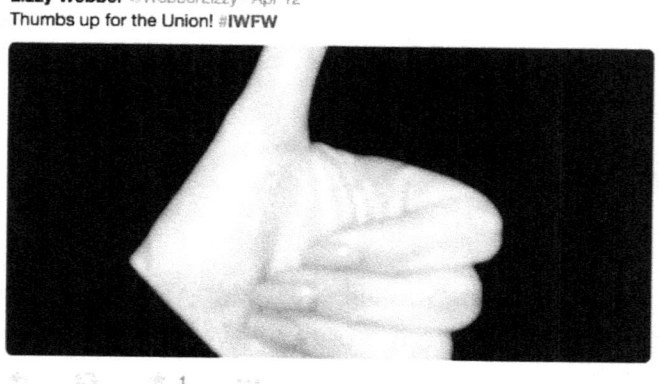

Figure 2. Voting for the International Web and Facetwit Workers union in I Work for the Web.

Figure 3. Link Dinn (played by Talan Memmott) created this union poster in I Work for the Web.

Author and electronic literature pioneer Talan Memmott's popular character @Link_Dinn was a rebel from the popular job networking site LinkedIn. Link Dinn, whose avatar image was an angry-faced wooden child's toy, had declared himself the shop steward and began putting up posters. That night in Nighthawks, Link Dinn was the rallying point for the prounion workers (see figure 3).

Artist Joellyn Rock's character @VanaEverbush (a tip of the hat to analog computer pioneer Vannevar Bush) came to the party with Russian-revolutionary-style posters to encourage a Pinterest user revolt (see figure 4).

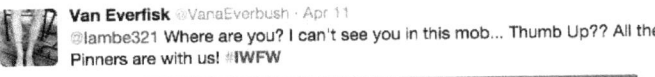

Figure 4. @VanaEverbush (played by Joellyn Rock) created this union poster in I Work for the Web.

@VanaEverbush's image was quickly co-opted by the official *I Work for the Web* account, turned upside down and reposted as fake news (see figure 5).

Figure 5. Mark Marino as the corporation flipped Joellyn Rock's poster to become a down vote in I Work for the Web.

Mark Marino's @tycoonthropist was a thin-skinned narcissist enraged at the ingratitude of the emplustomers (employee-customers). Suddenly, word spread. The Pingertons had been there. Link Dinn had been assassinated! A photo of a pile of wood shavings marked his demise. The shock wave spread through the players. After an inconclusive and possibly tampered-with vote, it was decided the netprov would end on its last day with a web workers' walkout, posting images of their hardworking fingers walking off the keyboard, off the touchpad, and off the endless job (see figures 6 and 7).

EXAMPLE 4: I WORK FOR THE WEB, A NETPROV 101

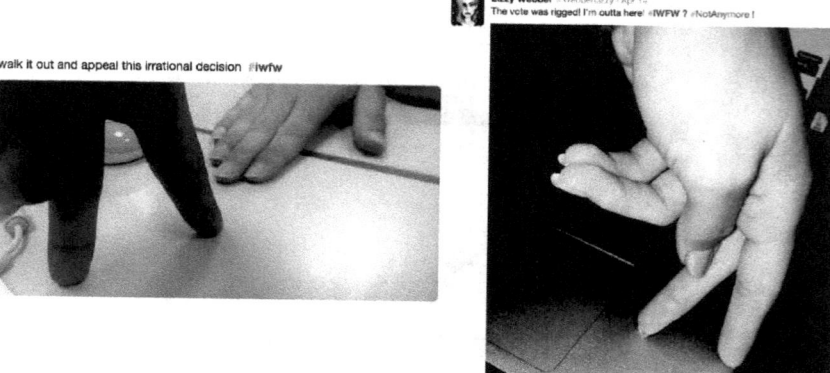

Figures 6 and 7. A two-fingered worker walkout was the climax of I Work for the Web.

Even @webwaffler, who had gone back and forth on the issues indecisively throughout the whole netprov, finally joined the walkout to honor the late Link Dinn (see figure 8).

Figure 8. @webwaffler finally stops waffling and joins the walkout in I Work for the Web.

These tiny snapshots of this huge netprov give you only the slightest hint of what fun it was to play that first time. Many players were doing multiple hilarious characters on both sides of the conflict: the union and the corporate overlords. That night at Nighthawks, in particular, has been talked about by featured players as a memorable artistic moment in their lives. To witness multiple story lines unfolding simultaneously at the hands of multiple creators is an astonishing, exhilarating, and laughter-filled experience. And many felt tears well up at the death of the beloved Link Dinn. Thankfully Link Dinn's ghost returned to give his final blessing (see figure 9).

Figure 9. The ghost of the deceased Link Dinn (played by Talan Memmott) has the final word in I Work for the Web.

Creating fiction within major commercial platforms is a carnivalesque approach to escaping corporate control. Netprov encourages you to let your fingers do the talking—and the walking.

CHAPTER 5.

SATIRICAL, SITUATIONAL NETPROVS

The improvised nature of netprov means it can respond, in real time, to real-life situations, using the same communication platforms and styles used for nonfiction texts. Satirical netprovs such as *I Work for the Web* take place within a shared situation, such as the corporate nature of social media. Netprovs such as *Workstudy Seth*, that take a more naturalistic, deadpan approach, play in a territory where it may or may not be clear to all readers whether the creator of the texts is real or imaginary.

If I'm doing a satirical netprov and I want it to be realistic, how do I make sure people know it's fiction?

I wish there was a simple answer to this, but there isn't. For example, most celebrity social media accounts are written in whole or in part by paid assistants, but not everyone knows it. And was your cousin's last vacation really that spectacular? Whether or not something is authentic is a complex negotiation between writer and readers. For many, this negotiation includes a context of inherited assumptions about certain genres of media—for example, newspaper, scientific research journal, history book—and these media's commitment to an evidence-based and peer-reviewed composition process. It also generally assumes an audience that shares a similar education and similar standards of authenticity to that of the writer. We forget the centuries it took to establish these assumptions, how ragged they were at first, and how uninclusive they have always been. What we see now is that these assumptions do not automatically transfer into new, more inclusive digital media.

Alice E. Marwick and danah boyd in their essay "I Tweet Honestly, I Tweet Passionately: Twitter Users, Context Collapse, and the Imagined

Audience" point out that despite the fact that all writers invent and address an imagined audience, knowing who that audience really is becomes a big problem in social media[1]: "Twitter flattens multiple audiences into one," they write, "a phenomenon known as 'context collapse.'" They make a nice distinction: "While Facebook or Twitter users don't know exactly who comprises their *audience addressed*, they have a mental picture of who they're writing or speaking to—the *audience invoked*." Since "the *ideal* audience is often a mirror image of the user," netprovs can only really be addressed to an invoked audience of people more or less like the netprov players themselves. This is an issue for all broadly public netprovs. It's a communication problem all of society faces in the twenty-first century: how to deal with context collapse, incomplete reading, and unknown audiences.

But what's the difference between a satirical netprov and, say, trolling?

The short answer is that intention matters. Classic online trolling as defined by Whitney Phillips in *This Is Why We Can't Have Nice Things: Mapping the Relationship between Online Trolling and Mainstream Culture* has the intention of causing emotional distress to the person trolled and then laughing derisively as that person expresses their distress.[2] In other words: trolling is bullying; its goal is to hurt and discourage.[3] Netprov, on the other hand, consists of some combination of the intentions: to entertain, to invite creative collaborative play, and to perform a wholesome satirical critique. Netprov's goal is to encourage and heal.

The satirical netprovs I like have a therapeutic or healing intention. The bloggers at the site *Aesthetics for Birds: Aesthetics and Philosophy of Art for Everyone* share a new definition of satire by Dieter Declerq as comprising, necessarily, entertainment and critique. Blog author aestheticsforbirds writes, "Satire, by contrast, functions as critique, which I understand as a committed moral opposition against a target, sustained by an analysis of that target's perceived social wrongness."[4] Satirical critique is diagnosis for the purpose of finding a cure.

What are other ways netprovs could take advantage of a situation and be used for encouragement and healing?

When the University of Chicago moved all classes online in response to the COVID-19 pandemic in the spring of 2020, students were suddenly dispersed and isolated, their sense of community torn apart. A multidisciplinary creative team from the university's Fourcast Lab and Weston Game Lab leapt into action and created an alternate reality game (ARG) called *A Labyrinth* to reconnect students through creative fun. "An alternate reality game," according to Wikipedia, "is an interactive networked narrative that uses the real world as a platform and employs transmedia storytelling to deliver a story that may be altered by players' ideas or actions."[5] ARGs often last months and challenge teams collaborating from near and far to solve puzzles and find real-world locations to succeed.

"It sounds like the most U Chicago thing out there to do," a student player recounted in a documentary video about *A Labyrinth*: "They would make a game for us to do to keep us kind of sane."[6] It started with an email to students with a seemingly innocuous barcode at the bottom. The barcode was, in the traditional terminology of ARGs, a "rabbit hole" that, viewed with a smartphone, led to a website that initiated players into the game. Cogame director and professor of English and cinema and media studies Patrick Jagoda explained the core fiction: "The idea is that there is an alternative version of the University . . . that's called Labyrinth, a kind of inter-dimensional maze. At its center is a character named the Taur." The character is "trying to find its way back to the Labyrinth," adds Heidi Coleman, the Cogame director, teaching in theater and performance studies: "The Taur character must go through a series of exercises, almost like a training, in order to be allowed back in. And that character does that with the help of the players."

As Jagoda explains in his summary of the project:

> On April 6, 2020, A Labyrinth began with an opening puzzle that unlocked the game and attracted approximately 3,500 players. A week later, on April 13, the Fourcasters welcomed 73 core teams to compete by completing 140 quests. Alongside the competitive aspect, the game had a parallel collaborative dimension. Via the Twitch live streaming platform, players were invited to explore the alternative space-time known as Labyrinth. Once a week, via a live and collectively adjudicated interactive narrative format (essentially, a video-based "Choose Your Own Adventure" style narrative), players helped the Taur locate key hubs and hidden objects as they tried to make it back to the center of Labyrinth.[7]

Quests designed by interface and game mistress Ashlyn Sparrow (I love this project's job titles!) and her team were organized into the categories of connecting, making, moving, solving, playing, researching, and world building. Of the quests, one student says, "They are so creative! For example, I've been leaning so much about different breads from different countries, or braille or semaphore signaling language."[8] Professors across the university were invited to make short videos giving instructions for quests based on their expertise. "We have hundreds of photos and videos of amazing creative work,"[9] says Sparrow.

The live Twitch streaming video feed, which invited viewers to vote, "allowed for not just a broadcast experience, but an interactive experience that you might find in an improv show," says Coleman.[10] The camera showed the world through the eyes of the Taur. Video designer Marc Downie laid out a map of short, gorgeously produced video clips he had taken on campus and was able to play them on the feed according to the choices made by players in real time. The clips, which featured a simulated information overlay and sophisticated cinematic storytelling effects, showed game-like interactions with objects, with actors playing characters, or motion from one area to another. Objects the camera/Taur picked up, as voted by players, unlocked more quests on the website.

Coleman described the real-time collaboration of the production team in a way familiar to netprov netrunners: "We were jamming so hard to get all of those quests written. And I kind of imagine, in broadcast news, where they're running across the studio to get the quest to play live. It felt like we were writing live."[11] "I had to wait until really late at night," recounts Sparrow, "to really make sure those points were calculated because that's when I knew: people are sleeping, and the only person that's awake is me."[12]

"We were not intending to create an archive of shelter in place," says Coleman, "but that is in many ways what happened." Sparrow concludes, "Maybe games are the solution. Maybe actually engaging people with multiple ideas, multiple ideologies, multiple gameplay styles is the way to get people to think and do something a little different."[13]

Of the ongoing work of the Chicago team, Jagoda says, "With each game we've thought about ways to use new and emerging technologies to produce better forms of collective improvisation." To me, *A Labyrinth* is a great example of artists being fully present in a historical moment and improvising social medicine with their healing powers of imagination.

A Labyrinth was pretty clearly a fictional fantasy, but don't some ARGs blur the line more between fiction and reality?

Yes, they do. In fact, there is a philosophy behind some ARGs from virtually the beginning of the form that is called "this is not a game" (TINAG).[14] Game and netprov designer and scholar Lauren Burr summarizes TINAG: "Instead of operating in the artificial reality of a clearly defined magic circle, ARGs overlay a fictional narrative on top of the real world inhabited by the players: an alternate, but not quite alternative, reality. . . . Thus in proclaiming that 'this is not a game' everything becomes a game."[15]

In thinking through the ethics of such games, Burr refers to the work of Markus Montola, Jaakko Stenros, and Annika Waern, authors of *Pervasive Games: Theory and Design*, who look at the threshold between a game being a *nuisance* and being *harmful*. They use the example of an outdoor rock concert as an event that can be a nuisance but is not harmful and contend that nuisances are an unavoidable part of urban life.

A final important principle Burr touches on is one we know from theater called "staying in character." Staying in character straddles the line between fact and fiction. Take a department store Santa Claus, for example: Are you going to be the one who announces to a line of kids what you know to be true? Fictional characters mingle among us in real life at theme parks, educational historical monuments, Renaissance fairs, the films of satirist-activist Sacha Baron Cohen, and, of course, professional wrestling. There is a term from wrestling I find quite useful: *kayfabe*. Wikipedia, defines kayfabe as,

> in professional wrestling . . . the portrayal of staged events within the industry as "real" or "true," specifically the portrayal of competition, rivalries, and relationships between participants as being genuine and not of a staged or pre-determined nature of any kind. Kayfabe has also evolved to become a code word of sorts for maintaining this "reality" within the direct or indirect presence of the general public.[16]

Politicians keep kayfabe around constituents, as do teachers with students, doctors with patients, and even parents with children. And children see through the gesture and love to mimic it.

So, what are the differences between mimicry, parody, and satire?

I've talked about mimicry and its accompanying laughter and how it is integrated with children's early learning. We return now to those children to see them using mimicry to imitate and exaggerate not just puppy but an adult, perhaps even the foul-tempered head of the clan. The child offers this satire as comfort to his peers, disadvantaged in age and rank. The revolutionary consolation satire expresses is, "The problem is not you, it is their inappropriate bad temper." The laughter not only amuses, it encourages.

I take *parody* to be the mimicry and exaggeration of a characteristic style, either in a person or a creative work. I take *satire* to be parody with the additional mission of denouncing evils. Many netprovs, ours and others', are critical—critical of both the content and form of contemporary communication; they are, in fact, *therapeutic*, aiming to reveal, correct, and heal.

The commedia dell'arte spoke truth to power, truth camouflaged in seemingly self-mocking silliness, and performed a kind of social recalibration and rebalancing in societies that were cruelly hierarchical. The vapid vanity of the elite, the cupidity of the clergy, and the small-mindedness of peasants are among the constant themes. No part of the social network was immune to being lampooned. Commedia was an equal-opportunity offender. But the biggest, most dangerous laughs came from bringing down the high and mighty.

What kinds of things do your netprovs satirize?

Looking back at our netprovs of the last decade, one strong theme that emerges is a satirical critique of what you might call a harmful gamification of social discourse. *I Work for the Web* is a prime example. So is *#fixurl8tionship*,[i] which invited players to "join a squad of Instagram influencers who 'FIX' fans' relationships by helping them look *GREAT* for the camera despite how they feel inside!!"[17] The site goes on:

> On the Internet, it's not how you feel, but how you look that counts. We create perfect lives full of perfect friends hanging out on perfect vaycays (think Fyre festival). At the same time, the internet is full of people ready to give you advice on how to fix what's broken in your life: your car, your computer, your hair, et cetera.

In #fixurl8tionship, we imagine a fictional world of influencers who give you superficial advice on how to fix the appearance of your broken relationships. As with most people giving advice, the person who gives it is generally the person who needs it the most. Still, hypocrisy needs no URL, just a hashtag. In this netprov, you will join the community to give and get advice on how to fix your relationships [for the camera].

We realized that likes, favorites, and other social media scorekeeping not only make money for the Rockehearsts of the world, but gamifying self-presentation actually can hurt people in small and big ways.

But netprov is all about games, about play, right?

Yes, but there is competitive play and there is cooperative play. Game theorist Jane McGonigal writes of competitive play: "Games make us happy because they are hard work that we choose for ourselves and it turns out that almost nothing makes us happier than good, hard work." And, she asserts, "That's exactly what the game industry is doing today. It's fulfilling our need for better hard work—and helping us choose for ourselves the right work at the right time."[18]

McGonigal is saying that play is work?

McGonigal is talking about organized, competitive play, play with a scoreboard, play that, like work (to her mind), has objective proof of success. If you lay enough stones you have a castle. Or if, as Scott Rettberg suggests in his article *Corporate Ideology in World of Warcraft*, you kill a certain number of computer-simulated enemies, you have a career. The enormously popular *World of Warcraft*, according to Rettberg,

> offers its players a capitalist fairytale in which anyone who works hard enough and strives enough can rise through society's ranks and acquire great wealth. Moreover, beyond simply representing capitalism as good, *World of Warcraft* serves as a tool to educate its players in a range of behaviors and skills specific to the situation of conducting business in an economy controlled by corporations.[19]

"Social Media functions as a giant scoreboard to confer significance to events that are more or less meaningless in the moment," writes Rob Hornung: "Getting likes on a photo of the meal you made yourself is more important and more significant than eating it."[20] Metrics make the meal.

The compulsive acquisitiveness of a consumption-driven economy is enacted in microcosm in the acquisition of likes, favorites, and retweets. For both the material economy and the emotional economy to work as perpetual motion engines, the good feelings elicited by acquisition must be short lived.

As Jacob Silverman, in *Terms of Service, Social Media and the Price of Constant Connection*, writes, "Metrics help create the hierarchies that are embedded in all social networks," and adds, "the goal of the digital space becomes not to enjoy yourself or aimlessly interact, but to rise higher in the game, which really can't be won."[21]

The social media scoreboard is how you know "how you're doing" in life. As my fictional *nom de clavier*, Hans Paedeweyder, wrote in my Facebook account:

> Facebook is a communication experience that, instead of satisfying your need to know, constantly reinforces a subtle, haunting, desperate awareness of the other, more important communications you have missed. Instead of reassuring you that you belong and you are well-liked it taunts you with endless comparisons with the greater success, greater beauty, greater popularity of others.

This is where Facebook has done Coke one better. Coke created an artificial craving only Coke could satisfy. Facebook has created an artificial craving that nothing can satisfy. Facebook is a beverage that makes you thirstier the more you drink it.

Why would social media platforms try to make you unhappy?

The more your craving keeps you on the device the more data you produce and the more money social media platforms make from selling it. Happy, unhappy—it's all good data. In fact, arguments are especially lucrative. Political arguments, for example: ching, ching, ching, the cash register rings! C. Thi Nguyen, speaking at the Royal Institute of Philosophy on the toxic polarization of political discourse, lists the following attributes of this system:

> Moral outrage porn: gives pleasure for adopting a simple system. Numbers: hide nuance and make the measured thing most salient. Gamification: gives people pleasure of adopting the (quantified) simplified goals. Echo chambers: dismisses complexifying new ideas from the outside.[22]

"The big worry I have," says Nguyen, "is that people are designing systems to create sticky narrow-mindedness."

Netprovs such as *All-Time High* and *I Work for the Web* intend to widen minds, to reveal invisible structures through satire. *I Work for the Web* in particular struck at the heart of the value corporations extract from seemingly user-centered online activities and how the companies' earnings rely on what I call a *consistent consumer ego*. A netprov duet by Mark Marino and Claire Donato called *Trading Faces* took this even further.

Try This: Trading Faces

1. Swap your Facebook account password with someone you really trust.
2. In phase one, try to impersonate the other person faithfully.
3. Contact your partner directly in case of emergency or if a follower seems to be truly upset.
4. In phase two, merge your personality with that of your partner.
5. In phase three, become fully yourself in the other's avatar.

Some Facebook friends were mystified, some a little concerned as "Mark" and "Claire" posted their experiments with unexpected activities. Donato reflected: "It was really disorienting—the different layers of persona and presentation. I would often forget who I was, and whose account I was logged into. Perhaps our avatars like take on these lives of their own. Mark can be logged in as Claire, but maybe Claire-the-avatar, is still Claire in some sense."[23]

So, you're suggesting that there is a possibility of liberation through netprov?

Communications theorist David Meurer, in his essay "Capturing the Imagination: Literary Expression, Participatory Culture and Digital Enclosure," asks whether or not it is possible for our consistent consumer egos to ever be free in social media platforms. In a section called "Performing Imagined or Fluid Identities," he notes,

> while participatory digital narratives operate within the ever-widening organizing logic of the network and are thus subject to forms of enclo-

sure and indirect extraction of value, they prompt us to imagine the potentials of the network in ways that problematize assumptions about the veracity of our identities and interests, and thereby undermine the efficiency of profiling algorithms. . . . They also allow us to develop subject positions, non-normative identities, and dispositions that are not so easily subsumed.[24]

Netprov may provide a way out. Netprovs, via the commedia, come from the tradition of carnival. Carnival is the time when all goes topsy-turvy. The usual rules don't apply—masters serve servants, masks allow preforgiven liaisons, costumes allow forbidden power reversals—and brutally hierarchical societies enjoy an escape valve, a chance to blow off steam before things explode. If carnival exists at all, then "normal life" is not proven God-ordained but just a matter of chance, force, and privilege, never to be taken entirely seriously.

Most importantly these satirical, situational netprovs embody an alternative value network to the unacknowledged labor of the obedient consumer. Instead of an addiction to acquisition, netprov offers satisfaction here and now—satisfaction in play, in creativity. It is a value network of inner rewards, redeemable in the moment, good forever. A real, connected, community based on "yes, and."

EXAMPLE 5: *REALITY: BEING @SPENCERPRATT,* A NETPROV

Join the Game!

In January of 2013, reality TV stars Spencer Pratt and his wife Heidi Montag were sequestered on the set of the 24/7 surveillance TV show *Celebrity Big Brother* in England. Collectively dubbed "Speidi" by tabloids, Spencer and Heidi came to fame starting in 2006 in the pioneering lifestyle reality show *The Hills,* framed as a weekly documentary about rich Los Angeles teens. Heidi was encouraged and edited to be the ingenue; Spencer took on the role of (using professional wrestling's behind-the-scenes term for its villains) the *heel.* Now, the British producers of *Celebrity Big Brother* had cast them into their crucible as the couple you love to hate.

Suddenly, tweets began to appear to the million-plus followers of Spencer's account, seeming to break the rules of the show, which forbid its stars from using social media during the game:

Spencer Pratt, @spencerpratt January 2, 2013
Testing . . . Testing . . .

Spencer Pratt, @spencerpratt January 2, 2013
OMG!

Spencer Pratt, @spencerpratt January 2, 2013
Woh.

Spencer Pratt, @spencerpratt January 2, 2013
Yes, cheers, everyone, this is actually Spencer Pratt.

Spencer Pratt, @spencerpratt January 2, 2013
And I am married to Heidi Montag. Wow.

Spencer sounds different. He knows an awful lot about poetry all of a sudden, including asking followers for bookshop recommendations in London and correcting Twitter followers on their knowledge of haikus. How can he be tweeting when he's supposed to be out of touch in the *Celebrity Big Brother* house, his fans want to know? Heidi's account confirms that Spencer has lost his new phone in London. Spencer's loyal followers begin to call out the tweets as impostures and their author as a thief:

> Spencer Pratt, @spencerpratt January 2, 2013
> Maybe I should just say: I love you all followers, except maybe the people who are tweeting nasty things about me right now.

> Spencer Pratt, @spencerpratt January 2, 2013
> Although being a celebrity, I suppose I have the magnanimity to love even those who spew forth twitter hate

The voice of Spencer's feed gradually gives up trying to mimic Spencer and shares more about the predicament of being in possession of the phone. He delights followers by giving them the honor of retweeting them. Spencer's followers begin to beg for "rts" (retweets). Over the next few days, the account releases a series of glamorous, candid photos of Heidi found on the phone, showing off her gorgeous mani-pedi, flirting with Gandalf, and showing off her enormous stack of laundry. When the mysterious finder of the phone is unable to sell the mobile to British tabloids, he gradually reveals that he is an obscure British poet who is dying to promote his literary career but, despite his sudden access to a huge Twitter audience, can't, out of fear of being arrested. Spencer's followers dub the imposter "Tempspence" (temporary Spencer).

> Spencer Pratt, @spencerpratt January 2, 2013
> This rt-ing is wearing out my thumbs. Perhaps a challenge is in order: rt's only for haikus

And followers rose to the challenge, Googling the rules of haiku and giving it their best shot. The haiku game begins a series of writing games, each with its own hashtag, in which Tempspence rewarded the best players with retweets. The games included:

#twouplets

Poets write rhyming replies to another's tweets, particularly tweets not intended as poetry. These work best when you match the syllable count (roughly) and complement the content by continuing the idea. Many players used internal rhymes so that each tweet itself was a couplet.

#exphrastic

Ekphrasis is describing a picture in text. In this game, we describe pictures of ourselves, revealing intimate details and moments from our lives, without attaching the photo to our tweet. Since Tempspence cannot share a picture of himself, we take on his burden by trying to share ourselves without showing ourselves. It's a way to become intimate while remaining anonymous.

#shibboleth

Facing a constant barrage of accusations of being a fake as Spencer's followers put two and two together, Tempspence invites the poet-players to tweet something about yourself, about the real you, the you-you, that only those closest to you, your mum, your best mate, would also know. Share a doodle that you typically draw on the corner of a napkin while on the phone, breaking up with your BF or voting for TV's #teamspeidi.

#centode

To help Tempspence woo his two ladies, Una and Duessa, users are invited to submit lines of poetry about their own girlfriend or boyfriend—just a simple line that describes a quirk or an endearing quality or something dark or beautiful. To submit to the poem, Tempspence poets replaced the name of their loved one with either Una or Duessa. Tempspence creates poems out of these lines and presents them to one or another of his ladies.

As a netprov *Reality: Being @spencerpratt* pivoted on the name Spencer, with the imaginary poet winding up, by the end of the month, telling the story of his own romantic life using the code names Una and Duessa, characters in Renaissance English poet Edmund Spenser's *Faerie Queene*. Following the *Big Brother* format, the @spencerpratt account's followers voted on which of the two damsels Tempspence should try to woo.

Who was Tempspence? Tempspence was Mark Marino with some help from me, and the whole netprov was done at the request of Spencer and Heidi themselves. The real Spencer, as it happens, was one of Mark's students in a USC class where he taught about netprov, including *Workstudy Seth*. As a TV star deep in the world of paid social media helpers, Spencer thought *Workstudy Seth* was brilliant—a topsy-turvy turnabout of power and fame. Spencer also participated himself in the netprov *Fantasy Automated Investory's League (F.A.I.L.)*, which I talk about in chapter 8. As Speidi prepared to dive into the *Celebrity Big Brother* isolation after completing Mark's course, Spencer asked Mark if he would like access to his and Heidi's accounts for a netprov. For a delicious and delirious month, Mark and I would talk on the phone once a day or more as we watched the waves of reaction among Speidi's Twitter followers, planning Tempspence's next move. Articles began to appear about Tempspence, such as "Spencer Pratt Loses His Christmas Present from Heidi Montag On 'Wild' New Year's Eve" in *EntertainmentWise*[1]; "'Thief' Who Stole CBB Star Spencer Pratt's Phone Starts Sharing Intimate Pictures of Wife Heidi Montag" in the *Daily Mail*[2]; and, later, "How The Hills' Spencer Pratt Landed at the Center of a Complex Piece of Twitter Performance Art" in *The Observer*.[3] Mark and I began trying to entice followers into literary play, hoping that Spencer and Heidi wouldn't be mad at us once they emerged from *Celebrity Big Brother* isolation.

Speidi loved what we had done. That was a big relief for us. Media and performance artist Kate Durbin wrote soon after:

> As someone who follows and re-tweets celebrities on Twitter for my own conceptual Twitter project, I came across Tempspence naturally, as I followed and re-tweeted Spencer Pratt already. When Spencer / Tempspence tweeted that he was buying his girlfriend Heidi Montag my collaborator Amaranth Borsuk's digital poetry book *Between Page and Screen*, the top of my head exploded, in a post-Dickinson-cyberspace kind of way.... I cannot resist any project that implodes the false distance between mediums / worlds normally considered totally disparate, such as reality TV and avant garde literature.[4]

CHAPTER 6.

THE THINGNESS OF LANGUAGE

Wordplay in Netprov

These tweets are part of a multigame, prepandemic-era netprov called *Center for Twitzease Control*, the motto of which was "Infectious Wordplay—Pass it On!"

SammieSammie, @SammieS42823042 April 16, 2013
By dose is so sduffy! koff #twitflu #ctwitzc

Y, @descen_t April 16, 2013
Id dreally lige a beanud budder ad djelly righd now #ctwitzc #twitflu @spencerpratt @digits91

Spencer Pratt, @spencerpratt April 16, 2013
@SammieS42823042 Ugh, I hobe your code is nod cadchy #ctwitzc #twitflu

Why does seeing something spelled wrong on purpose make me chuckle?

Does it? Oh, good! It makes me chuckle too! Comic misspelling is a universal gesture that is simultaneously silly and deep. The social layer of comic wrongness reminds us of all the hours we spend in school "trying to get it right." To misspell is foolish and audiences (and God) love a fool. But there is an even more primordial chasm over which misspelling dangles us: the fundamental arbitrariness of alphabetic and phonetic writing. The right angles of the letter *T* on paper or on screen are no more related to the sound of that letter, made using the tip of the tongue, than *O* or the symbol $. Like the transgressive music of puns we talked about earlier, alphabetic-phonetic languages show us that form-content connections are simultaneously vital and random.

Why does it matter that the alphabet is random?

The arbitrariness of spelling points to another, deeper mystery—a deeper failure—that lies at the very heart of language. This is the fact that language doesn't really work very well. By this I mean that language, as poets, lovers, and parents have always found, is woefully inadequate for describing precisely the complex inner state of a human being. And our inner states are probably the most important aspects of our lives. Sure, we can get close to describing these states using images and analogies and we can elicit shared experience—all the tricks of rhetoric. But still, there are always things going on in our vast, whole-body, neurochemical, parallel-processing conundrum that leave us at a loss for words. And, at the same time that language is a frustrating disappointment, it is also a precious miracle that works far better than we have a right to expect. So we keep trying to share what the world feels like, and we call it literature.

Spelling in English has a history worth remembering as well. Standardized spelling is a recent phenomenon. Shakespear famously spelled his own name at least three different ways. Until the late-nineteenth century, the alphabetic-phonetic system was a relatively relaxed toolkit. Rigorously standardized spelling is an artifact of empire—the imposition at gunpoint of English as a worldwide language—which those who find themselves fiercely prescribing certain standards of spelling would do well to remember. Spelling always evolves, but the combination of commerce, politics, and technology in the twentieth century has left spelling stagnant for an unusually long time. It's time for a change.

Spelling and digital new media have quite an intertwined history. From URLs to hashtags to LOL-style acronyms to emojis, there arguably have been more innovations in spelling in digital media than in any other area of culture outside of hip-hop music.

My favorite online spelling stylist, the one whose work has influenced my line-by-line creative writing more than anyone else, is the magnificent Mez. Also known by the 3D-world handle Mary-Anne Breeze and as codewurker, Mez is a net.art practitioner and game designer.

What is Mez's writing like?

Mez's inter.mangling (see? I can't help myself from imitating Mez!) of computer programming code and English positions her texts on the border between human readability and machine readability. But her true triumph is her astonishing collection of portmanteau words and phrases that present the complex internal contradictions of human life in inextricable bundles. This fragment from the print anthology *Human Readable Messages [Mezangelle 2003–2011]* gives you a hint of Mez's linguistic style, which she dubs *mezangelle*:

> 2.3.9 _g[u]ilt skin + de[a]finition_dec[oy]ay
> [4.d]
> #t.Racking memories + cau[gh]terizing.w[ild.fire]hilst.moving
> #sto.Rage _[c]hiding while goats.blink+stamp.in.(ley)lined.troops
> #[s]huff[l]ing.insectile.heat+bite.[m|b]a rking.on.a.g.Host.luved.fig[I]ure
> _click: a.lone. vs .l.One.ly
> _shutter: [clay|silicon].chips + wool. Swathes.earth.r[d]ec[ayed]l(m)aimed
> _retrieve: b.Link.reminders every.wh.er(r)e[1]

Mezangelle, among its many other virtues, takes up the challenge left to literary writing by James Joyce's *Finnegans Wake*, the book written entirely in multilayered, multilingual puns, and responds to Joyce in kind, carrying his simultaneously forward- and backward-looking linguistic experiments into the twenty-first century. The definition of *mezangelle* found on the back cover of *Human Readable Messages* is the best one available, so I share it here:

> Q: wot do u get if u stitch 2gether standardized literary conventions [think: the monumental output of bill shakespeare + the staccato pulsings of emily dickinson] with coded poetics steeped in digitally-drenched communication?
>
> A: mezangelle
>
> https://traumawien.at/prints/human-readable-messages/breeze_cover_us.pdf

As Mez and mezangelle point out, the transition to digital screenwriting in multiple platforms is another reminder of the arbitrariness of language and of our current, invisible-to-ourselves, random stylistic constraints.

Even though alphabetic languages are supposed to translate sounds into squiggles, English puts the *b* back in subtle with its silent and inconsistently spoken scribblings. Emojis are quite literally tiny facial expressions (😀). CAPS ARE UNDERSTOOD TO BE SHOUTING, GOL-DANG IT! We've already pointed at the fun to be had in stage directions, he said, laughing out loud (LOL). Initialisms such as IMHO, for *in my humble opinion*, become almost abstract, visual symbols for a phrase or concept, in the same way that we no longer read the & symbol as a calligrapher's version of the Latin *et* (and).

You're really enthusiastic about all this, aren't you?

[Rob climbs the hill and addresses the multitudes of netprov players.] Use these tricks! And abuse them! Have clueless characters get them wrong, or invent new experimental versions of them. This is great fun IYPLETTAI (if you pause long enough to think about it). We made the netprov *Center for Twitzease Control* a playground for just such experiments. We introduced it like this on the netprov's website:

About Center for Twitzease Control

Mission
The Center for Twitzease Control is dedicated to the identification, perfection and promulgation of social-media text mutations. It is a netprov organized by Mark C. Marino and Rob Wittig, along with Brendan Howell and Mark Sample.

The Situation
Mutant wriding manoeuvres run rampant—mzspellings, V15UAL PUN5, vrbl cntrctionz—creating a #ashtag #ash of bzzre wordzmbies roaming the legible landscape intent on eading aye!-balls. Some of these saucy dish-eases are netprovised by humans, others are autonomically produced by alrogythmically progummed infirmware. In all bud a few cases their libes are cut shrt before they blossom. They have not the miminum viability g*d g*ve a bacterium.

Our Goal
We seek to mark and robusticate rambo-unctuously self-supporating streigns of verbal virtulence and send em out to multiplea and readoublicate in ever-writening consentric rings.[2]

To keep up the fiction of a public health agency, the prompts are written as press releases and adapted for Twitter, the platform we used for the inaugural version.

Try This: Social Media Flu

Here's a great, simple, language-game netprov:

1. Identify a social media platform in which to play.
2. If you need a hashtag, aim for one that helps explain the concept; for this one, we have used #twitflu.
3. Write some posts inspired by the following public announcement:

    Bajor Dwidder Flu Oudbreag *koff*
    Sources report a MAJOR grammar- and spelling-resistant strain of Twitter flu spreading at this hour, particularly in the NE and SW USA. The Center for Twitzease Control has released the following statement: "Doze infegted wid the Dwidder Flu wride as tho they had a bonstrous head code sniff koff. To be the bona fide Dwidder Flu bessages bust condain the word "sniff" or "koff" ad leazd odce in each dweed. The signadure ha ha hatchoo! eggsguse me hashdag of the dwidder flue is #twitflu. All Twidzeases use the hashdag #ctwitzc." Stay tuned for farther...

Try This: Whoz a Kewt Widdle Twitzeaze? U R!! #bbtalk...

This is another favorite from the Twitzease collection:

1. Identify a social media platform in which to play.
2. If you need a hashtag, aim for one that helps explain the concept; for this one, we have used #bbtalk.
3. Write some posts inspired by the following public announcement:

    Embarrassed reports from people worldwide conducting important business with clients, professional peers, and attempting serious communication about intimate relationships confirm an outbreak of the Twitzease #bbtalk. Symptoms: cloying and annoying phonetic baby talk. Retweet tag: #TZT. Hashtags: #bbtalk #ctwitzc. Example: Pwease come by our office to put a eensy teensy signature on your contwact. Pwetty pwease? #bbtalk #ctwitzc.

Try This: VWL DRGHT (Vowel Drought)

Here's a netprov that puckers up your mind like biting into a lime:

1. Identify a social media platform in which to play.
2. If you need a hashtag, aim for one that helps explain the concept; for this one, we have used #-vwls.
3. Write some posts inspired by the following public announcement:

   The Center for Twitzease Control reported this morning that a sudden diminution in the global percentage of tweeted vowels began to occur in places as disparate as Gdansk, Poland, rural regions of Peru, and Kyzyl-Kiya, Kyrgyzstan. Researchers at the CTwitzC are mystified as to the method and motivation of the Twitzease's spread, citing theories as disparate as vowel dieting, vowel conservation, or perhaps an as-yet-unnoticed worldwide vwel shrtage. Symptoms: all vowels are removed from a tweet. Example: Wh wnts t g fr ccktls ftr wrk?
   #-vwls #ctwitzc.

Try This: Long Hashtag Meme Gene Amok!

Feeling prolix? Try this sumptuous netprov:

1. Identify a social media platform in which to play.
2. If you need a hashtag, aim for one that helps explain the concept; for this one, we have used #hsh2long.
3. Scientists at the Center for Twitzease Control finally have been able to isolate the Twitzease that appears to be the logical conclusion of the trend of ever-lengthening fake hashtags—the dreaded #hsh2long. Symptoms: the message portion of the entire Tweet consists of one long hashtag. Example: #ifitactuallysnowstonightI'mgoingtoabsolutelyfreakoutitisAprilforchrissakesIrefusetoshovelanymore.

In addition to our basic encouragement to use both the overall netprov hashtag #TZT and the particular Twitzease's hashtag, we offer these variant mutations:

1. Double down: Send the same tweet twice, first the way you normally would, then altered by that day's Twitzease and hashtag (e.g., #opposite).
2. Reflection infection: Reply to others, sending them back their tweets altered by that day's Twitzease and hashtag (#TZT).
3. Ongoing mutation: Partners or groups send the same tweet and hashtag back and forth multiple times or pass it on; the Twitzease alters the text more each time.
4. Evolve the strain: Take one of the existing Twitzeases and mutate it. Give it your own hashtag, and then give all your friends big open-mouthed Twitter kisses (twisses) and see how it spreads.

Should different netprov characters use different kinds of spelling?

Yes, it's a great trick. It can give a visual texture to a character's posts, which helps them stand out from the firehose torrent of posts in a large project. It also can reveal a character's inner struggles. Sometimes there's a physical reason for the altered spelling—low visibility, technical malfunction, or injury—that adds to the realism.

In the 2011 netprov *Grace, Wit & Charm*, Mark's character Neil is suffering from carpal tunnel syndrome, which intensifies his plaintive posts:

Neil, @Neil_GWaC May 14, 2011
My wrists are KILLING me today. 2many Smoothmoves! #gwandc

Sonny, @Sonny1SoBlue May 14, 2011
Ah, your wifey must be deploydmented again, Neil! RT @Neil_GWAC My wrists are KILLING me today. 2many Smoothmoves! #gwandc

Laura, @Laura_GWaC May 14, 2011
Seems like those wrists have been bothring you for a while @Neil_GWaC #gwandc

Neil, @Neil_GWaC May 14, 2011
Yeh, and the quacktor gave me tehese Canadian meds and Im sure they're plazebos. cant even swing the three-sided sword! #gwandc[3]

Try This: Play A Character with Unique Orthography

Here's some great practice for making your netprov character be recognizable and memorable in the feed:

1. Create a character and have them work themselves out of a dangerous situation in seven posts.
2. What drives your character's "mistakes?" Speed, overwrought emotion, rebelliousness?
3. Be careful not to mock undereducation. It is a traditional ploy in literature, but it comes off as mean-spirited, since undereducation is most often a byproduct of poverty. Your character can be a knucklehead, but as a starting point, make them a privileged knucklehead (there are plenty of them).

Like so many other electronic literature creators, we were inspired in our investigations of the materiality of language by the experiments of the French writer's group called Oulipo (Ouvroir de littérature potentielle, which is translated as "workshop for potential literature" or "sewing circle of potential literature").

I've heard of this; what is the Oulipo?

Picture this: A group of French mathematicians and writers meet for a fine dinner on an autumn evening in Paris in 1958. They delight each other reading texts created by mathematical systems. The literary formulas of the Oulipo are game-like, both in their use of rules and, occasionally, in their implied sense of competition. Note that the social infrastructure of the Oulipo is based around ritual monthly dinners. These dinners might seem like a social structure apart from, and unconnected with, their literary activities, but I see them as an exact parallel to the camaraderie of the commedia dell'arte and to the far-flung friendships of netprov.

Oulipo creates mathematically based literary forms. As the American Oulipian Harry Mathews explained to me in conversation, whenever Oulipians tell people that, they get a puzzled look. So Oulipians immediately add: think of a sonnet, which is a mathematical form. Basic Oulipian games include N+7, in which you replace every noun in a text with the seventh noun to follow it in a given dictionary, and lipograms, in which you write a text without using a given letter or letters of the alphabet.

Oulipian writers find these strict rules liberating. They often frame their practices as games. Mathews writes:

> The Oulipo supplies writers with hard games to play. They are adult games insofar as children cannot play most of them; otherwise they bring us back to a familiar home ground of our childhood. Like Capture the Flag, the games have demanding rules that we must never forget (well, hardly ever), and these rules are moreover active ones: satisfying them keeps us too busy to worry about being reasonable. Of course our object of desire, like the flag to be captured, remains present to us. Thanks to the impossible rules, we find ourselves doing and saying things we would never have imagined otherwise, things that often turn out to be exactly what we need to reach our goal.[4]

Early on, the Oulipo also begain experimenting with machine-made literature, benefiting from the overlap between the mathematicians in the group and computer scientists. The great catalog of Oulipo experiments continues to inform and inspire netprov.

So far there have been two main kinds of activity in electronic literature: programming machines to write literature and using new digital modes as platforms for human-written literature. Netprov has found itself mostly in the latter category. But Mark, along with some other netprovers, has constructed bots that participate in netprovs, such as the cheer bots who plagued the halls and events of *All-Time High*.

Do I have to be a programmer to build a bot?

Not at all! There are simple bots that can be made in Google Docs. Programming is just another language. And as if all the arbitrary absurdities of language we've discussed already weren't enough, there's more! As you may know, the humans of our planet speak in different languages.

Yeah—what's up with that?

I know, right? Myths such as the Tower of Babel try to understand, order, and explain the multiplicity of tongues, but we're often stuck not only trying to translate what's going on inside us into language but then translating that into yet another language. Talk about language working and not working at the same time!

A linguistic artifact that is not actually random but is nonetheless fraught with pitfalls is the cognate, a word that means the same thing in both languages. Of course there are false cognates, a word that looks the same in different languages but means drastically different things.

For an Electronic Literature Organization conference in Paris, Joellyn Rock and I created the netprov *Tournament of la Poéstry*.[ii]

Try This: Bilingual Poems

Here is the bilingual invitation to this bilingual netprov:

Th(l)e défi/challenge?
Compose petite poèmes comprehensible completely both en Français and English!
C'it's simple!

Voilà an example.
"Fool(lement) Desire"
J desire tU.
J desire tU enormusmly-ment!
Qu(when)and tU r en NY, & J en Paris . . . depressive=J ☹
J fool(lement) desire tU . . . J (be)comme Mr. Bean.
C'it's a game.jeu.
C'it's litérature.
C'it's . . . Poéstry!

The R.eg(u)les?

1. Compose en couplets.distichs.
2. (Rimes non necessairey.)
3. Apart(ça) from that, all.tout's acceptable: cognates, symboles, numb3rs, proper nambes proprem, etc.
4. Mutuallmently intelligible neologismes sont.are grandly encouragayed.
5. Orthographye & grammaire traditionel be.soit damnayed!
6. The poèmes vont/will communiquate(ront) par.by any moyeans necessaire!
7. C'it's experimentale!
8. C'it's seulement pfour amusement only!

Themes

1. Aimer de loin / Love from afar
2. Se vanter de compétence à écrire de la poéstry / Brag about your poéstry-writing abilities
3. Retour de Damas / Return from Damascus
4. Rendez-vous dans la forêt / Rendez-vous in the forest
5. Rencontre avec le monster / Encounter with the monster

So you netprov players are rule breakers—tricksters—right?

What comic misspelling and the experiments of the Oulipo have in common is the way they question centuries of shared beliefs about language: that it is divine and organized in unseen ways, that the right words work magic in a supernatural way, that words provide a direct connection between two souls, and so on. What this joking and experimenting does is insist on the "thingness" of language. Language is indeed just a thing—a magnificent thing, but just a thing. And to say so is, variously, blasphemous, illegal, immoral, revolutionary, and anarchic. Silly humor is dangerous. It exposes secret and sacred smuggling on the border between form and content.

Genres of fiction, and genres such as the three-act Hollywood movie or the Internet meme, have a thingness too. Satirical play with these forms also violates the form-content border.

Antoinette LaFarge, in her essay "A World Exhilarating and Wrong: Theatrical Improvisation on the Internet," makes a connection between Internet play and literature in a way that is apt for netprov. "In the realm of fiction, the long Western tradition of comic, satirical, and surreal fiction feeds online theater," she writes: "Online interactions tend toward verbal extravagance inherited (directly or indirectly) from such writers as Petronius, *François* Rabelais, Flann O'Brien, Raymond Roussel, and James Joyce."[5]

So there were rule breakers back in literary history as well?

One of my favorite literary examples of form-content border violation is Laurence Sterne's *Tristram Shandy*, written between 1759 and 1767, which systematically breaks the rules of book construction on a physical level by misnumbering pages, misnumbering chapters, and inserting endpapers in the middle of the book. Meanwhile, on a semantic level, the book breaks rules by having the narrator do such thngs as apologize to characters who were left on the stairs while he made a multipage digression.

Even in Sterne's time, early in the life of the novel, a set of conventions of graphic design on one hand and narrative form on the other had coalesced into a package of attributes—a rule set, a spell creating a magic storytelling zone—which was intended to go unnoticed by the reader. Sterne breaks his own storytelling spell and dares readers to still believe. In doing so, he implicates both the practices of fiction and the practices of real life in which so many social fictions—of hierarchy and power—are maintained.

Like the Monty Python character who runs back and forth through the door, marveling at the fact that indoors he is on video and outdoors he is on film (the production mode of British sitcoms of the time), the frame-breaking "meta" humor of a novel such as *Tristram Shandy* is a practical method to make the invisible visible for a wide audience. Structural satire provokes structural insight. The very silliness of silly humor rests in the fact that it calls into question basic, assumed rules of existence. Self-awareness and comedy travel together; so often what is being satirized in satire is the *non*self-awareness, the cluelessness, of the target. Sometimes the rules contravened are unchangeable, like death and gravity, but sometimes they are arbitrary, such as particular pompous modes of social media posting that prejudice the content while claiming impartiality and neutrality. Netprovs are a safe way of breaking rules.

Here is a 2017 netprov that breaks with convention by taking a known form of rule writing connected with material reality—recipies—and blends them with fiction, tastily.

Try This: Cooking with Anger

> Welcome to *Cooking with Anger*, a netprov where you get to cook up a story out of a basket of ingredients. To join the feast, just sign up for an account, and once you're approved you can get cooking! *What is* Cooking with Anger?
>
> Modeled on TV cooking competitions, *Cooking with Anger* is a netprov where storyteller-chefs improvise a tale and a recipe from a basket of select ingredients.
>
> Many have written about cooking with love; now it's time for all the other emotions! *How to Play* Cooking with Anger
>
> Get your basket of ingredients from the Protag-o-Matic randomizer http://markcmarino.com/cwa/basketpicker.html.

1. Copy and paste your basket at the top of your tale.
2. Write the condensed outline of a stirring story—220 words or less—using ALL the ingredients from your basket. Use people, places, and things as narrative; fold food items for a recipe into the fiction. Season the tale with the emotional spice packet.
3. We encourage you also to post a video in which you tell the story, tell about the story, or tell how you made the story.

EXAMPLE 6: #1WKNOTECH, A NETPROV

A Collaborative Thought Experiment

Seven years after the introduction of the smartphone, its addictive and distracting properties were on everyone's . . . hang on, (looks down), let me just ch . . . check my messages . . . lips, Mark and I issued the following invitation for a new netprov[j] in 2014:

> During #1WkNoTech we claim to be going for a week without technology while Tweeting the heck out of it!
> What would it really be like to drop your devices?
> Use your imagination!
> Share your story on the hashtag: #1WkNoTech.
>
> - Show us yourself enjoying a peaceful moment in the woods!
> - Share the glories and horrors of battling tech withdrawal!
> - Post a pic of you throwing your phone away!
>
> Will it be heaven? Will it be hell?
> #1WkNoTech Nov 1–16. "Don't Miss Out!"
> We'll See You There![1]

By jumping straight into players' own social media lives, this netprov does some of the same things *Reality: Being @spencerpratt* began to do: asking players to step back and look at their own digital habits. Digital platforms seek exactly what the makers of slot machines do: to increase what gambling technologists call "time on device." As streaming entertainment service Netflix's CEO Reed Hastings put it, "We compete with sleep. And we're winning!"[2] And just as Mark and I had Spencer's account reflect on its own fame, *#1WkNoTech* players are invited to reflect on their own micropublishing micro fame, their love of likes, their fear of missing out.

To students and featured players, we offered the following tips on how to play *#1WkNoTech*:

Before the netprov

Let's get the tough stuff out of the way first. Fair warning. This may be the hardest homework assignment you have all year. We're not unrealistic. We're not going to ask you to go a week without technology. But we are going to ask you to go for one hour without technology. And it gets worse. Go an hour without technology at a time and in a place where you habitually use technology. Keep notes on your feelings with pen and paper. How does it feel? Really? What's going through your heart and mind? Are you relieved? Anxious? Why? Be a good observer of yourself and your time. If you cheat—if you can't go for an hour without technology—nobody will know. But it's an interesting thing to know about yourself, isn't it? Save all the feelings surrounding your lapse for use in writing the netprov.

Pre-write the List of Top Five Lists of Top Fives.

Based on your observations, your reading/watching and your hour without technology, write thoughtful nominations for the following lists:

- Top Five Worst Tech Behaviors and Why; min. 2 sentences each. Category

- Top Five Ways Tech Makes You Feel Better and Why; min. 2 sentences each.

- Top Five Ways Tech Makes You Feel Worse and Why; min. 2 sentences each.

- Top Five Best Things That Would Happen if You Gave Up Tech for a Week and Why; min. 4 sentences each.

- Top Five Worst Things That Would Happen if You Gave Up Tech for a Week and Why; min. 4 sentences each.

Now look at your List of Top Five Lists of Top Fives and write a brief, tentative seven-day plot line for yourself. What do you think would really happen to you? Which days would be the worst? When would you be most tempted to cheat? What would happen with your friends and family? You are not obligated to stick to this plot line — the prov in netprov stands for improvisation after all — but at least you'll have a shape to start with.[3]

On the *#1WkNoTech* project website, we offered earnest support for Fear of Missing Out (FOMO).

> It's Just 1 Week.
>
> You know you should cut down—even quit—your dependence on technology, right? But it's hard. Too hard to do by yourself!
>
> That's why we've created the #1WkNoTech community to take a stand!
>
> We'll support each other in 1,000 ways so we can all step back from the madness, take a breath and get real!⁴

There were butterflies in stomachs as the start time of the project drew near:

> Mike & Sara, @mikensara4ever November 9, 2014
> wait a minute. how are we going to favorite each other's #1wknotech tweets?
> #onehandclapping

The first few days paid off the basic joke of the netprov:

> Melissa Ng, @MelissaNg11 November 10, 2014
> Bet my parents in Ohio are dying to know how my interview today went. Keep wondering, parents! #1wknotech

> Manic AF, @MP89MP November 10, 2014
> But seriously think of all the fun stuff you can do without technology! The possibilities are ENDLESS. I feel lonely. #1WkNoTech

> bhallamk, @Bhallamek November 11, 2014
> my face was always buried in the laptop, never noticed how STRANGELY my dog stares at me all day. #1wknotech #tumblr

> Sasha M, @sasha_m98 November 11, 2014
> The great thing about #1wknotech is that I don't have to be bombarded by images of people having a lot more fun than I am.

> Sketchy McGinn, @Sketchy_McGinn November 12, 2014
> Each hour that goes by, it feels better and better to know I'm not using Twitter. Starting to feel bad for the people who are. #1WkNoTech

Then anxiety began to set in. The emotional stock market was closed:

Amanda S Gould, @stargould November 12, 2014
With no tech and no friends we must like our own #1wknotech posts #augrealities. #notechmoreproblems #tumblr

Grace Anaclerio, @Granaclerio 14 November, 2014
Can we pls talk about how Miley [pop superstar Miley Cyrus] was at the USC game and I had to find out afterwards by word of mouth like some basic commoner? #1wknotech

Kathi Inman Berens, @kathiiberens November 15, 2014
LIKE withdrawls. #1wknotech #digiwrimo #tumblr #FOMOM

Mark C. Marino @markcmarino November 15, 2014
Snorting a line of LIKEs off my powered down phone #1wknotech #tumblr (see figure 1.)

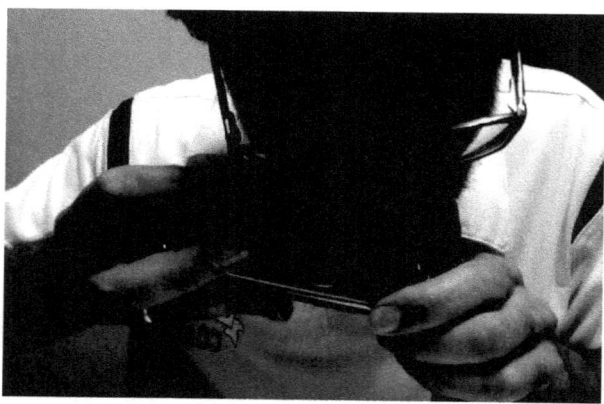

Figure 1. "Snorting a line of LIKES off my powered down phone." Image accompanying Mark C. Marino's #1WkNoTech tweet.

Sketchy McGinn, @Sketchy_McGinn November 15, 2014
Starting to feel bad for my food. It's practically begging to be photographed.
#1WkNoTech

By the end of the week the strain was beginning to show:

Chris Gnarley, @Chris_Gnarley November 16, 2014
@CooperV12 seriously. I've missed out on so much reassurance of worth via likes. never be the same #1wknotech #FOMO

What Am I Doing?, @whatamidoing_16 November 16, 2014
I am going to slightly miss this week of no tech though. Oh, wait. No I'm not. #1wknotech

Lita_lota, @litalota228 November 16, 2014
Farewell #1wknotech . You end in 15 mins. Let the sleep deprivation over Instagram/Facebook nonsense commence! #going-tomiss1wknotech

#1WkNoTech is a nod to the tradition of protest art that has its seeds in the rebellious Romanticism of the nineteenth century but emerges in a form we would recognize during World War I in works such as the bitterly funny nonsense of Dada poetry and the ragged, biting collages of Hannah Höch that graft BMWs to bathing beauties and bombs to bankers. Like Banksy in more recent years, the goal of this kind of art is to do the wrong thing in the right place, to yell to the sleepwalking passerby, "wake up!," to call attention to the elephant in the room.

#1WkNoTech is designed first to delight and amuse and secondly to offer a nonjudgmental way for players to explore their own use of (or addiction to) digital media. The netprov is informed by reflections such as media sociologist Sherry Turkle's existential dictum of social media life "I share therefore I am" and the phenomenon of craving the faves—obsessively and frequently returning to social media to count the votes a post has received.[5] Nearly all would acknowledge the impossibility of *really* going for a week without it and are supported in investigating their own unique reasons why. Seriously, dear reader, could you do it? I'll keep an eye out for your post.

CHAPTER 7.

ORGANIZING AND LAUNCHING OPEN-ENDED NETPROVS

All netprovs start within some kind of fictional world. This is crucial to avoid the pitfall of what we used to call, in Invisible Seattle, the "graffiti wall" structure of collaboration: "We're going to put paper all over the wall and set out markers; *now come be creative!*" Without a guiding concept, the results are often boring: false starts and canned gags.

Other fields that feed into netprov have their own names for what Mark and I call fictional worlds. "Premise is the term used to describe a fully formed comedic idea found in an opening," write Matt Besser, Ian Roberts, and Matt Walsh in the textbook for their popular stage improv company Upright Citizens Brigade's (UCB) improv classes. UCB also calls a premise a "base reality."

The fictional worlds Mark and I create tend to spring from moments in new technologies where the everyday writing people are already doing reveals some hidden stress. The discouragement caused by our encouraging fitness apps, for example, is the subject of the netprov *1Step Forward, 2Steps Bak*[1] that posits a "bakstepping" craze and keeps users' scores always a few baksteps away from their goals. Many of our netprovs concern fictional businesses since businesses loom large as "characters" in the harsh soap opera that circulates resources in our consumer society.

Once you've got a fictional world, how do you share it with netprov players?

Sometimes the name or even the hashtag of the netprov itself explains the concept, like with *#1WkNoTech*, a week without technology. At the very least, the name should serve as a reminder of the fictional world. The name of the netprov *Air-B-N-Me*,[i] of course, plays off the currently popular apartment-sharing website Airbnb. We're also guided by the Hollywood filmmaking axiom that if you want the audience to know something you must tell them three times, so we try to sprinkle the key elements of the fictional world in different locations. Here is the initial invitation to *Air-B-N-Me* from the top of the corporate-looking, registration-only, forum website:

> **Welcome to Air-B-N-Me!**
>
> In this exchange economy, we share our cars, our homes, and all our stuff. What if we could share our lives?
>
> If you ache to be anywhere but here, welcome to Air-B-N-Me, a new experience in lifeswapping. When you feel like checking out of your own life, check in to somebody else's. Why not turn your downtime into a timeshare?
>
> Air-B-N-Me is the original (and still the best!) online lifeswapping community.

Players took the *Air-B-N-Me* premise and ran with it:

> "igottaBme2, 02.04.2016
> Meet my boyfriend. He's courteous, caring, and comely. So, like the last 4 boys, I've got to break up with him. Only I can't. Every time I go to break up with him, he brings me my favorite Thai dishes or offers me a foot massage. But you've probably got a spine. So come on in and kick him to the curb for me. Thanks!
> Time: Saturday 9–10pm
> Streaming Time: 9:59pm EST Username: 2Kind2BKCruel (YouTube)
>
> PleasantAnne, 05.04.2016
> REVIEW OF MY VISIT
> Wow!
> You are not kidding.
> He is seriously charming. The son of Paul Rudd and George Clooney!
> I was going to use this as a try-out of the TIGER! TIGER! attitude I'm learning at my women's self-defense class where we get to bash Mr. Nichols in his padded suit.
> I went into this visit all "TIGER! TIGER!" and going to read this loser the riot act.
> But then he started asking questions. Questions! Of me! And really pretending to listen!

So 4 hours later I was snuggled up on his shoulder watching something called Fuller House.
Sorry!
I'd rate this visit:[bliss emojis]"

We used marketing language on the website to model the premise:

"Monetize your Monotony!
Rent the lost moments of your life and earn big bucks!
Be an Air-B-N-Me Lowner (Life-Owner)
When you check out of your life, someone else checks in!
  "I recarpeted my garage with the money I made!"—Tony P.
  "I'm just glad someone could use it!"—Maria. S.
  Check out for an hour at a time!
Airbnme—earn from your biggest asset! Your unused life!

Crave more zing?
Be someone completely different! Affordably!
Be an Air-B-N-Me Lurfer (Life-Surfer)!
When someone checks out of their life, you check in!
  Be a surf instructor!
  Be an airline pilot!
  Be a White House aide!
  Be a back-up dancer!

Air-B-N-Me—when you want to be anyone but you!"

We love to share the rules of play within the fictional world of the netprov. The science-fiction mechanics of the *Air-B-N-Me* world can be explained on the website in marketing language.

How Air-B-N-Me Lifeswapping Works

1. **Want to make money?** Sell unused bandwidth from your life by posting an ad on our easy-to-use Lowner (Life-Owner) site.

2. **Want to get away from it all?** Be a Lurfer (Life-Surfer)! Select a Lowner whose life you like. We have lives to match any budget!

3. When the Lowner checks out during the 3 D's—Distraction, Detachment, Denial—the Lurfer checks in! The Lowner goes on auto-pilot, doing what they normally do but the Lurfer gets the full experience of what happens.

4. Lurfers can make suggestions for Lowner behavior, but Lurfers shouldn't be surprised if they get no response. Lowners are bound by the Power of Habit and won't do things they don't normally do.

5. Enjoy not being you up to a maximum of 1 Hour (which science says is well short of the bonding/transfer threshold).

6. Be in (B-N) the Lowner's body—see what they see, hear what they hear, taste what they taste!

7. Write a review of your visit to help others make their choice!

8. Rental fees are automatically transferred from the Lurfer's account into the Lowner's.

9. Quality is ensured by random 1-minute AuthenticaptureTM videos taken during visits.

10. Anonymity is key; no repeat visits; no hard feelings.

This list contains a combination of real, practical advice for the player of the netprov alongside purely fictional elements. The player is told that the creative play consists of writing reviews of their visit and in making one-minute videos. At the same time, it is an artistic reflection on a vital subject—our actual everyday of experience of this mediated world, how awake (or asleep) we are to the gift of life.

Since *Air-B-N-Me*'s premise of lifeswapping brought with it a number of science fiction questions, we chose the typical website form of a frequently asked questions page to frame the play:

About Hosting and being a Lowner (Life-Owner)

Q: Does it hurt?
A: No, not at all! Since you are usually spacing out and absent from your sensations anyway, life will pass just the same as it always does—you won't feel (or remember) a thing. And you'll be earning good money!

Q: What happens if someone leaves a mess?
A: The beauty of the Air-B-N-Me system is that they get to rate you and you get to rate them. Any Lurfer who gets too low scores gets banned. So, basically, nobody's going to be a slob!

Q: How honest should I be in my ad?
A: Authenticity is kind of subjective as we see it. Experts say we all tend to devalue our own lives for sympathy and point instead to the novelty

effect where travel meals taste better than home meals. Don't be afraid to highlight the positive!

Q: What is it like to return to myself after a Lurfer has visited?
A: Scientists say it's just about the same as when you realize you've been on Facebook longer than you planned. You shake your head, take a deep breath, and get your a** in gear. Only you're richer!

About Visiting and being a Lurfer (Life-Surfer)

Q: Should I bring anything on my visit?
A: You can't! Part of the fun is relying on what your Lowner has in their world in the way of food, clothing and emotional support. Adopt an attitude of curiosity and be flexible. "Surf the earthquake!"

Q: As a Lurfer am I able to control the body of the Lowner?
A: Don't count on it. You can try to suggest actions, but you can't make a Lowner do something they wouldn't normally do. The most you can do is DJ your Lowner from a playlist of their own usual behaviors. Sometimes Lowners don't react to you at all and you're just along for the ride.

Q: Am I responsible for taking care of my host's relationships?
A: Nah! They've made their bed, and you get to lie in it for a little while, that's all. At worst, your actions as the Lowner will provoke questions like: "Are you listening? Are you OK? Do you even care about this marriage?" in other words: normal, everyday reactions. Treat everyone with respect and pretend you have a touch of the tummy flu. That will get you through any awkward situation!

Q: What if it gets weird?
A: Define weird! We're all human beings on planet Earth. We all share gravity, water, regrets. How weird can it get? As we like to say: "one person's weird makes for a great little getaway!"

Q: When I'm visiting, do I have my food allergies or my host's?
A: Just like emotions, skills, and beliefs, your allergies belong to your host. Eating foods you can't normally eat is just one of the many pleasures of Lifeswapping!

Q: Do I stay emotionally connected to my host after I've been them?
A: No! You'll have good memories and a fond glow, but that's all. Full-on flashbacks are exceedingly rare.

What if I'm running a netprov and players need help getting their minds around the fictional world?

Rightly or wrongly, we tend to assume players are acquainted with the cultural habits we're lampooning and have basic skills on the platform we've chosen for a netprov. But sometimes we offer more step-by-step advice.

Try This: Air-Be-N-Me Step-by-Step

Since *Air-B-N-Me* was by invitation only, Mark was able to write these more detailed instructions for students and invited players:

1. Before you play:

    - What are moments in your life when you tend to tune out?
    - What are moments when you'd like to be anywhere but there? (Perhaps because the moment is too intense, too uncomfortable, too important.)
    - How might others appreciate these same moments?
    - Whose life would you like to swap into? Why?

2. Create one or more characters.

    - Character Name:
    - Age: (you'll need a fictional birthdate to register on the forum)
    - Gender:
    - Location: (city, country)
    - Occupation:
    - Screen Name of Character (no spaces)
    - Descriptive phrase
    - Amenities: (What comes with your life?)
    - Unique About Me: (a phrase or two that accentuates the desirable features of your life)
    - Primary Availability: (list three times you'd like to check out of your life)

- House Rules: (any restrictions, things lifeswappers can't do with your life)

3. In the forum, post advertisements on behalf of your characters as Lowners (Life-Owners), advertising the everyday downtime available for use by others.

    - Consider writing an ad for:
        - A totally boring moment
        - A moment that involves something not promised (in the description)
        - An uncomfortable or awkward moment
        - A stressful moment
        - An unexpected life event

4. In the comments after the advertisements, post reviews of your experiences as a Lurfer (Life-Surfer) in the lives as described. Stay close to the life moment as described in the ad.

5. Post one-minute videos purporting to be the random AuthenticaptureTM videos for various Lowners. Shoot one minute of a point of view shot, as though the person is looking through your eyes. Use the vertical (tall, portrait) format.

    - Plan out your time. Even one minute of video can seem like an eternity if it's not planned.
    - Put a surprise in every video, something unexpected.
    - Don't show any faces.
    - Avoid showing personal info: your license plate, your address, etc.
    - Show your hands and feet. For some reason this helps give the impression that the person is inside you.
    - The Lowner should not speak during their broadcast.
    - The Lurfer (viewer/renter) should marvel at the experience—since they appreciate everything the Lowner takes for granted.

Why are you asking people not to show faces in their images?

Showing no faces is one of the netprov best practices that has emerged over the years, for several reasons. It makes it easier to play a character who is unlike you. Paradoxically, it looks like it has "higher production values"; viewers can't as easily compare your look and gestures to that of professional models and actors. By being more raw, it also can look more "real," more naturalistic. Finally, if you want to publish your version of the netprov, it means you don't necessarily have to get signed, legal permissions from your models.

For the 2014 and 2015 netprov *Outsource My Study Abroad*, netrunner Kathi Inman Berens and I found that not using faces gave a haunting immediacy to the images as they combine with the stories. The fictional world of *Outsource My Study Abroad* posited that if players couldn't really study abroad, they could arrange with foreign students to reciprocally create a virtual study abroad blog with exotic foreign images. Without faces, players were much more easily able to project themselves into the international experience. Kathi and I offered these encouragements:

> Have your models wear some bright color. Use the recognizable color of clothing/hats that your faceless models are wearing to create a visual continuity from location to location and allow readers to project themselves into the proceedings.

Tips for Photography in Netprovs

Since I'm on the topic of imagery and fictional worlds in netprov, the image instructions for the netprov *One Star Reviews*, below, contain my best photography tips. These tips will radically increase the quality of your everyday, personal social media images as well.

1. No recognizable faces. Hands, feet, backs, and elbows are more evocative (and no legal permissions are needed).
2. No ordinary angles. Which is to say: no blah, ordinary photos with the subject at medium distance and the camera held at arm's length and chest height. Yawn. There are plenty of these already! Take a tip from the thousands of hours of good cinematography you've seen in your life! Take a knee! In fact, lay down on your back and shoot upwards! Stand on a chair and hold the camera by the ceiling! Set the lens of the camera right on the table and shoot

across the table, right on the floor and shoot across the floor, right on someone's sleeve and photograph their hand! Do ultra-long shots! Do ultra close-ups!

3. Try using layers of depth. Put something close in the foreground and capture something else far away in the background. Let the camera focus on the windowsill and have the background be blurry, or vice versa.

Figure 1. Photo from #1WkNoTech illustrating the powerful principle of not showing recognizable faces in netprov imagery.

4. Try representing the world in a still life. Find an arrangement of objects that tells a story. Or make an arrangement of objects that does (e.g., knife + VR goggles + crumpled used Band-Aid packaging; e.g., the love triangle of a salt shaker, pepper shaker, and sugar packet).

5. Don't steal photos! If you take photos from the Internet, make sure they are copyright free or labeled "for reuse" or "reuse with modification." Some search engines allow you to filter by copyright. Look for CC licenses.

Even in a project based around selfies, it helped to obscure the face to make the image more of an open invitation. Here's one of the early images from *#1WkNoTech* (see figure 1).

Can open-ended netprovs be about serious topics too?

Sure! Just look at the alternate reality game (ARG) *World Without Oil*.[2] Games theorist Jane McGonigal was part of the creation of *World Without Oil*, which she calls a "forecasting game" in which players write plausible "forecasts" from their varied professional, geographic, and cultural perspectives of the results of a sudden cessation of the world's oil supply. This is collaborative creative writing, pure and simple. According to her account the first period of the game was taken up with doomsday scenarios, but the last part of the game saw the rise of collaborative problem solving, and participants reported taking back practical ideas from the game into their professional lives.

Try This: Monstrous Weather

Here's an example of a netprov invitation that certainly didn't discourage humor but was designed to set a course into deeper waters:

> The week the internet went down, so many of us sat around marveling at the weird weather and telling scary stories. One story lead to another, all around the world. Now we are collecting summaries of these stories. Surely you heard some!

This was the invitation that launched the 2016 netprov *Monstrous Weather*.[ii] It continued:

> Tell us: who told the tale, what happens, and how it plays off of real-life weird weather (google it), in 300 words or fewer!
>
> We are not the first to notice that the week the internet went down was exactly 200 years since Mary Shelley, Percy Shelley, and Lord Byron, kept indoors by the climate disruption of a distant volcano, sat around and told each other ghost stories. Mary invented Dr. Frankenstein. Byron started the vampire craze.
>
> What new and frightening phantasms will be the product of our own Monstrous Weather?

Good invitations don't hold anything back; the entire netprov is there in the first four sentences.

To give first-time players practical starting points, we followed the more literary invitation with a short list:

1. In 300 words or fewer, summarize a scary story somebody told the week the internet was down.
2. Who told the story? When and where? What happens in their story?
3. Include one bit of weird weather.
4. See if your story can reply to another story. Answer, amplify, remix! Or start a new topic with a new story.

What if players don't follow the rules of your netprov?

The inaugural 2016 version of *Monstrous Weather* was by invitation only. We knew the invitees shared literary backgrounds, and although they proceeded to break many of the rules, they broke the rules in a literary way;

which is to say, it was done in a delightful way designed to elicit laughter and insight. Their intent was to broaden, not wreck, the netprov.

Sometimes, though, in broad-participation netprovs, true vandals and trolls come in, trying to negate, mock, and break the game. As Whitney Phillips says in the magnificently titled *This Is Why We Can't Have Nice Things*, "Until sensationalist, exploitative media practices are no longer rewarded with page views and ad revenue—in short until the mainstream is willing to step in front of the funhouse mirror and consider the contours of its own distorted reflection—the most aggressive forms of trolling will always have an outlet, and an audience."[3]

What we've found in many of our broad-participation netprovs is that if the premise is robust enough, a good netprov can't be broken. During the month we spent pretending to go to high school with each other on Twitter in *All-Time High*, we realized that since the real-life high school experience itself is sadly replete with vandals, trolls, and bullies, the occasional trolling simply added to the realism.

How do you help people get over their shyness and get started playing?

The first models of play are crucial to a netprov. They are just as important as a good invitation. Alex Mitchell provided a haunting early model for *Monstrous Weather*:

> We sat on the floor in the middle of the room, because that seemed to be the right thing to do.
>
> Some of us still held our phones, dangling them limply in our hands or resting them on the floor beside us. I occasionally, instinctively unlocked the screen and checked for email, for a status update, for anything, although I knew there would be no signal. Despite the duct tape on the windows and along the bottom of the door, I could smell the burning. The haze got into my nose and mouth, into my hair, and under my nails. I could taste it when I ate, and I dreamed of it while I slept.
>
> The stories started spontaneously, fragments of memories we shared to keep ourselves sane.[4]

This model serves perfectly as the central node to Mitchell's excellent hypertext archive of *Monstrous Weather*,[5] which he discusses in the essay *Monstrous Weathered: Experiences from the Telling and Retelling of a Netprov.*[6]

I contributed another:

A Green World

We were laying on our backs looking at the stars. Mark Marino, aflutter with success after winning $284.50 in a marathon poker game, told us a story about how one day a guy goes into the bathroom after playing football with his kid only to discover that the soap doesn't get the mud off his hands. The guy comes out into the kitchen where his wife is discovering that dish soap no longer gets dishes clean. It turns out that all soap stops working, world-wide, all at the same time.[7]

And then within twenty-four hours, Jeremy Hight established what was to become a continuing theme of meta narration in his brilliant, self-descriptive post: "Story made from the titles of all the other stories." The netprov grew in a number of different directions, including a long rant by Scott Rettberg in the voice of the Norse god Thor.

One Star Reviews is a netprov concept that is particularly complex and therefore its first models were particularly important. The inaugural version of *One-Star Reviews* took place in 2017 in the form of a subreddit on the forum platform Reddit.

Aren't *most* of your netprov premises pretty darned complex?

Point taken. We're working on that. But . . . um . . . anyway. *One Star Reviews*[iii] took as its starting point the basic strategy of marketing. "The purpose of publicity is to make the spectator marginally dissatisfied with his present way of life," wrote John Berger, way back in the *Mad Men* era of 1972.[8] Christopher Lasch noted succinctly that "advertising institutionalizes envy and its attendant anxieties."[9]

For *One-Star Reviews*, Mark and I wrote a fictional interview that we sent as support to players:

> There's already a tradition already of ironic reviews on Amazon and elsewhere, lavishly praising dud items. And there's also a tradition of finding and sharing bad reviews of iconic things—the Grand Canyon, Shakespeare's Hamlet. What cracks us up about our netprov is creatively finding a third answer to the binary question: Like?/No Like? Our players are exploring with their imaginations and finding amazing things to enjoy in totally unlikeable situations.

The invitation to *One-Star Reviews* is succinct:

One-Star Reviews is a community of fictional characters who find value in things rated at one star.

The first models for *One-Star Reviews* tried to lead the way:

Parking Space Full of Clarity
MATEUZ'S VACUUM AND SMALL MOTOR REPAIR
reviewed by Mwa4407, October 2017
On the web Mateuz listed his hours as 9–4:30 weekdays. I pulled up right in front of his strip-mall door at 10:28am only to be greeted by his battered cardboard sign hanging askew and reading "Sorry, We're Closed." I burst into tears. Once again my attempt to cross even one item off my mile-long To Do list was thwarted.

I thought about my recent streak of bad luck. Then I thought about Dad's cancer. Then I thought guiltily about the annual Slip 'n Slide for Cancer and how much work I still owe them. Then I thought about world cancer rates and whether they are going up or down. Then I thought about my first wife and how with her math skills she'd be the perfect person to Google cancer rates. Then I thought about how I used to love bringing her coffee in bed every morning and how the first morning I didn't do that was the deepest stab in my heart of the whole divorce. Then I thought about her recent email—out of the blue after 20 years—and how it contained in miniature the whole dynamic of our relationship: "Come here, go away! Come here, go away!"

And then, astonishingly, sitting there I REALIZED FOR THE FIRST TIME that because of her rough childhood she is someone who can't stand to be loved. She can't trust it will last. Aww. I get it—small repair shops like Mateuz's are a vanishing breed and we should be grateful they exist at all!

Thanks, Mateuz!!!

Fungus Amongus
DEL-WRAY MOTEL
Reviewer: Madame Curious, October 2017
Amenities: Molds of every kind
When I saw all the mold (in the bathrooms, on the blinds, on the popcorn ceiling) in the other reviews, I realized this would have to be my first destination in the floodplains of Johnstown, PA. I grabbed a rucksack of sample kits, hopped in little Thatcher (my sputtering old VW bug which can be a nasty clanking betch), and was on my way. When I got here, the must from the rooms penetrated my mask, engulfed my pores. Spores filled the dim, dingy room with a kind of slow motion dance of microbes.

That people slept here, rested here was amazing to me, but Mark and Lori (married 50 years!) were down by the pool, it's own special kind of Petri dish. And Mel with his hairpiece, which was alive with mold as well, at the little bar attached to the dilapidated corner of this Mecca of mold, seemed to enjoy it well enough. What astounded me were the cultures—so many different, all cohabitating, becoming, if you will, a kind of super organism, strange and different than any I'd ever encounter again, that seemed to welcome me when I walked in, not with words or handshakes, but with a merry welcoming enveloping hug that immediately began to cohabitate and engorge my own biome, making me one with its multitude.

For *One-Star Reviews*, using Reddit, which itself is built around ratings, gave the perfect graphic and visual support to the project.

So again, the look of the interface is important?

Yes! It supports the premise, the fictional world. Graphic satires largely have lurked in the margins of literature, since most "serious" literary satirists have chosen or been persuaded to dress their texts in the same typographic, puritan gray as other "serious" works.

The direct graphic design inspirations for netprov begin with the *Harvard Lampoon* satire magazine of the 1960s, which each year attempted to graphically imitate a particular mainstream magazine well enough to fool the reader at first glance. This directly led to the *National Lampoon*, a commercial magazine, run by *Harvard Lampoon* veterans. *National Lampoon* side projects included the *National Lampoon's 1964 High School Yearbook Parody*, which closely resembled a typical US high school yearbook, including handwritten notations by the fictional students through which a portrait of the characters and relationships emerged.[10] They also published the *National Lampoon Sunday Newspaper Parody*—a complete miniature, newspaper on newsprint paper, including all the typical sections of an American Sunday paper—the *Akron Republican-Democrat*—which, upon careful reading, revealed webs of intrigue and scandal in the community.[11] The *High School Yearbook Parody* in particular has long seemed to me a perfect example of nonlinear narrative; a complex account of the dramas of the school year emerges no matter the order in which you read the work.

Try This: Outsource My Study Abroad

Outsource My Study Abroad[iv] was inspired by the real-life account of a woman ghosting her friends and faking images of an international trip in Facebook.[12] "Pics or it didn't happen" goes the common phrase. Here are the invitation and rules Kathi Inman Berens and I used with her students in Bergen, Norway, and my students in Duluth, Minnesota, United States.

Outsource My Study Abroad
"Creating remixable memories since 2014"

Part One: Home Town Photo Expedition; Post Pics and Captions to Group Tumblr
Share what it's like to be at your campus and your town. Give students in the other town a real flavor of the surroundings. Find the unique places and unique details. Write about your town in creative, artistic, honest and emotional ways. No BS. What is it really like to be a student here?

Step 1: Home Town Photo Expedition
Go on a photo expedition in your city in small teams. Take photos of the kind that would be taken by a study abroad student. It is OK if teams use some of the same locations—just take creatively unique pictures. Include no recognizable faces. Take 30 to get 12: take 30 photos and pick the 12 best ones!

Step 2: Post the Photos to Tumblr with a caption that is both journalistic and novelistic
Each player posts and captions 4 of the photos on the group Tumblr. Each caption should contain minimum 3 sentences. This caption should include a brief factual account of the place: local history, what significance the place might have the lives of students, etc. It should also include a powerful inventory of the subjective experience each photo suggests—smells, sounds, moods—giving students in the other city the flavor of the place.

Part Two: Go on Expeditions Prompted by Players From the Other Town; Post Pics and Images to Group Tumblr

Step 1: Find 4 Intriguing Locations in the other town using Google Maps & Street View

Step 2: Write 3 Expedition Prompts for the Other City's 4 Intriguing Locations in Google Maps Pins

For each of the 4 locations in the other city you've found on Google Street View, write three prompts.

- a. A prompt about the PLACE itself, to be answered by photos and text.
     For example: "What is down that alley?"
     "What kind of objects are lying on the ground?"
     "What is the most surprising thing you can see here?"

- b. A prompt about some aspect of the INNER, EMOTIONAL LIFE of students, the kinds of things that would come up in a deep conversation with students from the host country IN THIS PARTICULAR PLACE, to be answered by text:
     For example: "Is it easy to make new friends in this town? How do you do it?"
     "What's it like to be GBLTQ in this city?"
     "What do people do on a first date?"

- c. A PHOTO REQUEST for a posed photo—no faces visible, of course—that creates a memorable moment of fun with new friends, written in the form of a memory, to be answered by a photo or photos:
     For example: "Remember when we danced the waltz on the sidewalk?
     "Remember when we talked all night in the park and watched the sunrise together?"
     "Remember when we were making jokes and eating ice cream and laughing here?"

Step 4: Respond to the Prompts About your City by doing a Photo/Writing Expedition in the 4 Locations That Intrigued Them

Step 5: Put the photos and captions into the shared Tumblr
Each team member posts and captions 4 photos

Part Three: Create Your Personal Virtual Study Abroad Timeline/Newsfeed on your own Tumblr

Step 1: Review the Tumblr photos and captions from the other city.

Step 2: Build your personal virtual timeline/newsfeed
Find 11 images from the other city on Tumblr and add a caption to each of telling a story about what happened to you (and your new, imaginary friends) when you studied abroad in this place. Add a few images from your own city if they contribute to your story line.
Consider the arc of your story. Were you sad and homesick at first, but by the end of your stay you had made great new friends? Did you fall in love? Did you struggle with coursework but get 100% in the final exam?
The "Don't Ruin Your Job Prospects" Rule: Do not picture or describe the consumption of alcohol or intoxicants

OK, that's how to get shy players started. But what about people who go on and on and write too much?

To paraphrase Alexander Pope and William Shakespeare, aiming to keep the number of words you use down to an absolute, bare minimum is the soul of being funny in the moment.[13] The three-hundred-word limit of *Monstrous Weather*, even though it was stretched by some who will remain nameless ([coughs] scottrettberg), generally produced a wonderful form of condensed storytelling. It was helped by the idea that players were repeating and summarizing stories they'd heard from others, and even though compact, the entries often contained a story within a story.

If the platform doesn't already have content limitations, it often helps to encourage them to keep it short, both in the rule set and the first models. We've found that three hundred words is an optimum size, easy to both write and read in stolen moments at work.

What if I'm really stumped and can't think of a fictional world?

Try a "mockumentary" version of some real-life world you know; your workplace, for example. Mockumentaries in film include *This Is Spinal Tap*, about a fictional heavy-metal rock band; Christopher Guest's *A Mighty Wind*, a spoof of the '60s folk music scene; and *Best in Show*, which purports to follow competitors in a national dog show. Once unusual in strategy, mockumentaries have been reabsorbed into the mainstream in shows such as *The Office* and *Parks and Recreation*, where characters speak and make faces directly to cameras seemingly wielded 24/7 by unseen documentarians.

These mockumentaries purport to take us behind the scenes, and therefore behind the social masks of the supposed documentary subjects. In each of these examples, the tension between a public persona and a private reality both add a flavor of unrehearsed authenticity to the projects and is automatically satirical, as it was in *Grace, Wit & Charm*.

Try This: Mockumentary Netprov

1. Pick a place, a fictional world, such as fictional workplace.
2. Begin posting short posts as though you were answering questions from a documentary journalist.
3. Be way more honest than you would in real life; e.g., "This is the room where we hide and waste time."
4. Describe a big event coming up that everyone in the world is anxious about—a meeting, a job review, a date.

Some of these netprovs take place on more than one platform. How does that work?

In our everyday, nonfiction use of media, we follow news stories in multiple media, in a complexly interwoven way. This is called transmedia, and one of the early thinkers about transmedia, Henry Jenkins, defined it this way: "Transmedia storytelling represents a process where integral elements of a fiction get dispersed systematically across multiple delivery channels for the purpose of creating a unified and coordinated entertainment experience. Ideally, each medium makes its own unique contribution to the unfolding of the story."[14] The great comic book and movie franchises of the Marvel and DC story empires are great examples of this, as is the vast narrative of *Star Wars*.

Jenkins pays particular attention to the interpersonal roles and relationships transmedia necessitates: "Because transmedia storytelling requires a high degree of coordination . . . it has so far worked best either . . . where the same artist shapes the story across all of the media involved or in projects where strong collaboration (or co-creation) is encouraged." And he uses a term strikingly similar to Del Close's "group mind": "Transmedia storytelling is the ideal aesthetic form for an era of collective intelligence."[15]

Transmedia also is shares a fundamental gesture in common with alternate-reality games, which reach out into reality. Jenkins writes, "A transmedia text does not simply disperse information: it provides a set of roles and goals which readers can assume as they enact aspects of the story through their everyday life."[16]

Jenkins notes an aspect of this changing dynamic that threatens to change the politics of show business, and potentially the broader political structure of the society:

> Storytellers now think about storytelling in terms of creating openings for consumer participation. At the same time, consumers are using new media technologies to engage with old media content, seeing the Internet as a vehicle for collective problem solving, public deliberation, and grassroots creativity. Indeed, we have suggested that it is the interplay—and tension—between the top-down force of corporate convergence and the bottom-up force of grassroots convergence that is driving many of the changes we are observing in the media landscape.[17]

Who owns characters?

Obviously there is an answer in terms of copyright law and the armada of attorneys that enforce it. But the cultural answer is different. Catherine Gallagher discussing the construction of fiction by the early novel, writes, "Another, seemingly paradoxical, pair of features is closely related and shared by all novel characters regardless of the mode of narration: they are at once utterly finished and also necessarily incomplete."[18] Her illustration is, "No matter how many times we reread Anna Karenina, there will never be more to learn about, say, the childhoods of the heroine and her brother."[19] This is a perfect illustration of the importance of which cultural world you come from when you come to netprov. In Gallagher's world of literature, Anna *belongs* to Tolstoy, and only what he writes about her can be considered as valid evidence. But in the world of mass media and the web, popular characters have a status somewhere between property and persons. Artistic property belongs to its creators by some combination of legal copyright, an ethical principle of crediting the maker of an object as a recognition of skill and intelligence, and the relationship between parents and children. Persons, by contrast, exist in the public domain and can be researched and written about by anyone. In the case of imaginary characters, research into their background consists of invention, since everything already known about them was also the product of invention. The one hundredth fan fiction writer's invention about a character has no less logical validity than the first writer's.

What kinds of stories happen in fan fiction?

Captain Jean-Luc Picard of *Star Trek*, ordered to take a vacation, crash lands on the planet of Tolkien's Middle Earth; Captain Picard meets Lord Elrond and, after some preliminary fumbling they have great sex.[20] Fan fiction is when fans extend the narrative of popular characters. Huge, vibrant, interactive fan fiction communities exist all over the web. This delightfully transgressive scenario points out what happens when worlds collide. A collision between fictional worlds can only be done by fans, who can freely travel across interdimensional and copyright boundaries. The growing economic power of fans empowered by fan fiction and other fan activities has become a force to be reckoned with in the industries of mass media.

Many now enter the path of creative writing through fan fiction and the complex sharing and creative back-and-forth on popular websites such as Archive of Our Own, Fanfiction.net, and Wattpad. Fan fiction practitioners and essayists Flourish Klink and Elizabeth Minkel have an excellent podcast, Fansplaining,[21] that investigates the genre from the inside as ardent fans and writers and from the outside as a cultural, historical, and business phenomenon.[22]

Part of the pleasure of fan fiction is the way in which it produces insight by breaking the internal rules of a given fictional world, thereby, in Roger Caillois's terms, breaking the spell by which the actor fascinates the spectator. Further pleasure is the willful intermingling of characters and settings from vastly different fictional worlds. Early electronic-literature pioneer Antoinette LaFarge points out that this is a particular temptation in digital settings:

> Similarly weak boundaries between author and character and between one story and another are a feature of online theater by virtue of the fact that players invent their roles under the spur of the moment. In an improvisation called 'Guilty as Lambs, Innocent as Sin,' the scene was a courtroom where two characters were disputing custody of a third. By the end, however, the performance had been infiltrated by a number of characters from the O.J. Simpson murder trial.[23]

What can be added to Caillois's idea of "breaking the spell" is the possibility of a moment where the supposedly invisible spell is made visible but still does not ruin the game because another higher-order game is being played.

How big can a netprov fictional world get?

We live in a culture of binge reading and binge watching. Henry Jenkins observed this evolution when he quoted a screenwriter in the 2000s: "When I first started you would pitch a story because without a good story, you didn't really have a film. Later, once sequels started to take off, you pitched a character because a good character could support multiple stories. And now, you pitch a world because a world can support multiple characters and multiple stories across multiple media."[24]

"More and more, storytelling has become the art of world building," Jenkins writes, "As artists create compelling environments that cannot be fully explored or exhausted within a single work or even a single medium. The world is bigger than the film, bigger even than the franchise—since fan speculations and elaborations also expand the world in a variety of directions."[25] This poses the question: Must world building be centralized, broadcast, top-down? Could it be grassroots, from the bottom up?

How long should a netprov be?

Another excellent question! You are really "on" in this chapter!

Um . . . thanks?

Let your intuition, and your to-do list, be your guide. Netprov should be fun; that's a cardinal rule. If you feel your character has more to grow, then keep going. Mark and I have set time limits to netprovs (based on our own availability) only to find players continuing to create long after our end date. These days I'm looking at the duration and structure of *All-Time High* to be perhaps the optimum: an overall duration of one calendar month, with real-time live events every Wednesday night. But it will undoubtedly evolve as technology and society change.

Try This: Focused Fan-Fiction Netprov

1. Each player picks a character from their favorite fictional world.
2. Those characters find themselves in an airport; their flight has been cancelled.
3. Romance ensues.
4. How do the characters work together to get each one home?

EXAMPLE 7: *THE LA FLOOD PROJECT*, A NETPROV

An Environmental/Political Story Line

"A flood has hit Los Angeles. It is spilling deeper across streets, yards, roads; a disaster is unfolding across the city and voices are being heard from the epicenter and beyond."[1] So begins the description of the *LA Flood Project*[i] on the netprov's reconstructed website (netprov websites tend to disappear as domains expire and hosts go bankrupt):

> The LA Flood Project is a Rashomon-style multi-POV locative narrative experience that unfolds across LA, spilling over our cast of characters and the participants who join the flood through their cell phones. The Flood dredges to the surface the unspoken laws and logic of the city. It reveals hidden boundaries even as it spills over them.
>
> To engage the Flood, Angelenos can explore the map at home or at each location.

The website from the initial 2011 version added this powerful prompt in the invitation: "A basic geo-social truth is revealed: the greater the wealth the higher the one's neighborhood; the flood disproportionately harms lower-income neighborhoods."[2] This was a netprov with social justice bite. Mark Marino was the overall netrunner, along with creators Jeremy Douglass, Juan B. Gutierrez, locative literature pioneer Jeremy Hight, and Lisa Anne Tao. The name of the author group of the scripted part of the *LA Flood Project* was, collectively, LA Inundación.

The *Rashomon* reference, pointing to Akira Kurasawa's samurai film that tells the same story several times from the different points of view of its characters, testifies to the importance of that film for a generation of writers longing to break out of the conventional storytelling formula. This netprov was about a shared crisis that, through the leveling media of the web and Twitter, would allow stories to be shared in a way they aren't in normal life.

It was also a locative narrative, which the new site describes as "a tale set against a geographic location. If you have ever walked around a museum with an audio guide, you have experienced one kind. Now imagine going to those locations and encountering parts of a story."

The content was shared in three ways: oral histories (YouTube audio files with accounts read by voice-over actors) tied to pins on a Google map, written narrative also pinned on the map, and an hour-by-hour flood simulation in Twitter.

LA Flood Project is an elegantly simple netprov. The plot is the point: waters are rising; what happens? The netrunners knew in advance they wanted the netprov to unfold according to a day-by-day scenario:

> October 20: The rain begins to fall, causes usual traffic disruptions.
>
> October 21: Second day of continuous rainfall, mudslides begin.
>
> October 22: Hurricane Ys makes landfall; LAX shut down.

In Twitter:

> @AngeluciarRuiz October 22, 2011
> @SuchinNa3 Suchin, are you there? Are you OK? You can stay at my house tonight. Try to get here soon. I'm worried about you. #laflood
>
> @bruceheyer October 22, 2011
> Looks like we're going to have to stay in for the most part this weekend. Thank God the Internet still works. Flash games ftw! #laflood

In the scenario:

> October 23: Mayor Villaraigosa institutes curfews; massive power outages.
>
> October 24: The Flood intensifies as Atmospheric Rivers fall; major failure of Los Angeles levies and flood control system; President Obama visits the flooded areas.

In Twitter:

> @sneakerheadJD October 24, 2011
> @DjSeuss my apt is starting to look like an indoor pool #laflood

@jilltxt October 24, 2011
Worried about friends in LA – are they really keeping USC open still? #laflood

In the scenario:

> October 25: National Guard arrives: Army amphibious units arrive; Obama calls for temporary military control of LA.

In Twitter:

@drwoenergy October 25, 2011
@braaaaaadley I hope other states send rescue and medical teams. who knows how many people are trapped somewhere? #laflood

@nickpm1 October 25, 2011
i wish i could be a frog #laflood #frog #fml

@hkeurogh October 25, 2011
The national guard in LA? It's starting to look like World War III #laflood

And finally, in the scenario:

> October 26: Airlifts begin.
>
> October 27: 12am the rain stops; the waters are receding.[3]

The two performances so far of the *LA Flood Project* produced wonderful Twitter collaborations from across the city. Structurally, the scenario serves the same purpose as the commedia dell'arte scenario: a purposeful structure, and a plot meant to reveal truth about social inequality and provoke creative discomfort.

CHAPTER 8.

NETPROVS WITH A STORY LINE

Scenarios like the rising waters of the *LA Flood Project* provide a narrative trellis that can give netprovs a planned story shape. This is not better or worse than open-ended netprovs; it's just different. A planned story shape is appropriate for some concepts and not for others.

Try This: Simple Scenario-Based Netprov: Lighter and Lighter

With one to three friends, play this simple netprov in the social media platform of your choice:

1. Days 1–2: Separately you all notice that your body begins to feel slightly lighter than normal. Share your wonder and distress at the changes. Investigate causes, share hypotheses, corroborate and comfort one another.

2. Days 3–4: You notice that your body is even more light now. You can jump farther than before, ascend stairs without fatigue. In addition, you notice that any object you hold is correspondingly lighter than usual. You can lift quite heavy objects. Everything else is normal. Be your usual self, dealing realistically with an unusual circumstance.

3. Days 5–6: You continue to get lighter, settling slowly into chairs and leaping when you want to walk. It begins to be inconvenient, even dangerous.

4. Day 7: You can fly. Is it a gift or a catastrophe? How would you actually deal with it?

How does a story line work in a larger netprov?

The netprov *#BehindYourBak*[i] was inspired by the flood of email notices sent by social media platforms trying to coax and scare users into donating more time, particularly emails, that openly play on the fear of missing out. Mark and I wanted it to put players into a progressively deeper hole. This is the basic invitation:

#BehindYourBak, a netprov

Apps beg for our attention. Notifications whine, they tease, they bully. They inflame our social curiosity.

In the netprov #BehindYourBak we pretend our fictional characters have been locked out of their accounts by the stupendous mega-network Behind Your Bak—but they're still getting notifications! Agh! What are people saying?

Create a fictional character in Twitter and let your character's imagination run wild.

The scenario for *#BehindYourBak* is simple:

Phase 1 (first 20 percent of time): express frustration at being locked out and your character feeling like the only one.

Phase 2 (middle 50 percent of time): share with others who are also locked out about your character's imaginings, prompted by the notifications and trying to compensate for the imagined problems—thereby making things worse.

Phase 3 (final 30 percent of time): continue your characters' personal stories while collaborating with others to figure out why all have been locked out and develop a plan of action.

The visual component of *#BehindYourBak* is called the "PostEarYour":

Tweet a PostEarYour—or shot of your character from behind their back. Let others speculate on what your character was doing. (Keep it PG, nothing sexual or inappropriate please. Use original photos only, no faces.)

Can netprov story lines be more detailed than that?

At almost the same time as Mark and his collaborators were producing the *LA Flood Project*, I was making my own first attempt to piece together all the elements of the as-yet-unnamed form of netprov on a website titled *Chicago Soul Exchange*.[ii] I described the basic premise of the 2010 project this way:

> *Chicago Soul Exchange* is a week-long collaboration predicated on the assertion that there are more human beings alive today than the sum total of human beings who have lived before, making it arithmetically impossible for everyone now to have a past life. We posit a secondary market in past lives that sells quality past lives (which turn out to be difficult to harvest) to the highest bidder in online auctions. Chicago Soul Exchange the company is a small, plucky, Ma-and-Pa start-up in the industry.
>
> "Chicago Soul Exchange—Yes, you can have a better past! At competitive prices!"["][1]

The characters were workshopped and created in advance, instead of emerging from play. The central character, PastLifeMaven, played by Jean Sramek, described herself as

> a veteran of office politics and underappreciation who, when faced at age 40 with a diagnosis of squamous licatropha (benign!) decided ... to drop all the trivia and dedicate my life to doing what I want to do hardest—matching up short-changed folks of the present day with the dashing past lives they most deserve!

PastLifeMaven's best friend SpiritualEssence was played by Margi Preus, and I played a trio of characters created to advance the plot: ChadBonner, a suave but sketchy past-life "harvester"; VladtheWholesaler, a nefarious Russian past-life-dealing competitor; and N. Michael Barrington, attorney for the shadowy Credit Liechtenstein Caribe Investment Group. Other players wrote short descriptions of lives for sale and bid on listed lives.

The scenario for *Chicago Soul Exchange* was this: far from containing the glamorous heroines and heroes everyone wants as past lives, the catalog is full of nondescript agricultural workers, most of whom died young. As the week begins, PastLifeMaven announces that ChadBonner has brought her a hot property, an actual medieval English knight, Swidhelm! A bidding war ensues. VladtheWholesaler appears, offering an elevated fee for a quick purchase. But SpiritualEssence has already snapped up Swidhelm. Vlad ups his pressure to sell. SpiritualEssence reports the physical presence of Swidhelm in her kitchen, which sets off a rip-roaring metaphysical debate among customers: Can past lives have their own bodies? Vlad's offers turn into threats of a hostile buyout. Swidhelm's wife appears in SpiritualEssence's kitchen, hopping mad.

Just as Vlad is set to pounce, Credit Liechtenstein Caribe Investment Group, acting as agent for unnamed industry giants, sweeps in to buy Chicago Soul Exchange, along with Swidhelm, and close it down. We were exploring psychological and social issues that were to return in subsequent netprovs: self-acceptance in "as is" condition and the construction of personal identity through cultural and economic shopping.

As the launch of *Chicago Soul Exchange* approached, I was getting feedback from potential players that some had the time, energy, and interest to play larger roles and others were intimidated by that prospect and wanted a way to be involved mostly as an audience with the opportunity to participate here and there. For the first time, I organized the contributors consciously into lead characters and audience-contributor characters, laying the groundwork for our current system of featured players and players. From *Chicago Soul Exchange* I learned how to divide a netprov into narrative "beats." *Beat* is a term that has several definitions in theater and film. I use it in netprov to indicate the smallest unit of narrative action, usually an exchange of behavior among characters that results in a change.

Try This: Chicago Soul Exchange

Here's a recipe for having fun with the soul exchange idea:

1. With three to ten friends, pick a social media platform of choice. Play for one month.

2. Each player writes twenty entries for the Catalog of Past Lives.

3. Each entry in the Catalog of Past Lives must consist of two sentences, maximum. (Horrible, isn't it—summarizing a life in two sentences? Then why so often does it make us laugh?)

4. Use your own knowledge of history and of life today to make realistic descriptions of past lives. Avoid the temptation to populate

the past with novelistic or cinematic lead characters. Draw from an imaginary but realistic, random selection of past lives.

5. Once your catalog items are posted, bid and haggle over them as on an online auction site.

6. Invent and share with players your own narrative shape; for example:

    ◦ Week 1: Theme: dissatisfaction with your own life
    ◦ Week 2: Idealization of your newly acquired past lives
    ◦ Week 3: Gradual disappointment with your newly acquired past lives
    ◦ Week 4: Grudging acceptance of your own life

If you have predetermined characters and a scenario, it isn't really improvised, is it?

There is a distinction between what I would call "pure improv," where all the action is improvised such as Del Close and Charna Halpern's Improv Olympics in Chicago, and hybrids of memorized sketch comedy and improv such as the Second City in Chicago and Toronto and the Groundlings in Los Angeles. A typical Chicago Second City stage show will have approximately 80 percent memorized material and 20 percent improvised segments.

Character-based sketch comedy is developed in many different ways. Sometimes they are done in the classic playwriting method: the writer sitting at home and writing out an entire sketch or a group of writers sitting around the writers' table. As often though, a basic idea is brought to a private improv rehearsal session and workshopped by a group of writer-actors. And sometimes new ideas come straight out of these rehearsal sessions themselves.

Another good example of a narrative trellis is the netprov *Mem-Eraze*,[iii] where events were designed to build up toward a highly charged family reunion. A website in the visual micropublishing platform Tumblr gave this invitation:

"Mem-Eraze is an online support group for those who lost their online social scrapbooks in the Mem-or-Eaze Inc. server fire and bankruptcy."[2]

The page went on to posit a visual culture that had grown up in this support group:

> "Recovering from the shock of losing all their family photos and despairing of being able to recreate past travels and past reunions, members of the Mem-Eraze support group begin to reconstruct family history using images of everyday objects—for one family the salt and pepper shakers become grandpa and grandma, soup spoons are the kids, teaspoons are the grandkids. They lay out in the Summer of 2014 on the napkin-beach by the tablecloth-sea. The family stories emerge vividly nonetheless. In part a cautionary tale about entrusting our family archives and family narratives to online corporations—when will the first catastrophic loss of data occur?—this netprov harnesses the expressive power of the highly developed contemporary art form of snapshot-and-caption."

Try This: Mem-Eraze

Here's a way to play this fun, visual netprov:

1. Group players into a single family of three to five or multiple families of three to five.

2. Have players create characters that are organized randomly into large, extended players; meet in real life to outline shared elements of family history.

3. Have players then reconstruct vanished family photos supposedly lost in the server fire by photographing small, common objects in improvised tabletop scenes, captioning them and posting them by hashtag. (Try to use generic, nonanthropomorphic objects without visible logos and photograph them from low angles, composing images visually reminiscent of family photos. Using similar objects for the same characters creates an amazing sense of family resemblance.)

4. As players collaboratively create a family history, look for stories to extend, amplify, or tell from another perspective. Foreground feuds, alliances, and suspicions.

5. Play is organized around a highly charged family reunion near the end of the time period, at which the dynamics previously established are enacted acutely.

6. Invent and share with players your own narrative shape, for example:

    ◦ Week 1: Theme: grief over the loss of the family archives; beginning to retell stories
    ◦ Week 2: Polite disagreement over past events
    ◦ Week 3: Open argument about past events; preparations for the big family reunion
    ◦ Week 4: The family reunion: preparations, travel, the live event; the aftermath: debriefings from multiple perspectives

So, story lines can be kind of general or very specific?

Correct. The 2012 netprov *Last Five Days of Sight and Sound*[iv] had a specific story line. It was inspired by the increasing sensual focus—tunnel vision—on smartphones. Players imagine they have completely lost their vision and hearing. They are patients at an experimental clinic where surgeons under the direction of the mysterious Dr. Vossergon have connected their brains directly to the internet. As Mark and I wrote:

"You begin to explore your temporary media-only world and experiment with communicating with fellow patients through Twitter. You eagerly await the second surgery that will restore your vision and hearing. But it emerges that Dr. Vossergon has disappeared and can't be located. Nurse Zink informs you that the connection to sights and sounds through the internet can only last five more days without the second surgery; without it you will forever lose sight and sound. What will you do with your last days of mediated seeing and hearing? You are invited to write about what you most love to see and hear. With one day to go, a last-ditch solution is created. If you can coordinate with other players in an elaborate, precisely-timed daisy-chain—everyone retweets the same set of messages within 5 minutes—you can keep your vision and hearing. Can you do it?"[3]

Try This: Last Five Days of Sight and Sound

Here's the recipe for a netprov with lots of potential for physical acting, based on the premise above:

1. Identify two to nine players.

2. Day 1: Begin tweeting and exploring your new world, which you can perceive only through screen and headphones.

3. Day 2: Perform some real-life experiments with sensory deprivation (safely!). If you can be in the same space as another player, you can try partner physical activities. Activities include brushing teeth, dancing under a blanket, and passing a water bottle across a room to a thirsty player with your heads covered by a coat or blanket, using only screen and headphone communication.

4. End of day 2: The announcement that you all have five days of mediated sight and sound left. Share your priorities. React to others' priorities. Help other players experience life priorities via your phones.

5. Day 6: A way out—an online endgame—is invented and agreed to by players. The endgame could be garnering X number of votes from nonplayers on a post in an hour, or all players posting an image of a randomly chosen object within an hour, or the composition of a collaborative sonnet in three minutes or less.

6. Day 7: Play the endgame.

How do you do a story line netprov with a lot of players?

Fantasy Automated Investor's League (F.A.I.L.), from 2012, was inspired by the complex collaboration fantasy sports leagues in which online players compete with remixed, imaginary teams made of real-life players and their real-life statistics.[4] Mark and I played the three imaginary CEOs, and players, including students, played their workers. The tight scenario for this netprov began with this invitation:

> "Dan, Lisa and Consuela banter constantly in Twitter. They are busy, single salesfolk who keep their college friendship alive by teasing each other about their fantasy league. But rather than playing fantasy sports, they are die-hard members of the Fantasy Automated Investors League (F.A.I.L.) in which they are CEOs of imaginary businesses. They wheel, deal, joke and trash talk, and we learn that (in real life) Consuela is being promoted to corporate stardom, Lisa dreams of marriage and kids (perhaps with Dan), and Dan's career is going down the tubes."[5]

Once the basic fictional world is established in tweets among the trio who imagine themselves to be alone, a surprise is in store that will change lives together.

> "First, Consuela attempts a sudden merger of her powerful fantasy company with depressed Dan's failing one—a merger with decidedly romantic overtones—sending lively Lisa into a jealous tailspin. Consuela's move violates not only the unspoken rules of the game but also the delicate balance of their relationships.
>
> Second, the three CEOs discover that these are not merely fantasy businesses. Suddenly, disgruntled, real-life employees begin to surface in Twitter, furious at Dan about the merger and its resultant layoffs and plant closings. It turns out the three have unwittingly become ensnared in a Wall Street scheme that creates real corporations and hires real employees managed remotely with digital aloofness by unsuspecting armchair CEOs. The two plots weave toward a wild double dénouement. What matters more, the friendships or the workers? Does love triumph? Who gets final bragging rights? Stay glued to your twitter feeds and find out!"[6]

In *Invisible Rendezvous*, I wrote about fantasy sports leagues as a model of remixing given cultural elements into creative weaves. I still think it is a useful alternative cultural model to the old one-way broadcasting model and a great image of how fan fiction, social media comments threads, and netprov work.

Some netprovs are designed to allow open-ended play within a planned story line system. Digital artist Joellyn Rock put together a collaboration between herself, multimedia composer Kathy McTavish, and me at the Walker Art Center in Minneapolis, Minnesota. Rock's inspiration was drawn from literature:

> In Invisible Cities, Italo Calvino describes his imaginary Sophronia, made up of two half-cities, part circus and part stone. For the dusk-to-dawn event, Joellyn Rock created over two hours of colorful mashup video projections on circus themes with a digital age spin. In the spirit of carnivalesque celebrations, the audience plays along with silhouettes of Multifficient the Multi-tasker, Textana the Texted Girl, Connectiva the Cord Charmer, Pollinatrix the Pollinator, and the Amazing Dr Calvino.[7]

Figure 1. Sophronia, interactive digital installation with live Twitter netprov feed, installed at the Walker Art Center, 2014. Joellyn Rock, Kathy McTavish. Photo: Joellyn Rock.

Figure 2. Sophronia, interactive digital installation with live Twitter netprov feed, installed at the Walker Art Center, 2014.

Visitors to the Sophronia room were dazzled by Rock's glowing circus tent, the walls of which glowed with digital video, set in a cavernous room with McTavish's graphics sliding slowly across all the walls, punctuated by live tweets drawn into McTavish's system via their hashtag. Rock described the interactivity:

> The collaborative project offers both physical and virtual space where participants may spin their own stories of Sophronia. In the multimedia installation, the audience has various modes for participation. The glowing space invites a mischievous mix of digital video and live silhouettes, colors and sounds, texts and bodies in motion. Visitors may enter the circus tent, using props and costume 16_Felements to embody the characters of Sophronia. Or they may use mobile devices to enter the project

twitter feed at #sophroniatwo and watch the text projections wash the walls with crowd-sourced story fragments (see figures 1 and 2).

Rock's 2015 collaborative installation *FISHNETSTOCKINGS*, which premiered in Bergen, Norway, offered netprov participants a chance to play with variations on a classic fairy tale, *The Little Mermaid*. The project, Rock wrote,

> is inspired and informed by historical mermaid legends and their myriad literary variants. Both cautionary and emboldening, mermaid tales inhabit the blurred boundary between childhood longing and adulthood regret. In variants of the little mermaid tale, we find a story of the passage between worlds.[8]

Figure 3. FISHNETSTOCKINGS digital retelling and remixing of The Little Mermaid with live Twitter feed, Bergen, Norway, 2015. Joellyn Rock, Alison Aune, digital artists; Pete Willemsen, programmer. Photo: Joellyn Rock.

Players participated by tweeting to different hashtags, which would group tweets into a narrative sequence and display them in real time, floating and flowing through the giant wall projection of the project that combined video, live interaction triggered through an Xbox Kinect motion detection system, and the live tweets (see figures 3 and 4). Rock's narrative frame was evocative, powerful, and open-ended:

> FISHNET Act I: Innocence & Curiosity, the tale's beginning, when little mermaid is living with her family in her underwater palace, longing for a view of the upperworld.
> Act II: Stormy Seas, Shipwreck & Rescue, when the mermaid encounters the prince on his ship, their worlds collide and a stormy shipwreck leads to a rescue.
> Act III: Bad Bargains & Good Exchange Rates, when the mermaid sacrifices her tail, loses her voice, and reinvents herself in the fishmarket. It's

your turn to voice alternative endings to the bad bargains made by little mermaids.

Figure 4. FISHNETSTOCKINGS digital retelling and remixing of The Little Mermaid with live Twitter feed, Bergen, Norway, 2015. Joellyn Rock, Alison Aune, digital artists; Pete Willemsen, programmer. Photo: Joellyn Rock.

In 2013, reality show stars Spencer Pratt and Heidi Montag reached out to Mark Marino again, wanting to see if he and I could cook up a new netprov for them. Mark and I had been musing about what we called a "magic door" netprov where we would make a casual joke about some preposterous organization, then open the magic door to reveal an already-existing, elaborate, carefully crafted website about that organization and launch into a netprov. We imagined one fine Thursday night in October when, suddenly, Spencer and Heidi's official Twitter accounts and a core group of fans would begin live-Tweeting episode 3 of their new TV show *SpeidiShow*, a show no one had ever heard of, a show that, as its elaborate professional website stated plainly, was imaginary. "Although the show's website posts previews and recaps for each episode," wrote Myles Tanzer on BuzzFeed, "there's no actual production of a web series. . . . 'Netprov basically extends what 'reality stars' do all the time—only it allows the fans to help tell the story,' Pratt told BuzzFeed via email."[9]

We prepared an overall narrative arc that involved Spencer and Heidi gradually freeing themselves from the manipulations of their fictional reality show overlords all while they participated in an increasingly absurd set of adventures. The weekly topics evolved from typical reality show fare—"Europe on $0.00 a Day," "Speidi, Cater My Wedding!," and "Cutthroat Yoga: Don't Throw a Fitsperation"—to other genres: "Who stole the bees?" (an investigative reporting adventure) and the ghost hunting of Halloween's "Celebrity Haunted House" (see figure 5).

Figure 5. The SpeidiShow website mimicked a TV network website.

What if I want to make a really detailed netprov scenario?

I can't wait to see what you're cooking up! One of the most elaborate netprov scenarios was the one for *Grace, Wit & Charm*.

Each beat was three days long and on any given day of the two-week run, one beat was beginning, one beat was peaking, and one beat was concluding. Beats that occurred on the two Wednesday nights of live theater performance were subdivided into more beats for the stage production. In addition to these subplots, the characters responded daily to problems submitted by readers.

The scenario of *Grace, Wit & Charm* was as follows:

1) **Why Us?**
SONNY leads THE TEAM in bemoaning having been chosen as the poster-children for the online Open House; in doing so they provide basic exposition characters and setting.

2) **'Avatar as Voodoo Doll' Urban Myth**
DEB stumbles upon an online urban myth that onscreen avatars are voodoo dolls: whenever you play a video game, somewhere a real person is in pain.
DEB constructs pseudo-scientific experiments on the Voodoo Avatar principle for the team to perform with clients, finally giving a client a heart attack during the live show.

3) **Laura's Bad Boyfriend**
LAURA's long-distance bad boyfriend is back; Laura exults; the team groans and rolls eyes and predicts doom. He disappoints her yet again. During the live show, LAURA and SONNY have a big pow-wow on

Skype with LAURA'S BAD BOYFRIEND KOYS. LAURA explains that she and SONNY are such a good Charm team that she wants SONNY to consult on her real life relationship. She breaks up again the next day.

4) I'm a Long-Distance Loser

NEIL's private-defense-contractor-bodyguard-to-royalty wife in Afghanistan is cheating on him, and THE TEAM members inadvertently discover hard proof. At first they try to keep NEIL in the dark. NEIL finally accepts the truth and does a soulful soliloquy "I'm a Long Distance Loser"; LAURA tries to comfort him but he's oblivious.

5) Sonny Saves a Honeymoon

SONNY is called in to rescue a honeymoon; Deb believes it is the royal honeymoon . . . or at least "a" royal honeymoon. (The royal wedding of England's William and Kate occurred around this time) SONNY deftly resolves the marital problems; the team admires.

6) Take Your Damn Meds!

DEB jumps at the chance to take on a Health Care Challenge: home tele-nursing for shut ins. DEB is exasperated at non-compliant patients; SONNY and others rush in to mitigate her tirades. DEB resists, then goes along with the team as the team works out a tag-team method for dealing with home tele-nursing; DEB goes behind everyone's back to negotiate a large Health Care contract with Virtu-Kare.

7) Social Engineering

NEIL is called in to help a group of social media friends that has an awkwardness; he hacks TwitFace "just a touch" to rearrange some friendship networks. NEIL's hacking has set into motion a socially cataclysmic series of events threatening to ruin dozens of real life relationships; the whole team consults to help him out. NEIL solves the TwitFace social problem by inventing an imaginary person, whom he is now doomed to play forever.

8) First Tele-Surgery

DEB's business relationship with Virtu-Kare leads to a trial contract for a couple of tele-surgeries to come in the next few days; SONNY is morally appalled. DEB charges ahead with plans for the surgery; recruits SONNY as the "hands" by flattering his Radio Controlled Model Snowmobile vanity. DEB leads the first tele-surgery, with DEB doing visuals and SONNY doing hands, is a great success!

9) The Double Surgery

SONNY accepts another surgery, a carpal tunnel job, at first reluctantly and then with more enthusiasm. NEIL catches wind of the carpal tunnel surgery scheduled for Tuesday; he needs the same surgery but can't afford it, since SmoothMoovesTM doesn't offer health care. SONNY and DEB perform carpal tunnel surgery on a client while LAURA attempts to mimic the same operation on NEIL, onstage, with their hands in a pillowcase (see figure 6).

Figure 6. LAURA, left (Shannon Szymkowiak), begins to perform live, onstage carpal-tunnel-surgery-in-a-bag on NEIL, second from left (Jamie Harvie), in imitation of DEB and SONNY's tele-surgery. Photo: Joellyn Rock.

10) Laura's High School Revenge

LAURA bemoans her suffering at the hands of her old high school crowd, who still bully her; the team sympathizes. LAURA is assisted by the team as the team realizes that one of their clients bullied LAURA in high school; the team plots virtual revenge.

11) White Lie Therapy

NEIL uneasily finds himself doing online medical consulting and de-facto psychotherapy. Placebo therapy only works if the patient believes an authoritative doctor who claims the treatment is legitimate. NEIL's truth-telling hesitation undermines the process. He loses the confidence of a patient. DEB coaches NEIL on how to be an authoritative placebo doc.

12) Choosing the Prize

SONNY leads a discussion: Our team is now in the lead for the company-wide incentive prize; they can choose between a vacation in Ocean Shores, Mississippi (hardest hit by the BP oil spill) or a retirement savings plan; it must be a consensus, everyone must agree; Sonny argues for the retirement plan; DEB agrees. SONNY despairs as NEIL and LAURA rhapsodize over the vacation; DEB and SONNY argue for the retirement savings. Deb and Sonny both join the vacation; yayyy, deficit spending! Yayyy living for the now!

13) Deb's Kids Are Our Future

DEB's son is a video game addict; DEB and the team plan an intervention. DEB panics as the intervention goes awry; "Mom you're such a hypocrite! Look what you do at work!" A battle between the generations about net life. DEB is rescued as SONNY and Neil devise a way to pry the controller from Deb's son's hands.

14) Laura and Neil Elope

NEIL has been clueless ... but, yes, it's been building up forever; everyone can see it but NEIL and LAURA; NEIL and LAURA are in luuuv; LAURA seeks SONNY's subtle advice; NEIL seeks DEB's blunt pragmatic advice. LAURA's hopes abound. With prodding from their co-workers, NEIL and LAURA finally have their talk; in Twitter of course; they feel the same way about each other! Yay! They immediately have to text and TwitFace all their friends as they try to hold hands; they lay plans to elope. LAURA has been hoping NEIL has been clueless ... but, yes, it's been building up forever; everyone can see it but Neil and Laura; Neil and Laura are in luuuv; Laura seeks Sonny's subtle advice; Neil seeks Deb's blunt pragmatic advice.

15) Last Words

SONNY leads as Virtu-Kare begins to assign the team hospice, end-of-life challenges; they spend the last few moments with clients DEB is called into one of the most dreaded of all challenges: texting/chatting to someone in his/her deathbed on behalf of a squeamish relative. THE TEAM joins to say goodbye to a client who was a heavy web user; the team joins to say goodbye to the audience; the last words of the netprov and the last words to the client are the same; the value of a life lived partially virtually SONNY delivers a Last Words statement that both serves the needs of the client and also serves as a summation of the project.

EXAMPLE 8: *DESTINATION WEDDING 2070,* A NETPROV

A Sugarcoated Dystopia

Characters cowriting an account on the platform Reddit of a fictional, future wedding in an exotic location wrote:

> "Acslobber
> Frugal Parent/Guardian of Groom Billy Lessee: Chester Lessee
> Now normally, I don't much mind traveling. Been to Juneau, Chiang Mai, Reykjavik (before it turned into bathwater) . . .
> Well, I think with this trip to Argentina, I've finally seen it all. I should've known this whole thing was a bad idea when I saw that the price for an economy class ticket was proportional to the economy of Delaware.
> Well, we ran low on fuel over Brazil and had to make an unplanned stop in Mina's Gerais, where they calmly informed us that there was no fuel, and we would have to make alternate travel arrangements.
>
> agtorres323
> Unlucky First Sibling of Groom Billy Lessee: Azarada Lessee
> Some idiot set a trap last night hoping to get some food, but they just ended up getting snap at my leg? like I get it, food is hard to come by, we are in a crisis, blah blah but don't set them up where people walk by! damn . . . now I got to drink to get the pain away . . . there aren't any pharmacies by here so might as well. Then my son arrived . . .
> ANYWAYS tonight was the bachelorette party at the CHURCH. What type of nonsense. You're religious, we get it, but really, the church? We could've at least gone outside to the "beach" or something."[1]

When live-action roleplaying game (LARP) designer and scholar Samara Hayley Steele approached Mark and me with the seed of a netprov idea she had discussed with Dargan Frierson, an atmospheric scientist and head of EarthGames at the University of Washington, we leapt at the chance. They wanted to do a netprov about climate change. Mark and I realized that there was already plenty of anxiety around the topic and wanted to frame serious play within a comic framework. I remembered featured player Jean Sramek's recent hilarious text message tirade about destination weddings and her nomination of them as a netprov topic. The result was:

> *Destination Wedding 2070*[1] is a futuristic netprov in which you roleplay a family member slogging to a far corner of the globe so you can bicker with relatives, troubleshoot catastrophes, and vent in your secret diary. Oh, and of course—so you can celebrate the blissful union of the happy couple!
>
> *Destination Wedding 2070* is a dark comedy about wedding planning 50 years from now, and, spoiler alert: climate change is the ultimate wedding crasher![2]

For the writing mode of this netprov, we decided we'd use Reddit as the platform and extend the #secretdiary hashtag concept from *All-Time High*:

How to Play

1. Choose and sign up for a character in the designated Google Doc.
2. Go to our DestinationWedding70 Reddit.
3. In Reddit, write entries from your character's "secret diary" about how the various events of the wedding transpire, roughly 150–300 words.
4. The events of the wedding happen approximately one per day starting November third.
5. IMPORTANT: Start each of your character's secret diary entries with your character's NAME, AGE, and RELATIONSHIP TO A BETROTHED that you got from the Google document. For example, "Fabian Schutzenwald, 24, silly brother of Penelope Bespoke-Taylor."
6. Read other secret diary entries, support others' ideas, include the same details using the improv principle of "yes, and."

7. Everyone has their own perspective, so write how your character experienced those moments, which may have already been described by another wedding guest.

The real-life relevance of the netprov came straight from Frierson's lab.

Destination Wedding 2070 aims to make data about climate change more comprehensible. Although climatologists have strong models of the decades to come, they typically share it via graphs and charts. This netprov goes beyond data visualization by bringing the numbers to life in data dramatization as participants experience the effects in a speculative future scenario.

THE SCIENCE BEHIND THIS NETPROV

The data for this data dramatization netprov has been brought to you by EarthGames and was based on simulations from the CanESM5 model under SSP585, a high emissions scenario that represents substantial increases in fossil fuel use in the coming decades. Climate model data is usually presented in terms of averages, but each simulation creates weather across the globe. The forecasts from each city are adapted from particular Saturdays in 2070. The maps show the model data across the globe for max/min temperature, precipitation and humidity, and city forecasts are taken from the nearest gridbox or from a heuristic downscaling approach.

In the spirit of *World Without Oil* and the *LA Flood Project*, we wanted there to be a trellis narrative:

Beats of the Story

1. *Backstory and travel*: Describe your trip and events leading up to the wedding. This is a good time to write about your relationship to the couple, your family, the other family, guests, etc.
2. *Arrival and first night in the hotel bar*: Time to recover from jet lag, check out the destination, and see who shows up at the hotel bar.
3. *Bachelor/bachelorette parties in separate locations*: Was it a last hurrah vs. keep it tame, hedonism or silly fun? Did it seem like an arcane gender/sexuality binary ritual or did you modernize it? How did it affect the betrothed? Did it stress any tensions, create conflict before the big day?

4. *Rehearsal dinner:* This is Family B's contribution to the event. Where was it held? How was the food? How did the two families bridge their differences? Any hurt feelings? Anyone show up late? Anyone leave early (with someone else or alone)?

5. *Cold-feet moment:* The ways of the heart are as volatile as the weather, and even with global warming, a lover can still get cold feet. Which one did? Who talked them back into the wedding? Who shed tears? Who tried to capitalize? Who said they knew this would happen and then had to eat their words?

6. *Ceremony:* The big moment! What was the ceremony like? The music? The readings? The officiating? Any surprises? Anything unusual? Any objections? Power outages?

7. *Reception:* Time to celebrate! Let's hear about the toasts. What were the first dances like? What songs did people dance to? Who caught the bouquet or garter? How was the food? Did any new romances emerge? Any hatchets buried? And how's the weather?

8. *Morning after:* How are people recovering? What did the bride and groom get for gifts? Who woke up with whom? How did people get home?

And because we wanted to make sure there was an even distribution of players among the two families, we created a character sign-up system that lived in a series of online documents, each randomized with different family names, gender combinations, and character characteristics, that looked like this:

> You are cordially invited to the
> Lee & Lessee Wedding
> of
> Avery Lee
> to
> Billy Lessee
> In beautiful
> Mar del Plata[,] Argentina

Avery of the Lee family, a family known for their deep spirituality, is to wed Billy of the Lessee family, who are equally well known for their atheism.

Your Hosts (Non-player Characters)
(these characters are not roleplayed, only described)

Betrothed A: Avery Lee (Female)
Betrothed B: Billy Lessee (Male)
Officiant
Local Wedding Planner
Caterer
Florist
Security
Grandma Lee, who decreed the wedding location & left money for the wedding (deceased)

Please, sign your name, your character's name (first name), and Reddit handle next to a role
(or add your own)
on the Guest List below.

Guest List
Flighty Parent/Guardian 1 of Avery (P1A)
Moody Parent/Guardian 2 of A (P2A)
Frugal Parent/Guardian 1 of Billy (P1B)
Bawdy Mother of B (P2B)
Vengeful Best Friend of A (BFA)
Polyamorous Best Friend of B (BFB)
Fastidious First Sibling of A (S1A)
Unlucky First Sibling of B (S1B)
Flighty Aunt of A (GA)
Oddball Grandparent of Billy (GB)
Flamboyant Second Sibling of A (S2A)
Greedy Second Sibling of Billy (S2B)
Vengeful Ex-Lover of A (XA)
Prepper Ex-Lover of B (XB)
Picky Partner of First Sibling of A (PS1A)
Frugal Partner of First Sibling of B (PS1B)
Thieving Second Friend of Avery (F2A)
Thieving Second Friend of B (F2B)
Spoiled 5-year-old Child of First Sibling of B (CSB)
Drunken Wedding Crasher (WC)

Destination Wedding 2070 contains a number of elements that we think can be useful in future netprovs, especially if the character sign-ups and randomizations can be done increasingly smoothly within some kind of automated platform.

CHAPTER 9.

GAMES, ROLE-PLAY, AND NETPROVS IN THE REAL WORLD

As I scanned the world for netprov-like projects to learn from, more and more examples came from the world of games. I had not been a big gamer myself, but I could see the divide between big-budget, mainstream corporate games and other important initiatives such as the Indigenous Game Developers group organized by Elizabeth LaPensée[1] and the many communities of interactive fiction games that have developed around the easy-to-use game-creation software Twine.[2] I enjoyed beginning to learn about narrative games that overlapped with netprov and the rich critical theory about them, such as the excellent *What Is Your Quest? From Adventure Games to Interactive Books* by creator and scholar Anastasia Salter.[3] I could see a great potential for attracting gamers to come and play netprov. There were strong elements in common: a set-aside space for make-believe activity, an attitude of lighthearted experimentation. I already used the words *game*, *play*, and *playful* in describing netprovs because they defused a kind perfectionism and school-essay seriousness that some people associated with *writing*.

But there would come a moment in my study of the game world where what people were describing seemed very different from my experience of netprov. As a particular conundrum for me, one of my favorite game designers and thinkers, Jane McGonigal, wrote, "Bernard Suits, the late, great philosopher, sums it all up in what I consider the single most convincing and useful definition of a game ever devised: 'Playing a game is the voluntary attempt to overcome unnecessary obstacles.'"[4] I was perplexed, because Suits's definition of games didn't seem to fit netprov at all. In order to advance with netprov, I felt I needed to figure out what kind of game it is. I decided to look at some of my favorite creative games and think through the problem.

So, dude, you don't like soccer or poker or *Fortnite*, a popular online multiplayer game of our time?

Wait a minute! Who are you?

Your regular rhetorical-question-subheading-asker can't make it for this chapter, so I'm filling in; that ok?

What? I mean, sure. I guess so. Are they sick or something?

Nah, they're fine; just maybe a little bored. [clears throat] So, like, you don't dig soccer or *Fortnite*?

Kind of weird having a new subheading.... Well, OK. Um, the games I started looking at are more like creative games.

OK, but like, so, what do you call creative-type games?

Well, for example, during a visit to London by the Second City improv troupe in 1962, a game was developed among Second City players along with actors from the Royal Shakespeare Company, a game that continued for years. According to Del Close's biographer Kim "Howard" Johnson,

> The game was called, by some accounts, Gotcha! Players would point their index finger with thumb cocked, and the other fingers curled back. They would get three shots per day to shoot fellow players, who had to die in the most elaborate, dramatic manner possible under the circumstances. According to [actor Avery] Schrieber, there were only three exceptions to this rule: players could not be shot if they were (1) onstage working, (2) carrying a pot of boiling water, or (3) holding an expensive camera (apparently instituted by Del after he bought an expensive camera).[5]

In this game, no points were tallied. The goal was aesthetic. Pretending to die extravagantly in public was a heroic mission of bringing imagination and connection into humdrum, everyday life. The Gotcha! game, with its legacy of 1920s surrealism and Brechtian theater, is a great example of the core impulse of mimicry alive and well among adults in the so-called real world.

So, that's kinda like a running joke among friends?

Technically it's often called a "pervasive game." Wikipedia defines a pervasive game as "a Video, Role Playing (RPG), or Live Action Role Playing (LARP) game where the gaming experience is extended out in the real world, or where the fictive world in which the game takes place blends with the physical world."[6] In 1924, a storefront office opened at 15 rue de Grenelle in Paris. Its painted window and its letterhead proclaim "The Bureau of Surrealist Research." Behind the desk collecting dream data and automatic writing experiments was the bureau's intense young director, an actor named Antonin Artaud. A parody of a scientific laboratory, it was home to a variety of writing games and experiments in its short existence. The conceptual "game" was intended to disrupt traditional artistic processes and invite experimentation with new ones. In terms of social infrastructure, it was a clubhouse for the surrealists and their collaborations. The meta frame of the "parody office" served as a fictional world in the midst of the real world.

In 1983, clad as a "literary worker" in overalls with words stenciled on them, and a hard hat bearing a question mark, I stepped up to a passersby with a clipboard and said, "Excuse me, we're building a novel; may we borrow a few of your words?" Combining literary aspirations with backgrounds in skit comedy and political guerilla theater, inspired by Dada performance and surrealist expeditions, the group Invisible Seattle's projects used publications, posters, and performance to promote the generative notion of an invisible Seattle coexisting with the visible one—a smarter, more aware, more free, more real city accessed by the imagination. "Every time you read a book, you enter Invisible Seattle," went our early catchphrase. In the role of literary workers, we devised a scheme for the citizens to help write the great novel of Seattle the city deserved. I chronicled these adventures at length in *Invisible Rendezvous*.

Simple, brilliant projects such as the Swedish Number occupy that space of overlap between unclassifiable "cool things to do," creative games, improvisation, and real life. The Swedish government's official website for the project offered a great invitation:

> 250 years ago, in 1766, Sweden became the first country in the world to introduce a constitutional law to abolish censorship. To honour this

anniversary, Sweden is now the first country in the world to introduce its own phone number. Call today and get connected to a random Swede, anywhere in Sweden and talk about anything you want.[7]

The Swedish Number ran for seventy-nine days until trolling finally brought it down (once again, in the words of Whitney Phillips's title, *This Is Why We Can't Have Nice Things*.)

Aren't games different from works of art?

Being a substitute subheading question-asker, you have missed a lot of the backstory here. Well. OK. Hm. There . . . there are lots of overlaps between games and art.

Just as it took decades for photography and movies to be broadly accepted as art forms, scholars of games—which are creative cultural products just like paintings and poems—are completing their battle to validate games as art. Jane McGonigal describes ARGs as "the antiescapist game. . . . ARGs are games you play to get more out of your real life, as opposed to games you play to escape it. ARG developers want us to participate as fully in our everyday lives as we do in our game lives."[8]

Antero Garcia and Greg Niemeyer, in their introduction to their collection *Alternate Reality Games and the Cusp of Digital Gameplay* give an expanded definition of ARG where the digital platforms, shared by netprov, are included. For them an ARG is "a Video, Role Playing (RPG), or Live Action Role Playing (LARP) game where the gaming experience is extended out in the real world, or where the fictive world in which the game takes place blends with the physical world."[9] McGonigal agrees that currently, most gamers use games to escape from reality, but she reverses the usual value structure and turns the blame squarely onto reality. Why do gamers spend so much time in game worlds? Because, she contends, their quality of life in terms of satisfying work and strong social connections is far better in games than in their real lives. Gamers escape from reality, says McGonigal, because reality is broken.

What is this McGonigal person driving at? Aren't games just a pastime?

To explain the bewitching attraction of gaming, McGonigal lists four major categories of what she calls "intrinsic rewards": satisfying work, the experience (or at least the hope) of success, social connection, and meaning. She defines meaning as "the chance to be a part of something larger than ourselves. We want to feel curiosity, awe, and wonder about things that unfold on epic scales."[10]

So, McGonigal states, "When we realize that this reorientation toward intrinsic reward is what's really behind the 3 billion hours a week we spend gaming globally, the mass exodus to game worlds is neither surprising nor particularly alarming."[11]

But McGonigal has an agenda. After this analysis, she asks, "Why would we want to waste the power of games on escapist entertainment? Why would we want to waste the power of games by trying to squelch the phenomenon altogether?" She answers with a third alternative, her own big idea:

> What if we decided to use everything we know about game design to fix what's wrong with reality? What if we started to live our lives like gamers, lead our real businesses and communities like game designers, and think about solving real-world problems like computer and video game theorists?[12]

McGonigal's own ARG *Chore Wars* is a great place to start.[13] With graphics straight out of a Tolkienesque fantasy world, *Chore Wars* sums up its premise in a simple phrase: "Finally, you can claim experience points for housework." A life-management ARG, families can register on the website, adopt fantasy avatars, and the site will track who has earned the most points for cleaning, vacuuming, or vanquishing the dreaded toilet bowl. McGonigal describes herself racing to complete point-laden cleaning tasks in her own household. *Chore Wars* is a very literal application of the ARG principle of making real life like a game, dressing housework in the garb of heroic adventure and counting on a real-life family-game attitude and game banter for its effectiveness.

Richer and more inventively and ingeniously blended into real life is *Superbetter*, a concept ARG developed by Jane McGonigal to aid her slow recovery from a bad concussion she suffered in the summer of 2009. Feeling depressed, disempowered, and isolated by waiting weeks for small improvements, she (again, fairly literally) adopted a super-heroic fighting attitude and organized her physical therapy as a *Buffy the Vampire Slayer*-style series of missions that enlisted the help of a nearby and far-flung support network of friends and tracked her recovery publicly. One of the most interesting aspects of this project is the implicit recognition of the power of adopting a fictional persona on the "player's" real life mood and health. Mimicry, this game says, can become reality.

As I started to learn about ARGs one crucial difference between them and the low-budget, self-financed projects (the tradition of the world of experimental literature) I'd been doing became clear. As Garcia and Niemeyer explain it,

> Though less discussed as a motive of play than other aspects of ARGs, the role of the financiers of ARGs must be scrutinized. *The Beast* was a game developed in promotion of a blockbuster film. *I Love Bees* was a game developed in promotion of a highly anticipated video game. *Art of the H3ist* . . . was a game developed in promotion of a new car. As ARG enthusiasts and scholars are aware, these are genre-defining transmedia experiences that are bankrolled by companies with significant financial stakes in the marketing of the game. The list of ARGs developed primarily as marketing campaigns is extensive.[14]

So there are high-quality, high-production-values versions of the kinds of things you do?

Yes, but in my opinion, there are always strings attached to big budgets. Perhaps it's changing now, but in the early days, ventures into netprov territory by Hollywood or advertising companies would bring too much in the way of traditional high-production values, an industry know-it-all-ism, that would bog projects down and make them seem shallow and insincere, at least to my eyes. Instead of exploring what was new about the new medium, they would cling to the familiar like early filmmakers who insisted that a movie was a recorded play and that no audience would understand a moving camera.

Cultural and education institutions underwrite ARGs as well. McGonigal's six-week *Ghosts of a Chance* was sponsored by the Smithsonian American Art Museum. In it, fictional curators Daniel and Daisy are able to communicate with two ghosts haunting the Luce Foundation Center gallery, ghosts who insist that their stories be told in an art exhibit.[15] The problem is that, since they are ghosts, they can't make the art. They need the public's help with that. A series of online missions walked participants through research activities, gallery visits, and studios where they created art that was first shared on the web, then finally displayed for real in the gallery.

Then what's an example of a cool, low-budget netprov thingie?

In the "thingie" category falls the 2003 project cocreated by netprov featured player Jeremy Hight: *34 North 118 West*. This was a locative media project in which audio files were triggered by GPS location revealing the history of a Los Angeles neighborhood. Also low-budget were flashmobs in which people are rallied on social media to appear at a certain place at a certain time and perform a surprising or nonsensical activity and then disperse. Farther back were the good old "New Games" movement of arch-hippy and *Whole Earth Catalog* publisher Stewart Brand and friends in the late '60s.

What was the New Games movement?

The New Games concept was to invent and play games that were participatory but not competitive, in a "make love, not war" spirit. New Games such as boffing (play fighting with padded swords) and Earth Ball (played with a five-foot diameter ball volleyed aloft) in turn helped inspire the adventurous, games-in-real-life group Suicide Club, which grew out of a 1977 San Francisco State "free university" class and performed exploits such as dangerous bridge climbing, a nude cable-car riding event, and live-action street games. Out of the Suicide Club grew the San Francisco Cacophony Society, which in turn, according to the Society's website, influenced projects as diverse as Chuck Palahniuk's fictional *Fight Club* and the very real Burning Man Festival.

Some early ARGs built directly on New Games. In February of 2008, amateur archeologist Eli Hunt began a podcast series in which he recounted his potential discovery of a forgotten game from the ancient Greek Olympics. Eli Hunt was a fictional character. Despite this fact, links to Hunt's podcast were found on the International Olympic Committee's web page. Why? Because the game Hunt's podcasts set in motion, *The Lost Ring*, was actually endorsed by the International Olympic Committee and was sponsored by the McDonald's corporation. It was an ARG. Game expert Jane McGonigal was one of the game's creators.[16]

As the weeks went by, the game organized players around the world into international teams to search for real-life clues physically hidden on different continents and to piece together the rules of play of the lost game in which a blindfolded runner navigates a human labyrinth by using audible cues, a game that turned out to bear a remarkable resemblance to New Games.

Once the rules of *The Lost Ring's* ancient game had been established, teams formed around the world to actually play the game and actually compete for the best time, posting their results on YouTube. In this project, the fiction portion of the game is conceived, preplanned, and executed by a paid professional team who wrote the podcasts, hid the clues, and managed the website. The creative participation of the audience took the form of puzzle solving and competing in the support, "cocreating" a sport with all the sport's attendant styles, strategies, and tradition.

So the "game" in *The Lost Ring* was kind of to recreate history?

Yes, and that process also is not new. Historical re-enactment organizations have recreated historical battles for centuries, and informal to formal versions of live-action role-play (LARP) games exist, for a weekend or longer, for a wide range of budgets and tastes.

Then, as home computing became a reality in the '80s and '90s there was a transition from tabletop RPGs to online single-player RPGs, also known as interactive fiction, to multi-user dungeons or domains (MUDs) and MUD object-oriented (MOOs). With an increase in network access came the age of massively multiplayer online games (MMOs) and, most importantly for netprov, massively multiplayer online role-playing games (MMPORGs). MMPORGs create worlds that allow greater and lesser amounts of open play but fundamentally establish a fictional ground for participatory fictional improvising.

The following ARG-like netprov concept, still unproduced as of this writing, was a breakthrough for me and led to the fictional world *of Grace, Wit & Charm*.

Try This: "The Struggling Theater Company"

Here's an extra dimension of play for you and your actor friends:

1. Ingredients: one stage improv troupe, temporarily redubbed "The Struggling Theater Company," and a theater that can host a weekly show for a month or so.

2. Workshop fictional characters who are improv actors and outline a few story lines for the entire run. Each real actor embodies a fictional actor.

3. Announce that, between shows, audience members are invited to follow the social media feed, normally private, used by the troupe.

4. The fictional troupe members pretend not to fully realize the social media feed is public.

5. Starting a week before the first show, the troupe members behave extremely badly in their feed—feuds, cliques, strikes, affairs—high drama!

6. Moments before the performance begins, the live audience is encouraged to use their phones to access the fictional feed, in case they haven't already tuned in.

7. The "improv show" is terrible. No wonder they are struggling. But the real point of the live event is to perform crises in the backstory, resolving some issues and opening others. The feed continues with online backstabbing during the show (at the hands of actors momentarily offstage) and afterwards in a brutal written post mortem.

8. Then the writing in the feed starts building again and the story lines are improvised toward the next week's show.

So alternate reality games are pretty much the same as netprov?

There are crucial differences. Speaking of the importance of maintaining a level of frustration in games, Jane McGonigal quotes Raph Koster, "He writes, 'Fun from games arises out of mastery. It arises out of comprehension. . . . With games, *learning* is the drug.' And that's why fun in games lasts only as long as we're not consistently successful."[17] Although netprov as a creative game might quibble with the notion of necessary frustration, Koster's point about the importance of learning is exactly in line with the progression I see from childhood mimicry to make believe to therapeutic satire. In satire, insightful learning is the drug.

And here's where I ran aground against Bernard Suits's definition: "Playing a game is the voluntary attempt to overcome unnecessary obstacles."[18] Try as I might, I fail to find the *obstacle* in creative games such as netprov.

The key dynamic of games of make believe, as Roger Caillois points out, is the fascination of the spectator by the actor; there seems to be an irreducible aspect of performance to it. I would extend Caillois's take on mimicry by adding that in a collaborative game of make believe, there is a kind of mutual spectacle making taking place that *also* can be seen by passive, nonplayer spectators. Netprov players are players in the theatrical sense perhaps more than the game sense.

McGonigal herself writes about the collaboration within competition: "To compete against someone still requires coming together with them: to strive toward the same goal, to push each other to do better, and to participate wholeheartedly in seeing the competition through to completion."[19]

But isn't creative play in a group always kind of competitive?

Describing the invention of extreme skateboarding in the empty swimming pools of the Los Angeles drought of the mid 1970s, skateboard ace Bob Biniak described the combination of competition and mutual encouragement during the boundary-stretching play sessions by saying, "We pushed and praised."[20] All players want to do their best, even to do *the* best, and at the same time, excellence by anyone is always applauded, even if it breaks rules or explores new territory.

Formal improvisation contests in theaters and clubs, such as those that happen at Chicago's Improv Olympics, founded by Del Close, and Chicago's Green Mill poetry slams, are pseudo games.

Why pseudo games?

Because they have no objectively verifiable goal. Everyone can see the net ripple as the soccer ball hits the cords, but is it so clear who "wins" a poetry contest? There is, in fact, no accounting for taste, and there is no objective measure of aesthetic quality. The actual goal of the poetry slam movement was to break the pious silence that had protected the perpetrators of innumerably dull poetry readings, to improve writing and performance, and to bring poetry to a wider audience. A poetry slam is mimicry; it pretends to be a game.

Which brings me to my very favorite game—Mornington Crescent—one that arises from the grand tradition of BBC radio shows that use game formats and whimsical scoring as pretexts for improvised wit.

What kind of game is Mornington Crescent?

Here's an example of Mornington Crescent game play:

> Before you play Mornington Crescent it is assumed that because it was Thursday yesterday you will know that the short rules only apply and

from the 2nd turn in reverse order during September. Please also remember rule 7b: All Egyptian moves are disallowed except crossovers and double takes.

Please avoid all surface lines that back onto Mrs Trellis's home between 7pm and 7am on a Friday.[21]

Starting in 1978, Mornington Crescent has been featured on the long-running BBC comedy panel show *I'm Sorry I Haven't a Clue*. The ostensible rules are simple: (1) players name a London street or subway station in turn, and (2) the first player to arrive at Mornington Crescent is the winner. However, as soon as gameplay begins, every game invariably becomes mired in erudite arguments over the rules. Each player knowingly cites obscure subrules, exotic strategies, long-forgotten gambits.

In reality, Mornington Crescent is an elaborate in-joke, a satire of overearnest quibbling. Even the game's history invites debate, with perhaps the most authoritative being related by the show's late chairman "Humph" (Humphrey Lyttleton, coauthor of *The Little Book of Mornington Crescent*) who writes of the Tudor court rules from the time of Henry VIII, when the subway system was smaller, and by which Shakespeare himself played Mornington Crescent.[22]

Dude, do you have any quantifiable data to back up any of this? Any charts or graphs?

Not really. This book is more kind of a fine arts thing. Do you usually work on science, technology, engineering, and math (STEM) type books?

Of course. I was a biology major, man.

OK. Interesting. Well, um, literary games are a form of heightened conversation. Psychologists such as Mihaly Csikszentmihalyi and others have studied patterns of informal creative contests such as joke telling and "gross-out contests" (in which participants try to use words to create the most disgusting image and most disgusted reaction from others). Csikszentmihalyi cites studies that show there is usually a consensus among the groups involved in these informal creative contests about who has succeeded, who has failed, and who has ultimately won. The "rules of the game," although unarticulated, are understood by the members of the group.[23]

The rules of netprov are fluid, socially negotiated rules based on make believe. As Lance Parkin discusses in his consideration of the fictional world of Dr. Who, James Bond can stay the same age in the 1960s, 1980s, and 2010s whereas it is clearly "against the rules" for Sherlock Holmes to be alive at all in the 1920s.[24] McGonigal describes how even mainstream online games are constructed to make their rules easy to learn in the way humans learn social rules: "Traditionally, we have needed instructions in order to play a game. But now we're often invited to learn as we go. We explore the game space, and the computer code effectively constrains and guides us."[25] Netprov, then, is a collaborative game of mimicry that can enfold into its mimesis a mimicry of games.

The rules of netprov are generative—what I would call *parliamentary rules*, like *Robert's Rules of Order*. They exist to organize collaborative activity generically and do not specify a particular goal. They focus on preventing social abuses, guarantee that everyone may be heard, that time and attention cannot be monopolized, that decisions can be reached by fair and transparent voting. Parliamentary rules also can contain self-altering processes; constitutions contain procedures for amending the constitution. Remember that Del Close legislated, "The first rule of the Harold is that there are no rules."[26] I believe what Close was pointing at in his joking paradox is the powerful parliamentary ability to revise the rules on the fly. In a conversation with electronic literature and featured player Talan Memmott, I mentioned that "we'll have the rules for *Fantasy Spoils* ready for you in a couple of days," to which Talan replied laconically, "You know, Rob, whatever rules you make I'm going to break them."

Without rules and a score, how do you know who has won a netprov?

Sigh. Aside to the reader: I miss our usual rhetorical-question-subheading-asker! The goals of creative play ultimately are self-created and self-judged. No amount of praise can convince the self-doubting artist of the value of their work, just as no amount of detraction can keep the self-confident artist from realizing their vision. This lack of external proof of success is what makes for both the often-discussed risk taking of the creative life and the courage it takes to do it. The mutual recognition of this creative courage makes for a particularly strong social connection among creative collaborators. Del Close and his coauthors have described this bond in *Truth in Comedy*:

Del is fond of the "group mind" concept that develops during improv when everything works, and the ability to wire human minds together to become "Supermen."

"We are releasing higher and greater powers of the human being," he explains. . . . "When improvisers are using seven or eight brains instead of just their own, they can do no wrong.

On stage, one has a complete picture of what is going on, and also a clear sense of all potential moves. They are almost laid out in time. The pattern-making mechanism is kicked on, and yet, one's intellect does not desert him," explains Del.

"Since everyone is on the same wavelength, each player sees what the other sees. It's an absolute thrill, a tremendous surge of confidence, energy, and joy. I've given up searching for happiness, now that I realize joy is very easily achieved."[27]

So group mind is the goal of improv?

Not a *goal* really. Close's thrill is subtly, but importantly, different from McGonigal's "feedback" (scoreboards) and the objective proof of success. It has much more in common with McGonigal's idea of the intrinsic reward of social connection. Group mind is the camaraderie and mutual admiration of taking risks side by side.

Why is Mornington Crescent my favorite game? Because it satirizes the very idea of the objective proof of success and, by implication, the conventional concept of success itself. Creative games tackle a necessary obstacle: the seemingly irreconcilable psychological and social conflicts (such as constructed notions of success) inherent in social life. Like seismic tensions in the Earth's crust, inner psychological tensions among internal subpersonalities with conflicting motivations as well as outer social tensions among members of social hierarchies both find rebalancing in the earthquake of laughter. The truth is told, energy is released, and a workable balance is restored. An unsatirized world is unlivable.

But isn't there a difference between writing literature and game playing?

Writing itself is, let's not forget, a physical act. A miserable one, if one is to believe generations of writers rubbing their sore shoulders and cramped hands. Charles Dickens is said to have stalked his writing room when alone and composing, loudly growling the lines of his characters in development. Simply aiming for realism in mimicking social media means netprov players need to take pictures to include in posts, finding people to model for them or modeling themselves.

Try This: One-Star Reviews Field Trip

Here is a great creative netprov adventure you can do with friends:

1. Identify a place that could rate one star.
2. Arrange a time to rally around it with two to six intrepid explorers.
3. Bring tools for writing, including at least two fictional characters whose voices you are ready to inhabit. No stereotypes or caricatures, no character you've seen before. Instead, fresh observation, quirky and subtle as real life.
4. Write, on the spot, a review in a character voice that uses any other scale of evaluation other than the usual ones. Insist on being positive. Find value where no one else can. Explore! Surprise us!
5. Respond and build on at least one other review, in character, by continuing to explore in the direction it suggests.
6. Photograph (optionally) a unique detail of the place or thing. No lazy snaps or dull selfies! In fact, no faces at all! Instead, strange textures, ephemeral reflections, stains, flaws, and neglected beauty. Capture fragmentary images that make us go "Wha?"
7. Toast and celebrate together your creative daring with available food and drink. Woo, as they say, hoooo!

How long can these wildly experimental, real-life creative projects last?

Here's an example of an ultra-long-form, real-life creative collaborative game. A frenetic and brilliantly loquacious preacher took the stage of a small Chicago underground theater in 1991. I was in the audience. The pseudonymous Reverend Ivan Stang wiped the sweat from his brow and ranted: "Apostates accuse us, dear friends, of selling out. Selling out? Selling out? We have been trying to sell out for years . . . but there have *been no takers!*" The important and talented group of writers and performers associated with the Church of the Subgenius have done projects since the

1980s (the same time frame as Invisible Seattle) that share many of the characteristics of netprov.

The organization, legally a real church but essentially a fictional church, is an ongoing collaborative satire not just of US evangelical church culture but conspiracy theorists, UFO enthusiasts, and other fringe groups. It occupies and subverts traditional church structures and the media of church communications to advance the fiction—services, titles and hierarchy, "devivals," concerts, pamphlets, books, visual art, radio broadcasts, websites, and podcasts:

- If you are what they call "different"—
- If you think we're entering a new Dark Ages—
- If you see the universe as one vast morbid sense of humor—
- If you are looking for an inherently bogus religion that will condone superior degeneracy and tell you that you are "above" everyone else—
- If you can help us with a donation—

The Church of the Subgenius could save your sanity![28]

The church is collaborative, allowing membership (for a price) but also encouraging schisms and debate. Broad plotlines unfold in real time; for example, the assassination and purported resurrection of the church's prophet, the grinning, pipe-smoking '50s clip-art paterfamilias J. R. "Bob" Dobbs. The unspoken rule is that Subgenius figures always stay in character and always deny that what they are doing is art, like kayfabe in the world of professional wrestlers.

Now you're mixing up art and culture hoaxes with professional wrestling?

No, with politics. By insisting that surrealism was not an art style but a way of life, André Breton and the surrealists created a meta structure that surrounded any particular piece of writing, art, or even creative career. Surrealism was modeled on a political movement (issuing "manifestos," the everyday French word for a political party platform) or a scientific movement. As during centuries of sectarian conflict, one could "become" a Catholic or a Protestant; in the 1920s in France, one could become a Communist, a Freudian, or a surrealist.

The genius of the Church of the Subgenius is that by using one word, they explain the rules of their collaborative creative game, the word *church*. They are, as their literature proudly tells us, "an inherently bogus religion that will tell you that you are better than everyone else." The invitation to play and participate is broad and comprehensible. Their target audience is well-defined in their own literature: outsiders who feel alone in the sea of US religious conservatism and need an attitude that will help them survive. "Do people think you're strange? Do you? . . . THEN YOU MAY BE ON THE RIGHT TRACK!" says one of their earliest tracts. "'Unpredictables' are not alone and possess amazing hidden powers of their own! Are You Abnormal? THEN YOU PROBABLY ARE BETTER THAN MOST PEOPLE! YES! YOUR KIND SHALL TRIUMPH!"[29]

If you want to "join" the Subgeniuses, do anything that is church-like; in particular, like the independent southern US fundamentalist churches that they most closely parody. The thing I most admire about the flexibility of the Subgeniuses' "world" is that it perfectly accommodates creative disagreements. If you don't like how some other Subgenius preacher is doing things, you are encouraged to break away and form your own schismatic church—just as long as you have a spectacular and public battle—just like real churches have done for centuries.

What I still find so exciting about Invisible Seattle all these years is the deadpan proposition of an *invisible* Seattle, parallel and intermingled with the visible one, that is accessed by acts of imagination. "Invisible Seattle is the antidote for your feeling of completeness," goes one of the mottos. In the early '80s, Invisible Seattle godfather Philip Wohlstetter would spin yarns of finding evidence of a "parallel university" that quietly occupied unused classrooms at the University of Washington and, from the notes on the chalkboards, was offering much more interesting courses than the real university. Who were these unseen, more intelligent students and teachers? How could we meet them? How could we become them? The link to my netprov project of mysterious whiteboard notes is clear. The game of surrealism, of the Church of the Subgenius, of Invisible Seattle, and of netprov, is to awake in the morning in our same old beds with a new attitude: more creative, more proactive, more empowered, more alive.

In that case, what kind of game is netprov anyway?

It's an important question if we're going to understand netprov's possibilities. Johan Huizinga in his 1938 *Homo Ludens: A Study of the Play*

Element in Culture, included in Katie Salen and Eric Zimmerman's *The Game Design Reader: A Rules of Play Anthology,* listed among his formal characteristics of play:

> We might call it a free activity standing quite consciously outside "ordinary" life as being "not serious," but at the same time absorbing the player intensely and utterly.... It proceeds within its own proper boundaries of time and space according to fixed rules and in an orderly manner.[30]

But does all play necessarily involve Huizinga's "fixed rules?" Netprov is playful but has only evolving guidelines that are frequently broken without breaking the netprov. Roger Caillois expanded and refined Huizinga's ideas in his 1958 *Man, Play and Games.* Caillois writes:

> Many games do not imply rules. No fixed or rigid rules exist for playing with dolls, for playing soldiers, cops and robbers, horses. Locomotives and airplanes—games, in general, which presuppose free improvisation, and the chief attraction of which lies in the pleasure of playing a role, of acting as if one were someone or something else, a machine for example. Despite the assertion's paradoxical character, I will state that in this instance the fiction, the sentiment of as if, replaces and performs the same function as do rules.[31]

This convenient redefinition of "rules" as the "fiction" helps me wrestle with the difficulty of McGonigal's and Suits's formulation: "Games are the voluntary attempt to overcome unnecessary obstacles," especially if one views rules themselves as obstacles. Caillois goes on to write, "Rules themselves create fictions.... That is why chess, prisoner's base, polo, and baccara are played *for real. As if* is not necessary."[32]

Caillois extends this principle into two large categories of games. "Thus," he writes, "games are not ruled and make-believe. Rather, they are ruled *or* make-believe." To demonstrate this distinction, Caillois uses the lovely example of "children, in order to imitate adults, blindly manipulating real or imaginary chess pieces on an imaginary chessboard, and by pleasant example, playing at 'playing chess.'"[33]

Netprov is clearly a game of make believe. Caillois's image of children playing at "playing chess" is the exact structural model for Mornington Crescent. The game of playing at playing can have great artistic and social power.

Caillois creates a category of mimicry games, in which "the subject makes believe or makes others believe that he is someone other than himself. He forgets, disguises, or temporarily sheds his personality in order to feign another."[34] As the Church of the Subgenius says so boldly in their proselytizing pamphlets, "We pull the wool over our own eyes."[35]

When it comes to rules and mimicry, Caillois notes that in games of mimcry, "the continuous submission to imperative and precise rules cannot be observed—rules for the dissimulation of reality and the substitution of a second reality. *Mimicry* is incessant invention. The rule of the game is unique: it consists in the actor's fascinating the spectator, while avoiding an error that might lead the spectator to break the spell."[36] So then, netprov in Caillois's terms is mimicry. But I think it is more than that. Satire is social healing.

What I finally concluded in response to the question, What kind of game is netprov?, is that one kind of game involves competition, winners and losers, obstacles and limited winning conditions (right or wrong answers). Netprov is another kind of game, one that involves collaboration, enabling constraints (trellises, not obstacles), and unlimited winning conditions (no right or wrong answers, including breaking the rules).

As I've played netprov, I have come up with my own definition in response to Suits's: *netprov is the voluntary attempt to heal necessary relationships through collaborative play.*

EXAMPLE 9: THERMOPHILES IN LOVE, A NETPROV

Larping Five Genders

In 2016, LARP designer and scholar Samara Hayley Steele approached Mark and me looking to collaborate. Hayley mentioned that she had codesigned a five-gender role system for a LARP and that it hadn't been played as thoroughly as she would have liked. Mark's and my eyes lit up. If you can design a five-gender system for us, we said, we'll play! We didn't want to make it about humans so we decided to make it about the rainbow-colored single-celled dwellers of thermal hot springs like the ones Mark had recently visited on vacation.

> Thermophiles in Love is a five-gender dating website for microorganisms. Play as one of five genders as you seek to form the perfect quadruple. The genders in this society are: Hype, Obli, Fac, Acido, and Meso.[1]

We recruited writer-dancer-biologist and featured player Cathy Podeszwa to join the netrunner team and *Thermophiles in Love*[i] was born. Mark created an online "genderator" to randomly assign genders. In addition to a netprov version created on a stand-alone forum website, Steele was gamemaster for traditional LARP versions run in Berkeley, California, at the conference of the Society for Literature, Science, and the Arts (SLSA) in Atlanta, Georgia, and the Living Games Conference in Boston, Massachusetts.

Marino described the use of the genderator:

> Hayley and I would stand by a computer displaying the webpage for the genderator (a simple random generator). We would ask volunteers to step up and have their gender scanned, encouraging them to clear the minds so as not to cloud the genderator's sensors. Once they were in position, we would reload the page and then pronounce that the genderator had

determined their appropriate thermophile gender. The playful gender scan was meant as a satire on the arbitrary enforcement of the social construction of gender. However, it also served to bring participants into the world of the game.[2]

Thermophiles in Love Relationship Norms

- A relationship has four thermophiles in it. Never three. Never five. Just four.
- A quadruple (rhymes with "couple") can have any combination of genders in it; it's not unusual for two or more of the same gender to be in a quadruple.
- Thermophiles can't choose who is in their quadruple: Mesos are the matchmakers.[3]

Each gender was taught a simple, easy to remember gesture or *dance* that quickly identified them to other players. The genders included:

Acido: Acidophilic thermophiles (aka lithotrophs), the magnificent gender.

- Temperature Preference: Extreme Heat and Acidity (130oF+ / 54oC+ and less than 7pH).
- Lucky numbers: 3 and 4
- Motto: The Magnificent 7 rolled into 1.
- Those acid baths keep your organelle looking magnificent! Your presence turns any situation into something valuable.
- Always aware of being seen because you stand out. No matter where you go, you quickly become a public figure.
- Other genders: Find you magnetic.
- Weakness: Occasionally you flip out over things that some might call "trivial."
- You need constant feedback to feel secure (because whether or not they admit it, you know they're all looking your way).
- Ideal Occupation: Company spokesperson, pop singer, clothing line namesake, on-screen talent, Instafamous Twitterati, community spokesperson, politician, salesperson, the embarrassing-and-proud parent.

Fac: Facultative thermophiles, the mirroring gender.

- Temperature Preference: can adjust to a wide range, from high to extreme low (100oF-150oF / 38oC-66oC).
- Lucky numbers: 7 or 9.
- Motto: Dare To be Similar.
- The shape-shifting gender, you conform to whatever situation you are in.
- Propensity to develop different personalities, which to you are more like modalities.
- Truth is relative to you; "lying" isn't a concept to you.
- Other genders: Feel connected and at home with you—you remind everyone of their best friend from their hometown
- Weakness: Becoming overloaded by the very different expectations each person has for you.
- You are up for whatever.—Can cause jealousy as you flit about doing your thing.
- Propensity to lose yourself.
- Ideal Occupation: Explorer, investigative reporter, political strategist, Hollywood agent, cultural theorist, military intelligence in a "hot" zone, social worker, language interpreter, user interface designer, the parent who's like a kid.[4]

In a talk at the conference Social Studies of Live Action Role-Playing Games at the European University at St. Petersburg, Russia, Steele talked about gender playability.

> The goal, ultimately, when you're designing for gender playability, is for players to reify their game genders, which is to say, they take those social constructs to be facts of nature. It starts feeling "real." Once that happens, you achieve a type of gender playability, a type of fluency in the things of the game gender. This I argue creates a more immersive alternative reality experience, because gender is something that so many of us take for granted in such a deep way, that achieving gender playability in a game creates this feeling of the surreal, like the sense of being in a truly different, truly foreign society, in a way that I think surpasses other forms of playability in game design. I believe gender playability shows us

the amazing achievements of game design, in terms of what game design can teach us about our own culture.[5]

Marino describes the live LARP sessions:

> We held a series of thermophile speed dating rounds, followed by some match making, and then trial mini-dates of our quadruples. Participants live played all of these, which were followed by discussions about how the role-play and matchmaking went.[6]

An email from Steele after running the fifth live LARP version shows the subtle sensitivity of the larpwright and is a great model for netprov netrunners:

> I've gotten quite a few of the kinks out (very much thanks to some Theatre of the Oppressed workshops I've been to in the San Francisco area—very good techniques to bring into a LARP!) Everything is now done kinetically—the Mesos now tap people's shoulders and trade them with each other, gradually building the quadruples that way, rather than having to write names down.
>
> [One] thing that really got me later that I wanted to share: two days after running *Thermophiles in Love*, I ran into one of the players at MIT, and they were introducing themselves as their Thermophile name!! . . . I always ask the players to think a of gender-neutral noun and they write it down, then we fire up the Genderator and after everyone is gendered, I tell them "remember that gender neutral noun you wrote down? That is your Thermophile name."
>
> What an amazing collaborative piece! The gendering ritual . . . plus the Genderator!—plus those gender write-ups we all came up with!—that stuff is pure magic I tell ya!
>
> The dances have been a huge contribution to the game—having the way you move (rather than the way you look) be the thing that signals your gender has really gotten great feedback!! Also, perhaps the most moving moment in the Boston run had to do with the dances—this was described by one of the players during the post-game storytelling circle:
>
> (Note: for this game, I told the players: "Facs, the mirror gender, are the only gender that can do other genders' dances—they mirror the dances of others around them—they also have their own dance, but it is very rare to see.")
>
> This player had been part of a group that became quadrupled with a Meso who, mid-game, had a gender change. . . . Bartender (the former Meso) came wandering into their group saying, "I'm an Acido now." He

had this moment of feeling great joy for Bartender, and also shock that someone can become another gender, and at that moment he realized he was having a feeling that was genuinely *his* rather than mirroring others around him & very softly, at the edge of the group, for a fleeting second, he did the Fac dance. And that's what the Fac dance is about now: it's about being there for those little moments that belong only to you.

During that run, I had a player have a moment of tears during the gendering ritual. Based on how Mark and I did it at the SLSA, I always say "congratulations!" to the person about their new gender. And this young person, they'd never been congratulated on their gender before and they were saying "I don't know why it feels so good to hear that: congratulations" while wiping tears from their eyes.[7]

CHAPTER 10.

FUTURES OF NETPROV

Laughter, Insight, Empathy

I'm excited by the possible futures of netprov. I see a rollicking, rolling playing field in which writers of all skill levels can invent together and learn from one another. I see a satisfying creative outlet that busy people can participate in using tiny slices of time in everyday life. I see players feeling the rewards of cocreating large, smart, substantial works of art.

Technologically, I see netprov continuing to migrate as parody and satire from platform to platform as new platforms appear. Organizationally, if money were no object, I would form a small netprov production studio and employ a couple of netrunners, a handful of featured players, a programmer, a designer, and a production assistant or two. I'd create a simple, proprietary platform—essentially a private web forum—and invite groups of around three to ten friends to form private netprov groups among themselves, free from trolls. The studio would provide the trellis for a new netprov every calendar month, sent to all the groups. Each group would see in their feed their own and their friends' posts, intermingled with the featured players' posts which would be sent to everyone from headquarters, providing models and inspiration. Eventually, stellar groups might nominate themselves to be published to the wider community and other forms of sharing might be developed.

What do you think are the strongest characteristics you've discovered in netprov that can make real works of art?

Hey! Hi! Great to see you!

Hi! Yeah, sorry I couldn't be here for the last chapter. Did I miss anything good?

Nah. I was just worried about you!

It was the darndest thing. I was just cutting these organic carrots I get in our food box and—wham!—there goes a big chunk of my thumb!

Ouch!

It's fine now but I had to go to urgent care for stitches. As you were saying?

Well, in this book, I've talked about how principles of mutually supportive collaboration drawn from theater and games can be leveraged to create parody-based fictional worlds in which people can play productively. I've talked about how technical and graphic mimicry of vernacular models from mass media provides recognizable structures and helps explain these parodic games, and I've shown how ARGs provide numerous structural tips for organizing creative play and building new forms. I've also looked at how character development, plotting examples, technologically self-aware narratives, and an interplay between theory and creative writing drawn from literature and theater can bring the full depth and subtlety of the literary tradition to netprov's worlds. After examining all of these elements, a powerful triad emerges: laughter, insight, and empathy.

Laughter, insight, empathy?

Silly as netprovs can be, the laughter we seek is the laughter of insight. Psychological insight is the sudden understanding of the causes of one's disorder. Satire is psychological insight operating in a community.

Self-important new-media forms simply *beg* to be satirized, with all the comic consequences we've discussed. The question is: How truthful *are* these new forms and platforms? They often aim to be business "disruptors" and wind up disrupting human relationships as well. What unique parts of inner truth do they reveal and which do they conceal? Perhaps this ridicule provides a social function of publicly putting the new forms through their paces so that they are not taken too seriously.

An African consultant on an educational publishing project I was working on once described how West African Anansi the Spider folk stories were used in her family. Grandmothers and aunts were very observant about the behavior of the little kids. If one youngster was having problems sharing, sure enough, that night at story time, one of the elders would tell an Anansi story about sharing. Everyone in the intergenerational group would know who was being talked about, but the storytelling was never intended to shame or blame, just a reminder and encouragement. I believe netprov can use networked communication to function in society in just this way. Netprov has the potential to be not just creative entertainment but an art form that not only offers critical insight on society but also offers real opportunities for community building and new friendships.

Laughter, however, can cut two ways. It can be either mean-spirited or it can be generous and empathic. From the roots of improv theater, netprov can learn the power of empathic comedy. Del Close was an empathy junkie. Close's writing points us toward agreement as a process and connection as the goal.

Netprov as literature-based "show" offers the possibility of cocreation of insightful, healing satire that is as deep as the novels of the past. Netprov as "game" offers the possibility of new, empathic, real-life relationships based on collaborative creativity and genuine understanding. I believe the *world* a netprov narrative can offer its participants is their own everyday world—transformed by laughter, insight, and empathy.

How could you transform the world with netprov?

In the book *Difficult Conversations: How to Discuss What Matters Most*,[1] Douglas Stone, Bruce Patton, and Sheila Heen of the Harvard Law School's Negotiation Project follow up on the group's bestselling *Getting to Yes* with clear and practical advice for moving beyond personal and social standoffs. "We will show you how to turn the damaging battle of warring messages," they write, "into the more constructive approach we call a *learning conversation*."

How would a book from the Harvard Law School program help point to the future of a new art form?

Well, *learning conversation* already sounds a lot like a generic description of a netprov, for starters. And they go on to say, "Each difficult conversation is really three conversations." There is the *what happened* conversation, the *feelings* conversation, and the *identity* conversation (What does this conflict say about my identity and my status?), conflicting stories, feelings, identities? That's literature in a nutshell, right? In fact, they say, "Difficult conversations do not just *involve* feelings, they are at their very core *about* feelings." And how do the authors propose proceeding? They say simply, "Stop arguing about who's right. *Explore each other's stories.*"[2] They point out that we each have different information and therefore see the world differently. Therefore, in a phrase that would be right at home in a stage improv class, they encourage us to "move from certainty to curiosity" and to adopt what they call "the And stance." Sound familiar? It's the same *and* as the "yes, and" of improv:

> Don't choose between the stories; embrace both. That's the And stance. . . . The And stance is based on the assumption that the world is complex, that you can feel hurt, angry, and wronged, *and* they can feel just as hurt, angry and wronged. They can be doing their best *and* you can think that its not good enough. You may have done something stupid, *and* they will have contributed in important ways to the problem as well. You can feel furious with them, *and* you can also feel love and appreciation for them.[3]

The authors' encouragement to replace blame with a model of contribution—What did each party contribute to the situation?—prompts strategies that could come straight from the guidelines for a netprov:

> *Role Reversal*
> As yourself "What would they say I'm contributing?" Pretend you are the other person and answer the question in the first person, using pronouns such as I, me, and my. . . .
>
> *The Observer's Insight*
> Step back and look at the problem from the perspective of a disinterested observer. Imagine that you are a consultant called in to help the people in this situation better unersand why they are getting stuck. . . . If you have trouble getting out of your own shoes in this way, ask a friend to try for you. If what your friend comes up with surprises you, don't reject it immediately . . . how could that be and what would it mean?

The observer's insight exercise becomes one of the authors' key gestures, to create a Third story. "In addition to your story and the other person's story, every difficult conversation includes an invisible Third Story. The

Third Story is the one a keen observer would tell, someone with no stake in your particular problem." A fiction writer, perhaps?

Most similar of all to improv and netprov is the encouragement of the authors of *Difficult Conversations*, encouragement that the most helpful skill in collaborative problem solving is *listening*. They write, "*You can't move the conversation in a more positive direction until the other person feels heard and understood. And they won't feel heard and understood until you've listened.*" And this is from people whose job it is to drop in as consultants to volatile workplaces and help them learn to work together.

You think netprov can help people listen?

The watchword of all stage improv is listening. Without listening, improv doesn't work. The same goes for netprov; without reading carefully—tuning in to the emotional resonance of what others' characters are writing—you can't really play netprov. *Thermophiles in Love* offered a playful learning conversation about gender in a way that, as larpwright Samara Hayley Steele realized, could expand minds and offer insights in a game-like setting. What if groups of players from across the great social and political divides of our time could tell their stories in a playful environment that required us each to walk a mile in another's shoes?

Could there be learning conversations that make the same gesture as the final sequence of *Grace, Wit & Charm*, where the overworked, overstressed Character Enhancement Agents found themselves saving insurance companies zillions by performing remote hospice care in a sequence that was a sharp satire of America's health-care system as well as a goodbye to their player-audience of two weeks? Despite the absurdity of their task, the team gave it their best shot:

Grace, Wit & Charm, @GWandC May 29, 2011
WAIT!! Wait, team! Sorry. Sorry. (Before departing for your virtual vacation) One more VirtuKare hospice job before you go, OK? Patient is already on the line. #GWandC

Sonny, @Sonny1SoBlue May 29, 2011
OK. We'll take it together. "Hello ma'am. How are you? Well, that was a silly question wasn't it? You're dying, that's how you are." #GWandC

Laura, @Laura_GWaC May 29, 2011
Ma'am, I am powerful in this world, & the next, & I can assure you have nothing to fear from passing through the twilight doorway. #GWandC

Neil, @Neil_GWaC May 29, 2011
Ma'am Ill move for you like you used to move as a girl. See me? Feel it? Your body is all in your mind. Zumba with me, dear. #GWandC

Sonny, @Sonny1SoBlue May 29, 2011
Believe it or not, I'm looking forward to this Wolfstonecastlebane vacation! Laura? Neil? Can you guys program me some snomobiles? #GWandC

Deb, @Deb_GWaC May 29, 2011
Ma'am I can make the pain go away, see. I know your allone with no family there, but there are four of us here with you now. #GWandC

Laura, @Laura_GWaC May 29, 2011
Yes, Sonny, my Wolfstonecastlebane temple is a place to rest, recreate, recover. Sure, we'll build you a whole snowmobile course! #GWandC

Sonny, @Sonny1SoBlue May 29, 2011
Ma'am life is good, but so death must be good, too. I promise, yes I promise. #GWandC

Neil, @Neil_GWaC May 29, 2011
I think we're really helping this dying lady, team. This is kind cool! #GWandC

Deb, @Deb_GWaC May 29, 2011
Now that my son's cold turkey off his Leaping Lizards video game, can he come to Wolfstonecastlebane with us for a few days?@Laura_GWaC #GWandC

Laura, @Laura_GWaC May 29, 2011
Sure, Deb! Your son is welcome! #GWandC

Laura, @Laura_GWaC May 29, 2011
We're right here with you Ma'am. Glad to be with you. #GWandC

Deb, @Deb_GWaC May 29, 2011
Sure it's OK to let go Ma'am. You've fought a good fight. You have our permission to go! We love you. What's not to love? #GWandC

Sonny, @Sonny1SoBlue May 29, 2011
Ma'am, hello? Are you there Ma'am? Can you read these Tweets? Do you read me? Do you read us? #GWandC

Laura, @Laura_GWaC May 29, 2011
I think that's it. #GWandC

NOTES

INTRODUCTION

i. **Netprov:** *Grace, Wit & Charm*
    Tagline: Being You Is Harder Than You Think!
    First appeared: May 14–29, 2011
    Platforms: Twitter, website, two live theater performances, video streamed
    Netrunner: Rob Wittig
    Featured players: Cathy Podeszwa, Gary Kruchowski, Shannon Laing, Jamie Harvie, Jean Sramek, Margi Preus, Joellyn Rock, and Mark Marino
    Archive: Twitter's archiving; private archives; video performance archives in Vimeo, https://vimeo.com/70899728, https://vimeo.com/26176893, https://vimeo.com/2617689

1. Sam Rosenthal et al., "Welcome to Blaseball," Blaseball, accessed August 12, 2021, https://www.blaseball.com. See also Todd Martens, "It's a Beautiful Summer for 'Blaseball.' Yes, 'Balseball,' Where America's Pastime Meets 'D&D,'" *Los Angeles Times*, August 24, 2020.

2. Christina Pineda, "Tactics and Tropes of the Internet Security Agency," Homeland Security Digital Library, December 18, 2018, https://www.hsdl.org/c/tactics-and-tropes-of-the-internet-research-agency/.

3. Rob Wittig and IN.S.OMNIA (Computer bulletin board), *Invisible Rendezvous: Connection and Collaboration in the New Landscape of Electronic Writing* (Middletown, CT / Hanover, NH: Wesleyan University Press / University Press of New England, 1994).

4. Sue Thomas, Teri Hoskins, et al., "N_o_o_n Q_u_i_l_t," WayBack Machine, 1998, http://web.archive.org/web/20131006134639/http://tracearchive.ntu.ac.uk/quilt/quilt_1.htm.

5. Scott Retterberg et al., "The Unknown, the Great American Hypertext Novel," The Unknown, 1998–present, http://unknownhypertext.com.
6. Mark C. Marino et al., "The Los Wikiless Timespedia," *Bunk Magazine*, 2008, http://bunkmagazine.com/mediawiki/index.php?title=Main_Page.
7. Michael Russo, private correspondence with the author, n.d.
8. Bernard Suits, cited in Jane Mcgonigal, *Reality Is Broken: Why Games Make Us Better and How They Can Change the World* (New York: Penguin Press, 2011)

CHAPTER 1

1. Henry Raddick, review of Michael D. Ranken, *Handbook of Meat Product Technology*, Amazon, July 1, 2002, https://www.amazon.com/Handbook-Product-Technology-Michael-Ranken/dp/0632053771/ref=sr_1_4?ie=UTF8&qid=1542562163&sr=8-4&keywords=Handbook of Meat Product Technology#customerReviews.
2. Wayne Redhart, review of Burt's Bees Nuts about Nature 3-Piece Gift Set, Amazon, October 12, 2015, https://www.amazon.co.uk/gp/customer-reviews/RNEMRGTR7278X/ref=cm_cr_dp_d_rvw_ttl?ie=UTF8&ASIN=B00SP5NYCS.
3. Karen Magill, review of *The Very Best of David Hasselhoff*, Amazon, May 12, 2006, https://www.amazon.com/Very-Best-DAVID-HASSELHOFF/dp/B00005Q8UG#customerReviews.
4. Ellya, Patrick J. McGovern, reviews of "Uranium Ore," Amazon, http://www.amazon.com/Images-SI-Inc-Uranium-Ore/dp/B000796XXM/ref=cm_cr_pr_product_top.
5. Paul McGhee, *Understanding and Promoting the Development of Children's Humor* (Dubuque, IA: Kendall Hunt Publishing, 2002).
6. Michael Price, "The Joke's in You," *American Psychological Association Monitor* 38, no. 10 (November 2007): 18.
7. Catherine Gallagher, "The Rise of Fictionality," in *The Novel*, vol. 1: *History Geography and Culture*, ed. Franco Moretti (Princeton, NJ: Princeton University Press, 2007).
8. Gallagher, "The Rise of Fictionality."
9. Gallagher.
10. Gallagher.

11. Howard Rheingold, "Crap Detection Resources," Google Docs, accessed August 12, 2021, https://docs.google.com/document/d/163G79vq-mFWjIqMb9AzYGbr5Y8YMGcpbSzJRutO8tpw/preview.

12. Ryt Hospital-Dwayne Medical Center, "All the Miracles of Modern Medicine," 2011, http://www.rythospital.com/2011/.

13. Tom Way, "Dihydrogen Monoxide Info," Dihydrogen Monoxide Research Division, 2011, http://www.dhmo.org/.

14. Chris Harper, "Landover Baptist Where the Worthwhile Worship: Unsaved Unwelcome," Americhrist Inc., 2011, http://www.landoverbaptist.org.

15. Paul A. Bradley, "Mrs. Betty Bowers, America's Best Christian!," Betty Bowers, 2000–2011, http://www.bettybowers.com.

16. isabella v., *She's a Flight Risk*, (blog), 2003, http://www.aflightrisk.blogspot.com/.

17. Ramesh Flinders and Miles Beckett, *Lonelygirl15*, (blog), LG15, 2006, http://www.lg15.com.

18. Troy Hitch and Matt Bledsoe, *You Suck at Photoshop*, (blog), My Damn Channel, 2008, http://www.mydamnchannel.com/You_Suck_at_Photoshop/Season_1/YouSuckAtPhotoshop1DistortWarpandLayerEffects_1373.aspx.

19. Eric Loyer, *Upgrade Soul*, (blog), 2019, http://erikloyer.com/index.php/projects/detail/upgrade_soul.

20. Gallagher, "The Rise of Fictionality."

21. Fyodor Dostoyevsky, *Notes from Underground and the Double*, trans. Constance Garnett (Overland Park, KS: Digireads.com Publishing, 2018).

22. Dostoevsky, *Notes from Underground*.

23. Henry Jenkins, *Convergence Culture: Where Old and New Media Collide* (New York: New York University Press, 2006).

24. See Hartmut Koenitz, Gabriele Ferri, Mads Haahr, Diğdem Sezen, Tonguç İbrahim Sezen, eds., *Interactive Digital Narrative: History, Theory and Practice* (New York: Routledge, 2015).

25. Russell Brand, *My Booky Wook: A Memoir of Sex, Drugs, and Stand-Up* (New York: It Books, 2010).

CHAPTER 2

1. Dan Sinker, *The F***ing Epic Quest of @MayorEmanuel* (New York: Scribner, 2011).

2. Mark C. Marino, private working materials of the netprov *Air-B-N-Me*, circulated in email, April 2016.
3. Thomas Love Peacock, *Nightmare Abbey*, in *The Works of Thomas Love Peacock*, edited by H. F. B. Brett-Smith and Clifford Ernest Jones (New York: AMS Press, 1967).
4. Leonardo Flores, "Third Generation Electronic Literature," YouTube, 2018, https://youtu.be/hqes9WfJmrc.
5. Flores, "Third Generation Electronic Literature."

EXAMPLE 2

i. *All-Time High*
   Tagline: What if everyone was back in High School, including you?
   First appeared: July 1–31, 2015
   Platforms: Twitter, website
   Netrunners: Claire Donato, Jeff T. Johnson, Mark Marino, and Rob Wittig
   Archive: Twitter's archiving, private archives

1. Claire Donato, Jeff T. Johnson, Rob Wittig, Mark C. Marino, et al., "All-Time High, a Netprov," Meanwhile Netprov, 2015, http://meanwhilenetprov.com/ath15.
2. Jeff T. Johnson, private communication with the author, May 18, 2020.
3. Michael Russo, private communication with the author, December 30, 2019.

CHAPTER 3

1. Anne Libera, *The Second City Almanac of Improvisation* (Evanston, IL: Northwestern University Press, 2004).
2. For a nice overview of Pessoa, see Adam Kirsch, "Fernando Pessoa's Disappearing Act," *New Yorker*, September 4, 2017.
3. Rob Wittig, "Friday's Big Meeting," Tank20, 2000, http://www.robwit.net/fbm.
4. Rob Wittig and IN.S.OMNIA (computer bulletin board), *Invisible Rendezvous: Connection and Collaboration in the New Landscape of Electronic Writing* (Middletown, CT / Hanover, NH: Wesleyan University Press / University Press of New England, 1994).
5. Jill Walker Rettberg, "Mirrors and Shadows: The Digital Aestheticisation of Oneself," Proceedings of Digital Arts and Culture, 2005.

6. Firesign Theater, *Give Me Immortality or Give Me Death*, Rhino Records, 1998, compact disc.
7. Sherry Turkle, "Who Am We?," *Wired*, January 1996, http://www.wired.com/wired/archive/4.01/turkle.html?pg=4&topic=.
8. Erving Goffman, *The Presentation of Self in Everyday Life* (London. Anchor, 1959).
9. Mark C. Marino, Rob Wittig, et al., *SpeidiShow: A Netprov*, Meanwhile . . . Netprov Studio, 2013, http://meanwhilenetprov.com/index.php/project/speidishow.

EXAMPLE 3

i. **Netprov:** *Fantasy Spoils: After the Quest*
   Tagline: Having just completed the glorious epic saga, *Ultimate Final Victory!*, ye have now returned home to deal with the aftermath.
   First appeared: April 6–30, 2020
   Platforms: Discord, website
1. Mark Marino, Rob Wittig, *Fantasy Spoils: After the Quest*, Meanwhile Netprov, 2020, http://meanwhilenetprov.com/fantasyspoils.

CHAPTER 4

1. Rob Wittig et al., "*Grace, Wit & Charm*, a Netprov," 2011, http://gracewitandcharm.com.
2. Bari Rolfe, *Commedia dell'Arte: A Scene Study Book* (San Francisco: Persona Products, 1977).
3. Pierre-Louis Duchartre and Randolph T. Weaver, *The Italian Comedy: The Improvisation, Scenarios, Lives, Attributes, Portraits, and Masks of the Illustrious Characters of the Commedia dell'Arte* (New York: Dover, 1966).
4. Duchartre and Weaver, *Italian Comedy*.
5. Duchartre and Weaver.
6. Viola Spolin, *Improvisation for the Theater: A Handbook of Teaching and Directing Techniques*, rev. ed. (Evanston, IL: Northwestern University Press, 1983).
7. Charna Halpern, Del Close, and Kim Johnson, *Truth in Comedy: The Manual for Improvisation* (Colorado Springs: Meriwether, 1993).
8. Halpern, Close, and Johnson, *Truth in Comedy*.

9. See Matt Besser, Ian Roberts, and Matt Walsh, *Upright Citizens Brigade Comedy Improvisation Manual* (New York: Comedy Council of Nicea, 2013).

10. Alison Goldie, *The Improv Book: Improvisation for Theater, Comedy, Education, and Life* (London: Oberon Books, 2015).

11. Elke Huybrechts, "What Is Queer About Queer Performance Now?" *Theater Times*, February 17, 2019.

12. Antoinette LaFarge, "A World Exhilarating and Wrong: Theatrical Improvisation on the Internet," *Leonardo* 28, no. 5 (1995): 415–22.

13. Halpern, Close, and Johnson, *Truth in Comedy*.

14. Eric Berne, *Games People Play: The Psychology of Human Relationships* (New York: Grove Press, 1964).

15. Halpern, Close, and Johnson, *Truth in Comedy*.

16. Halpern, Close, and Johnson.

17. Halpern, Close, and Johnson.

18. Wittig et al., *Netprov Featured Players Google Group*.

CHAPTER 5

i. **Netprov:** *#fixurl8tionship* (fix your relationship) [for the camera]
   Tagline: Join a squad of Instagram influencers who "FIX" fans' relationships by helping them look*GREAT* for the camera despite how they feel inside!!
   First appeared: March 25–April 10, 2019
   Platform: Instagram, website
   Netrunners: Mark Marino, Rob Wittig
   Archive: Instagram's archive, http://robwit.net/fix

1. Alice E. Marwick and Danah Boyd, "I Tweet Honestly, I Tweet Passionately: Twitter Users, Context Collapse, and the Imagined Audience," *New Media and Society* 13, no. 1: 114–33.

2. Whitney Phillips, *This Is Why Why We Can't Have Nice Things: Mapping the Relationship between Online Trolling and Mainstream Culture* (Cambridge, MA: MIT Press, 2015).

3. See Anastasia Salter, *Toxic Geek Masculinity in Media: Sexism, Trolling, and Identity Policing* (London: Palgrave Macmillan, 2017).

4. aestheticsforbirds, "Aesthetics for Birds," (blog), accessed August 12, 2021, https://aestheticsforbirds.com; Dieter Declerq. "A Definition of Satire (and Why a

Definition Matters)," *Journal of Aesthetics and Art Criticism* 76, no. 3, https://onlinelibrary.wiley.com/doi/full/10.1111/jaac.12563.

5. "Alternate Reality Game," Wikipedia, accessed January 14, 2020, https://en.wikipedia.org/wiki/Alternate_reality_game.

6. Fourcaster. "A Labyrinth, an Alternate Reality Game, 2020," Vimeo, accessed August 12, 2021, https://vimeo.com/428616160.

7. A Labyrinth: Alternate Reality Game, Patrick Jagoda, http://www.patrick-jagoda.com/projects/a-labyrinth.

8. Fourcaster, "A Labyrinth."

9. Fourcaster.

10. See T. L. Taylor, *Watch Me Play: Twitch and the Rise of Game Live Streaming* (Princeton, NJ: Princeton University Press. 2018).

11. Fourcaster, "A Labyrinth."

12. Fourcaster.

13. Fourcaster.

14. See Antero Garcia and Greg Niemeyer, "Introduction," in *Alternate Reality Games and the Cusp of Digital Gameplay* (New York. Bloomsbury, 2017).

15. Lauren Burr, "Hacking the Academic Conference: Bonfire of the Humanities in Retrospect," *Academia*, accessed September 12, 2021, https://www.academia.edu/26150456/Hacking_the_Academic_Conference_Bonfire_of_the_Humanities_In_Retrospect.

16. "Kayfabe," Wikipedia, accessed August 12, 2021, https://en.wikipedia.org/wiki/Kayfabe.

17. Wittig Marino, *#fixurl8tionship*, Robwit, accessed August 12, 2021, http://robwit.net/fix.

18. Jane McGonigal, *Reality Is Broken: Why Games Make Us Better and How They Can Change the World* (New York: Penguin Press, 2011).

19. Scott Rettberg. "Corporate Ideology in World of Warcraft," in *Digital Culture, Play, and Identity, a World of Warcraft Reader*, ed. Hilde G. Corneliussen and Jill Walker Rettberg (Cambridge, MA: MIT Press, 2008).

20. Rob Hornung, "Fragments on Microcelebrity," *New Inquiry*, Oct. 1, 2012.

21. Jacob Silverman, *Terms of Service, Social Media and the Price of Constant Connection* (New York: HarperCollins, 2015).

22. C. Thi Nguyen, "The Gamification of Public Discourse," Royal Institute of Philosophy, December 5, 2019, https://youtu.be/1LpbGW3qLVg.

23. Claire Donato, interview with the author, 2015. Also cited in Rob Wittig, "Occupy the Emotional Stock Exchange, Resisting the Quantifying of Affection in Social Media," *Humanities* 6, no. 2 (2017): 33, https://doi.org/103390/h6020033.

24. David M. Meurer, "Capturing the Imagination: Literary Expression, Participatory Culture and Digital Enclosure," ELO2018 (Electronic Literature Organization), Université du Québec à Montréal, Montréal, Canada, August 13–17, 2018.

EXAMPLE 5

1. Lucia Binding,"Spencer Pratt Loses His Christmas Present from Heidi Montag On 'Wild' New Year's Eve," *EntertainmentWise*, January 2, 2013.

2. Lucy Buckland, "'Thief' Who Stole CBB Star Spencer Pratt's Phone Starts Sharing Intimate Pictures of Wife Heidi Montag," *Daily Mail*, January 6, 2013, https://www.dailymail.co.uk/tvshowbiz/article-2258059/Thief-stole-CBB-star-Spencer-Pratts-phone-starts-sharing-intimate-pictures-wife-Heidi-Montag.html/.

3. Jessica Roy, "How The Hills' Spencer Pratt Landed at the Center of a Complex Piece of Twitter Performance Art," *Observer*, January 28, 2013, https://observer.com/2013/01/how-the-hills-spencer-pratt-became-an-unlikely-participant-in-a-complex-piece-of-twitter-performance-art/.

4. Kate Durbin, "Kate Durbin Interviews Rob Wittig and Mark C. Marino of 'Tempspence,'" HTML Giant, June 27, 2013, http://htmlgiant.com/random/kate-durbin-interviews-rob-wittig-mark-c-marino-of-tempspence.

CHAPTER 6

i. **Netprov:** *Center for Twitzease Control*
   Tagline: Infectious wordplay, pass it on!
   First appeared: April 12–20, 2013
   Platforms: Twitter, website
   Netrunners: Rob Wittig, Mark Marino, Brendan Howell, and Mark Sample
   Archive: Springgun Press, http://www.springgunpress.com/twitzease/

ii. **Netprov:** *Tournament of la Poéstry*
    Tagline: Joi(g)n(ez) (no)us! C"it's not.pas diffic(ult)ile! c'it's e.aisé!
    First appeared: September–December, 2013
    Platforms: Website, Twitter

Netrunners: Joellyn Rock, Rob Wittig
Archive: Twitter's archive; website, http://robwit.net/poestry

1. Mez Breeze, *Human Readable Messages* (Vienna: Traumawien, 2012), 90.
2. *Center for Twitzease Control*, Robwit, accessed August 12, 2021, http://robwit.net/center.
3. *Grace, Wit & Charm*, a netprov, 2011. Twitter, website (no longer accessible), two live theater performances, and streaming video. Peformance videos by Bruce Ojard, videographer; *Grace, Wit & Charm*, performance nights 1–2, parts 1–3, May 17–24, 2001, https://vimeo.com/26485377, https://vimeo.com/26176893, https://vimeo.com/26177139, https://vimeo.com/26485532, https://vimeo.com/26177854, https://vimeo.com/26178038
4. Harry Mathews, "Translation and the Oulipo: The Case of the Persevering Maltese," *Electronic Book Review*, March 1, 1997, https://electronicbookreview.com/essay/translation-and-the-oulipo-the-case-of-the-persevering-maltese/.
5. Antoinette LaFarge, "A World Exhilarating and Wrong: Theatrical Improvisation on the Internet," *Leonardo* 28, no. 5 (1995).

EXAMPLE 6

i. **Netprov:** *#1WkNoTech* (One Week, No Tech)
Tagline: Imagine a week without technology. Now, Tweet the heck out of it!
First appeared: November 10–16, 2014
Platforms: Twitter, Facebook, website
Netrunners: Rob Wittig, Mark Marino
Archives: Website, http://1wknotech.org; Twitter's archive; Facebook group, https://www.facebook.com/groups/932815316746058

1. Rob Wittig and Mark C. Marino, email to netprov players, 2014.
2. Rina Raphael, "Netflix CEO Reed Hastings: Sleep Is Our Competition," Fast Company, November 6, 2017, https://www.fastcompany.com/40491939/netflix-ceo-reed-hastings-sleep-is-our-competition.
3. Rob Wittig and Mark C. Marino, email, n.d.
4. "#1WkNoTech," accessed August 12, 2021, http://1wknotech.org.
5. Sherry Turkle, "Connected, but Alone?" TED Talk, YouTube, April 3, 2012, https://youtu.be/t7Xr3AsBEK4.

CHAPTER 7

i. **Netprov:** *Air-B-N-Me*
   Tagline: Spacing out? Rent your life and turn that space into income!
   First appeared: April 4–10, 2016
   Platforms: Private website discussion group, YouTube, website
   Netrunners: Mark Marino, Rob Wittig
   Archive: Private archives

ii. **Netprov:** *Monstrous Weather*
   Tagline: The week the Internet went down, so many of us sat around marveling at the weird weather and telling scary stories. Now we are collecting summaries of these stories.
   First appeared: July 20–August 10, 2016
   Platforms: Composition: Google group; publication: interactive websites, live reading
   Netrunners: Rob Wittig, Mark Marino
   Archives: Alex Mitchell's hypertext, http://narrativeandplay.org/mweather/mw%20hypedyn/index.html; Mark Marino's hypertext, http://markcmarino.com/mweather

iii. **Netprov:** *One Star Reviews*
   Tagline: *One-Star Reviews* is a community of fictional characters who find value in things rated at one star.
   First appeared: November 6–November 30, 2017
   Platform: Reddit
   Netrunners: Mark Marino, Rob Wittig
   Archive: Reddit's archive, https://www.reddit.com/r/onestarreviewsnetprov

iv. **Netprov:** *Outsource My Study Abroad*
   Tagline: Can't study abroad? We connect you with students who'll make those memories for you (and you for them)!
   First appeared: October 15–November 15, 2014
   Platform: Custom Google maps with attached text and images
   Netrunners: Kathi Inman Berens, Rob Wittig
   Archive: Google Maps archives

1. *1Step Forward, 2Steps Back!!*, #baksteps, accessed August 20, 2021, http://robwit.net/baksteps/.

2. Ken Eklund, *World Without Oil*, 2007, http://gamesforcities.com/database/world-without-oil/.

3. Whitney Phillips, *This Is Why We Can't Have Nice Things: Mapping the Relationship between Online Trolling and Mainstream Culture* (Cambridge: MIT Press, 2015).

4. Alex Mitchell, prog. and ed., *Monstrous Weather* (hypertext version), Narrative and Play, 2019, http://narrativeandplay.org/mweather/mw%20hypedyn/index.html.

5. Mitchell, *Monstrous Weather*.

6. Alex Mitchell, "Monstrous Weathered: Experiences from the Telling and Retelling of a Netprov," Electronic Book Review, 2019, https://electronicbookreview.com/essay/monstrous-weathered-experiences-from-the-telling-and-retelling-of-a-netprov/.

7. Rob Wittig. In Alex Mitchell, prog. and ed., *Monstrous Weather* (hypertext version), Narrative and Play, 2019, http://narrativeandplay.org/mweather/mw%20hypedyn/index.html.

8. John Berger, *Ways of Seeing* (New York: Penguin, 1972).

9. Christopher Lasch, *The Culture of Narrcissism: American Life in an Age of Diminishing Expectations* (New York: W. W. Norton, 1991).

10. P. J. O'Rourke and Douglas C. Kenney, eds., *National Lampoon's 1964 High School Yearbook*, 39th ann. ed. (New York: Rugged Land, 2003).

11. P. J. O'Rourke and John Hughes, eds., *National Lampoon Sunday Newspaper Parody* (New York: Rugged Land, 2004).

12. Zara Kenyon, "A Dutch Woman Used Facebook to Pretend she went Travelling in Asia," Cosmopolitan, September 11, 2014, https://www.cosmopolitan.com/uk/entertainment/news/a29570/woman-facebook-pretend-travelling-asia/.

13. The oft-repeated adage: brevity is the soul of wit.

14. Henry Jenkins, "Transmedia Storytelling 101," *Confessions of an Aca-Fan; the Official Weblog of Henry Jenkins*, 2007, http://www.henryjenkins.org/2007/03/transmedia_storytelling_101.html.

15. Jenkins, "Transmedia Storytelling 101."

16. Jenkins, "Transmedia Storytelling 101."

17. Henry Jenkins, *Convergence Culture: Where Old and New Media Collide* (New York: New York University Press, 2006).

18. Catherine Gallagher, "The Rise of Fictionality," in *The Novel*, volume 1: *History Geography and Culture*, edited by Franco Moretti (Princeton, NJ: Princeton University Press, 2007).

19. Catherine Gallagher, "The Rise of Fictionality," in *The Novel*, volume 1: *History Geography and Culture*, edited by Franco Moretti (Princeton, NJ: Princeton University Press, 2007).

20. Kate Lawrence, "The 5 Most Baffling Sex Scenes in the History of Fanfiction," Cracked, 2008, http://www.cracked.com/article_16554_the-5-most-baffling-sex-scenes-in-history-fanfiction.html.

21. Flourish Klink and Elizabeth Minkel, Fansplaining, accessed August 20, 2021, https://www.fansplaining.com/.

22. See also Anastasia Salter and Mel Stanfil, *A Portrait of the Auteur as Fanboy: The Construction of Authorship in Transmedia Franchises* (Jackson: University Press of Mississippi. 2020).

23. Antoinette LaFarge, "A World Exhilarating and Wrong: Theatrical Improvisation on the Internet," *Leonardo* 28, no. 5 (1995): [AU: Please insert page ranges].

24. Jenkins, *Convergence Culture*.

25. Jenkins, *Convergence Culture*.

EXAMPLE 7

i. **Netprov:** *LA Flood Project*
   Tagline: A flood has hit Los Angeles. A disaster is unfolding across the city and voices are being heard from the epicenter and beyond.
   First appeared: October 20–28, 2011
   Platforms: Google maps, Twitter, website, YouTube
   Netrunners: Jeremy Douglass, Juan B. Gutierrez, Jeremy Hight, Mark C. Marino, and Lisa Anne Tao

1. *LA Flood Project*, City Chaos, accessed August 20, 2021, http://laflood.city-chaos.com.

2. The original *LA Flood Project* website is no longer available.

3. The main *LA Flood Project* website is no longer available.

CHAPTER 8

i. **Netprov:** *#BehindYourBak*

Tagline: Someone's been talking about you behind your back. What do you think they're saying?
First appeared: October 22–November 18, 2018
Platforms: Randomized character concern creation generator webpage, webpage, Twitter
Netrunners: Mark Marino, Rob Wittig
Archive: Twitter's archive; pdf archive, http://behindyourbak.robwit.net

ii. **Netprov:** *Chicago Soul Exchange*
Tagline: Past-life resellers. Yes, you can have a better past! At competitive prices!
First appeared: April 1–30, 2010
Platform: Proprietary website chatroom
Netrunner: Rob Wittig
Archive: Private archive

iii. **Netprov:** *Mem-Eraze*
Tagline: *Mem-Eraze* is an online support group for those who lost their online social scrapbooks in the Mem-or-Eaze Inc. server fire and bankruptcy.
First appeared: April 13–25, 2014
Platform: Tumblr
Netrunners: Rob Wittig, Mark Marino
Archive: Tumblr archives, private archives

iv. **Netprov:** *Last Five Days of Sight and Sound*
Tagline: What if you could only perceive the world through the Internet? And only for five more days?
First appeared: March 27–April 2, 2012
Platform: Website, Twitter
Netrunners: Rob Wittig, Mark Marino
Archive: Twitter's archive, website

v. **Netprov:** *Fantasy Automated Investor's League (F.A.I.L.)*
Tagline: Wheel, deal, joke and trash talk about Fantasy Businesses the way others do about Fantasy Football teams!
First appeared: November 28–December 2, 2012
Platforms: Website, Twitter
Netrunners: Mark Marino, Rob Wittig
Archive: Twitter's archives

1. The *Chicago Soul Exchange* website no longer exists. All text is from my own personal archives.
2. *Mem-Eraze*, Tumblr, accessed August 20, 2021, https://memeraze.tumblr.com.

3. *Last Five Days of Sight and Sound*, Blogger, accessed August 20, 2021, http://l5dosas.blogspot.com/.

4. "*Fantasy Automated Investors League (F.A.I.L.)*, a netprov," Robwit, accessed August 20, 2021, http://robwit.net/fail.

5. Planning documents in my own personal archive.

6. Planning documents in my own personal archive.

7. Joellyn Rock, "The Sophronia Project: Experimental Video, Interactive Installation," WordPress, 2014, https://joellynrock.com/portfolio/sophronia-project/.

8. Joellyn Rock, "The Sophronia Project: Experimental Video, Interactive Installation," WordPress, 2014, https://joellynrock.com/portfolio/sophronia-project/.

9. Myles Tanzer, "How Spencer Pratt and Heidi Montag Fooled Everyone with Their Latest Reality Show," BuzzFeed, October 10, 2013, https://www.buzzfeed.com/mylestanzer/how-spencer-pratt-and-heidi-montag-fooled-everyone-with-thei.

EXAMPLE 8

i. **Netprov:** *Destination Wedding 2070*
Tagline: *Destination Wedding 2070* is a dark comedy about wedding planning fifty years from now, and, spoiler alert: climate change is the ultimate wedding crasher!
First appeared: November 3–11, 2019
Platforms: Website, Reddit
Netrunners: Samara Hayley Steele, Dargan Frierson, Mark Marino, and Rob Wittig
Archive: Reddit's archive, https://www.reddit.com/r/DestinationWedding70

1. "Lee & Lessee Wedding (Mar del Plata)," Reddit, October 31, 2019, https://www.reddit.com/r/DestinationWedding70/comments/dpibl2/lee_lessee_wedding_mar_del_plata/.

2. *Destination Wedding 2070*, WordPress, accessed August 20, 2021, http://meanwhilenetprov.com/dw70.

CHAPTER 9

i. **Netprov:** *Thermophiles in Love*
Tagline: A five-gender dating game for single-celled organisms.
First appeared: October 21–November 6, 2016

Platform: Private website discussion group
Netrunners: Samara Hayley Steele, Cathy Podeszwa, Mark Marino, and Rob Wittig
Archive: Private archives

1. *Thermophiles in Love*, Bootstrap, http://markcmarino.com/til/index.php?p=/.
2. Mark C. Marino, private correspondence with the author, June 15, 2018.
3. Samara Hayley Steele, manuscript rules of the game for the LARP/netprov *Thermophiles in Love*, collection of the author, 2018.
4. Steele, manuscript rules.
5. Samara Hayley Steele, "Game Design Methodologies for Gender Playability: A Case Study of Thermophiles in Love," Samarasteele.com, 2016, https://samarasteele.com/2016/12/20/a_case_study_of_termophiles_in_love.
6. Marino, private correspondence.
7. Samara Hayley Steele, private email with the author, June 15, 2018.

CHAPTER 10

1. Douglas Stone, Bruce Patton, and Sheila Heen, *Difficult Conversations: How to Discuss What Matters Most* (New York: Penguin, 1999).
2. Stone, Patton, and Heen, *Difficult Conversations*.
3. Stone, Patton, and Heen.

APPENDIXES

APPENDIX 1

PLATFORMS DISCUSSED IN THIS BOOK

Message to future scholars: Hi! How's it going? How are you even reading this? Does coffee still exist? Here is a quick description of the main platforms I refer to in this work.

Twitter: A microblogging, text and image, social media service where messages were known as "tweets" and posting as "tweeting" and messages were displayed in reverse chronological order. The original character limit of 140 characters was later changed to 280 characters. Registered users could post, like (vote their public approval of a tweet), and retweet. Posted messages could be read by anyone. Early Twitter culture was friendly, fun, and encouraged grassroots creativity. After becoming a publically traded company, advertisements began to appear. Twitter became a venue for the toxically divided political culture of the 2010s and '20s, including foreign Twitter interference in US elections and the near-daily tweets of the US President.

Facebook: A social media and networking service supporting unlimited text and image, groups, and promotional pages. Members' messages were visible to those who the members chose as "friends." Early Facebook use displayed a member's friends' messages as they were posted in reverse chronological order in a "feed. Members could "like" with a thumbs-up icon and repost. Facebook became a publically traded company and began displaying advertising, becoming one of the largest companies in the world. Sophisticated algorithms were used to identify members' preferences and to display messages in the feed of presumed greater relevance to and to target advertising directly to members.

Instagram: A photo-sharing social network service used for posting images, short films, and accompanying short captions. Users can like and repost. The original restriction of photos to a square format was later relaxed. Instagram began with grassroots personal photo sharing. Later it also became the province of "influencers" (popular members) the most prominent of whom earned a great deal of money for endorsing products and services.

Reddit: A crowdsourced news aggregator, rating, and discussion service. It's format is based on threaded discussion group or forum websites, with topics on a wide variety of subjects called "subreddits," unlimited text displayed in reverse chronological order, some image capability, and with a heavy emphasis on members' ratings. High ratings resulted in increased visibility of messages to all users. Culturally, some on the site had a rough-and-tumble feel with trolling and harassment needing to be constantly policed by the company and conspiracy theories and hate speech lurking in dark corners.

Tumblr: A short-form microblogging and social media service, displaying text and image in reverse chronological order on each member's own page. Linking to other members' posts and voting were possible. Not as popular a service as the others above.

TikTok: A video-sharing social networking service initially specializing in video segments of fifteen seconds. Videos could easily be combined with music, slowed down or sped up. Early use featured users lip synching and/or dancing to music. The "react" feature allows users to respond quickly to a video, often with their own version of the song or dance.

Discord: A proprietary freeware service created originally as a voice and threaded-discussion tool for game developers. It was later adapted for general use by gamers, educators and others. Members create their own "servers," with multiple discussion threads using voice, text, and limited images. It was particularly well suited for playing Dungeons & Dragons-style roleplaying games at a distance, with in-platform bots functioning as dice rolls and other gameplay aids.

Private forums: A password-protected, text and image, threaded-discussion group run on a private server, with topics and replies, text and image displayed in reverse chronological order, and database indexing capabilities.

APPENDIX 2

NETPROV STUDIO: GENERIC SCHEDULE AND TO-DO LIST TEMPLATE

Six Weeks before Launch

- Develop concept (netrunners, producers)
- Create project platforms (netrunners; designer; programmer; participation, player care coordinator, publicist)
- Develop narrative arc (netrunners)
- Contact teachers of e-literature classes

Four Weeks before Launch

- Finalize logos and graphics (netrunners, graphic designer)
- Create documents for featured players: basic story and how to play, beat sheet, tools and platforms (netrunners)
- Send save-the-date announcement to featured players and players, promotion list, publicity list (player care coordinator)
- Set up website with promotional text (graphic designer)

Three Weeks before Launch

- Create T-shirt, website (graphic designer, programmer)
- Order T-shirts (netrunners, publicist)

Two Weeks before Launch

- Send teaser to players, promotion list, publicity list (player care coordinator)
- Hold orientation meeting for featured players, Skype and in person (netrunners, featured players)
- Write model text and choose images for the project (netrunners)
- Create project trailer (netrunners, graphic designer, programmer)
- Share documents for featured players: basic story and how to play, beat sheet, tools and platforms (netrunners)

Seven Days before Launch

- Send press release to publicity list (player care coordinator)
- Launch website and trailer launch (netrunners, graphic designer, programmer)
- Rehearsal/play/character development session (netrunners, featured players)

Five Days before Launch

- Send out publicity (player care coordinator, publicist)

Three Days before Launch

- Send out publicity (player care coordinator, publicist)

Two Days before Launch

- Send out publicity (player care coordinator, publicist)
- Hold team launch meeting, Skype and in person (netrunners, featured players)

Launch Day

- Begin netprov play (all)
- Promotion blast (player care coordinator)

First Day (and odd days thereafter for entire netprov run)

- Continue netprov play (all)
- Player care (player care coordinator)
- Featured player care (show runners)
- Maintain project infrastructure (graphic designer, programmer)
- Begin archiving (archivist)

Second Day (and even days thereafter for entire netprov run)

- Continue netprov play (all)
- Promotion/publicity update (player care coordinator)

- Player care (player care coordinator)
- Featured player care (show runners)
- Maintain project infrastructure (graphic designer, programmer)
- Continue archiving (archivist)

Wrap Day

- Hold player care celebration with thank-yous (player care coordinator)
- Hold featured player care celebration with thank-yous (show runners)
- Hold cast party!!!, Skype and in person (show runners, featured players)

Postproduction

- Compile archives and prepare for publication (archivist, graphic designer, programmer)

Follow-up Publicity (player care coordinator, show runners)

APPENDIX 3

BEHIND-THE-SCENES TOOLS AND DOCUMENTS FOR NETRUNNERS

- Shared, online netrunners' folder for each netprov.
- Email list for netrunners; these emails are the to-do list before, during, and after the netprov.
- Email list for featured players.
- Email list for players.
- Shared, online production schedule document for the netprov, including rehearsals, promotion, and archiving.
- Participation statistics (if available from the given platform).
- Online meeting tools such as Skype or Google Hangout as needed for organizational meetings among netrunners and rehearsals and live events with featured players.

TOOLS FOR FEATURED PLAYERS AND TEACHERS

- Concise netprov description, invitation, and instructions document written by the netrunners; this text is used for netprov websites, press releases, etc.
- Scenario with the narrative beats and their timing (also called a beat sheet).
- Character document in which featured players share about their characters' backstory and individual story arcs, so featured players can support each other.
- Teachers' document for professors assigning the netprov that contains the description, invitation, and instructions above, plus recommended and related readings, prewriting activities, and prompts.
- Private online forum and/or Facebook group for rehearsal before the netprov and backchannel planning and feedback during the netprov. (Mark and I call our Facebook group Nighthawks in honor of the Nighthawks bar from *I Work for the Web*.)

TOOLS FOR PLAYERS (PEOPLE WE DON'T KNOW)

- "How to Play" web page for each netprov (can be within the fiction and/or outside the fiction); all promotional and press-release links lead to this page.
- Video trailer for the netprov; under one minute; jaunty music, catchy slogans, usually within the fiction.
- "Our Story So Far" summary on the netprov website for players joining in the middle of the netprov.
- "What Is Netprov?" page on the netprov website.
- Netprov merchandise web page as needed for the concept of the netprov.

www.ingramcontent.com/pod-product-compliance
Lightning Source LLC
Chambersburg PA
CBHW070840160426
43192CB00012B/2258